Anton
OLIVER
INSIDE

Anton
OLIVER
INSIDE

with Brian Turner

Hodder Moa

Photographic credits

Fotopress: 17, 20, 25, 27, 28, 44, 45, 46, 50, 52, 66, 71, 72, 73, 74, 75, 79, 81 (bottom), 82, 84, 86, 87, 88, 91, 94, 98, 100, 101, 103, 105, 106, 110, 111, 114, 115, 116, 120, 122, 123, 131, 133, 136, 139, 140, 143, 148, 151, 153, 155, 157, 160, 169, 172, 175, 176, 187, 192, 194, 197, 206, 207, 208, 209, 210, 218, 220, 224, 226, 230, 232, 236, 239, 240, 241
Photosport: 48, 49, 59, 61, 63, 64, 81, 133, 134, 214, 216
Anton Oliver: 32, 38, 41, 128, 161, 165, 166, 180, 182
Otago Daily Times: 165, 188, 189
John Selkirk: 57, 68
Peter Bush: 21
The Marlborough Express: 42
New Zealand Rugby Museum: 37

National Library of New Zealand Cataloguing-in-Publication Data
Turner, Brian, 1944-
Anton Oliver inside / Brian Turner.
ISBN 1-86958-991-2
1. Oliver, Anton, 1975- 2. Rugby Union football players—New
Zealand—Biography. 3. Rugby Union football—New Zealand.
4. Professionalism in sports—New Zealand. I. Title.
796.333092—dc 22

A Hodder Moa Book
Published in 2005 by Hachette Livre NZ Ltd
4 Whetu Place, Mairangi Bay
Auckland, New Zealand

Designed and produced by Hachette Livre NZ Ltd
Printed by Tien Wah Press Ltd, Singapore

Contents

Authors' Notes and Acknowledgements

I am sincerely indebted to all of those who offered their time or thoughts and allowed themselves to be interviewed by a strange, inquisitive, bearded man who would call unerringly at the most inconvenient of times! These collective accounts provided invaluable material to the creation of this tome: quite simply without your contributions there would be no book.

I must thank Kevin and Warren from Hachette Livre for their understanding in an ever-changing climate, sometimes dictated by selectors, sometimes by my own uncertainty. You have made business not seem like business and for that I thank you both.

I also thank the NZRU, in particular the two Steves, for their trust and support in some uncomfortable legal matters — it could have become a multi-headed leviathan, but it didn't — cheers.

To Jane, who helped transcribe four chapters or more early on. She did this without remuneration or hesitation and was the first to see *Inside*. 'Fanks' Aunty.

Thanks also to Grahame for the cover shot, advice and support. If only rugby players could earn the mountains of loot that artists enjoy for sitting on their backsides painting pretty pictures!

My little mud-brick cottage deserves a bouquet for always being there for me when the cumulus crowded. Most of my best writing was done within its cosy four walls: a safe haven-home.

I must also acknowledge Chris for his recent legal work, and Warren and Kevin for their contributions.

Most importantly, I would like to thank Brian Turner.

In what has ended up most accurately described as a collaborative effort, Brian was a patient, wise and accommodating teacher. He did a mountain of work, pecking assiduously away at his Mac in the back room of a small house in a southern hamlet called Oturehua — from spring to spring then threateningly close to another spring again.

Brian knows more about me than any other person: my fears, insecurities and all other matters private, and yet I am not perturbed by his extensive knowledge. He is a good honest man, as straight as is humanly possible and our friendship is now eternal; separated by 30 years of age but in all other aspects joined by mutual respect for each other's opinions and shared, rigorous thought.

Brian, we have many hills to climb, trout to catch, vino to drink and interesting discourse to traverse before the sun sets for one of us.

Thanks mate.

The absurd notion of an autobiography by a 29 year old has been an ever-present companion; always perched on my shoulder challenging my thoughts about the book's validity. This book is a selective account of my life to this premature point and I am well aware of the oxymoron that exists in a description of one's life at the age of 29 — I have had to get over this fact and hope that you, the reader, can do so too.

If I had known about the amount of time, effort, thought and diligence required to produce a book I would have been far less cavalier in accepting an offer from a publisher. However, I have found that most things that I truly value in my life have taken time: to learn, grow or forge. The lessons learnt from this book are many and varied, and so deserve their place in my 'life lessons lexicon'.

Therefore, I would, if offered the chance, do it all again.

Anton Oliver
July 2005

This book has been no mean adventure. My thanks to Anton for his openness, his rigour, his candour, and for putting so much faith in me. He is a remarkable, good man. The best thing about working with him on this book has been finding a new, true friend.

In the course of researching and writing this book with Anton many people were helpful and forthcoming. They provided insight, advice and information, and for that I am most grateful. If I've overlooked anyone, my apologies.

Among those I wish to thank — in no particular order — are: Tony Gilbert, Wayne Smith, Graham Henry, Steve Hansen, John Hart, Robbie Deans, Ken Hodge, Kevin Gloag, Peter Sloane, Greg Cooper, Phil Young, Wayne Graham, Sir Brian Lochore, Paddy O'Brien, Andrew Martin, John Sturgeon, John Graham, David Rutherford, John Hornbrook, Russell Gray, Monty Wright, Roger Clark, Russell Gray, Des Smith, Steve Martin, Steve Cumberland, John Mayhew, Gilbert Enoka, Steve Bentley, Simon Mayhew, Peter Gallagher, Matt Blair, Alex McKenzie, Phil Handcock, Mike Anthony, Bevan Grant, Donny Cameron, Lipi Sinnott, Martin Toomey, Rob Nicholson, Peter Sinclair, Mark Henaghan, John Hansen, Warren Alcock, Diccon Sim, Frikkie Erasmus, Lloyd Jones, Chris Laidlaw, Steve Davie, John Matheson (the journalist), Keith Quinn, Brent Edwards, Craig Page, Nathan Burdon, Kip Brook, James Funnell, Matt McIlraith, Wynne Gray, Ron Palenski, Jamie Mackay, Dave McLaren, Phil Taylor, Roy Colbert, Glenn Turner, Grahame Sydney, Dave Callon, Grahame Gladstone, Winston Cooper, Philip Temple, John Dean, Mike Kavanagh, Barry Becker, Peter Kirk, Neil Purvis, Neville and Mary Hore, Ian Smith, Rob Nichol, John Matheson, Colin Weatherall, Phil Hope, Alan Harper, Graham Cooney, Kieran Keane and John Rodgers, Frank Oliver, Tana Umaga, Andrew Hore, Tom Willis, Mark Hammett, Peter Bowden, Colin Meads, Andrew Mehrtens, David Latta, Kelvin Middleton, James Arlidge, Josh Blackie, Duncan Blaikie, Jeff Wilson, Mark Robinson, Kees Meeuws, Josh Kronfeld, Carl Hoeft, Simon Maling, Ben Hurst, Sam Harding, Brendan Cannon, Tony Brown, Marilyn (Anton's Mum), Brent Oliver, Ellie Henderson, Shona Neehoff, Jenni Hunter, Oke and Helen Blaikie, and Raylene and Justin Pigou.

My thanks to Kevin Chapman and Warren Adler of Hachette Livre NZ Ltd for their patience and tact.

Brian Turner
July 2005

Preface

In 2002, after I'd written a new book on that grand and grizzled icon Colin Meads, I thought, 'That's enough about rugby and rugby players for me.' I wanted to get on with more of my own work — poems, essays, the occasional column, other books I'd kept skirting, and so on. Having written three books with my brother Glenn, a cricketer and coach of note, and then books on Meads and another engaging individual rugby player, Josh Kronfeld, I'd said I'd done enough literary ventriloquy.

Well, clearly, I hadn't. Perhaps this is because, of all the players and others I talked to in 1998–99, when I was writing Kronfeld's *On the Loose*, none struck me as more interesting than Anton Oliver. I found Oliver unusual and intriguing, clearly sharp and intelligent. Oliver also struck me as a man genuinely concerned for the welfare of others. That's not as common in rugby as it used to be: professional sport tends to shift people towards the selfish rather than the altruistic end of the field.

Back in 1998 I saw him as tough, kind, emotional, combative — in the sense that he enjoyed a contest and wouldn't just agree unthinkingly. I thought, 'This guy's nobody's patsy.' I liked that. But at the time I had no idea that, one day, I would be working with Oliver on an account of his life and times.

Nor did I know that it would turn out to be as interesting and controversial. There are some strong, stubborn personalities involved. A few would rather only their side of a story was presented; some would prefer that certain issues not be discussed at all. Others wouldn't talk because . . . ? I'm not sure. Perhaps because if they said what they truly thought, and why they acted the way they did, it wouldn't show them in a very good light. Perhaps they'd prefer not to have certain observations made known. Perhaps . . .

I find the politics of rugby, and sport in general, fascinating and, at times, infuriating and distasteful. Needless to say it is volatile. There is a lust for power and control in some quarters, though few would admit it. Most still assert that they are in it solely for 'the good of the game'.

The thing that astonished me most, overall, was the amount of praise so many people were prepared to bestow on Oliver. In Peter Sloane's case he says, 'I just love the guy. So does my elderly mother. She gave me some shortbread to give him after what we all thought would be his last game at Eden Park in October 2004. I wanted to get into it myself but I couldn't, she'd taped the package up. And there'd have been a letter inside, I'm sure of that.'

There is absolutely no doubt that Oliver is widely liked and respected and that those who count themselves among his detractors are very few in number. One, though, is former All Black, Otago and Highlanders coach Laurie Mains.

Mains spoke to me but not at length. He said he was legally debarred from talking about matters to do with what went on in the Highlanders in 2003. Laurie is seen as a resolute individual, admired in some quarters and not in others. Taine Randell declined my requests too; he said that he was a mate of Laurie's and didn't want to say anything that might damage Otago rugby. He was into 'letting sleeping dogs lie'.

John Mitchell didn't want to discuss his experiences of Oliver.

Before I started working on this book I was one of those who inclined to the view that tails shouldn't wag dogs. And I still think that. I saw players as privileged, sometimes pampered, and in many cases overpaid relative to what many others in our society receive for their labours. I thought there was a fair chance that some players were a bit too precious and that, often, they were at too great a remove from life's harsher realities. What I found that the players I talked to were, most of them, far from precious; that most were insecure; that turmoil, intrigue, back-stabbing, self-delusion, long-standing enmities and rivalries, and so on and on, were the — often astonishing — reality of Otago rugby. Shakespeare would have loved the rugby world, not just in Otago, but throughout New Zealand. For it would be a big mistake to believe that the friction associated with politicking and factionalism in rugby is unique to Otago.

Sport and politics don't mix? Rubbish. Political animals are political animals. And there are plenty of them in rugby (and cricket too) in New Zealand. Since the advent of 'professionalism' it may have got worse. Why 'professionalism' in quotes? Because a lot of what goes on is anything but professional. As former All Black manager John Sturgeon said to me, in rugby, 'Disputes have got worse since money became a driver. Two things bring out the worst in men — women and gold.' Sturgeon was one who found it very hard to believe that Oliver was a so-called troublemaker.

In 2003, soon after John Mitchell had told Oliver what he'd sensed earlier, which was that he wouldn't be in the All Black team to play for the 2003 World Cup, I rang Oliver and said that when people opined that 'all will be forgiven if New Zealand wins the World Cup,' one could retort, 'Ends don't necessarily justify the means.'

I was thinking, as were many of Oliver's fans, of how previous All Black coaches Smith and Gilbert had been grooming him to be their World Cup captain. Gilbert in particular believes that he could have been New Zealand's equivalent of England's Martin Johnson, and that an Oliver-led All Black side would not have been seen as 'lacking maturity', which was how they were infamously described after the competition by the man responsible for them, John Mitchell.

At the time the World Cup team was chosen I was rereading John Mulgan's *Report on Experience*, an account of his time fighting with Greeks during the German occupation of Greece in the 1940s. In it he said that New Zealanders tended to think that 'Rugby football was the best of all our pleasures: it was religion and desire and fulfilment all in one.

'This phenomenon is greatly deprecated by a lot of thinkers who feel that an exaggerated attention to games gives the young a wrong sense of values. This may well be true, and if it is true, the majority of New Zealanders have a wrong sense of values for the whole of their lives.'

Also, 'Most New Zealanders can look back on some game which they played to win and whose issues then seemed to them a good deal more important than a lot that has happened since.'

I mulled over that. In Mulgan's time, rugby was a much more pervasive part of the wider community than it is today. But isn't his view still clung to by so-called rugby traditionalists, those who believe that, for all its faults, rugby still has a cohesive value that strengthens the social fabric of localities? I think that rugby's diehards, those of my generation (born in the 1940s) especially, still hold to these views, but the reality is that the values — and the ethos if you like — that underpinned rugby for decades in New Zealand have been rapidly breaking down.

The more I thought about it, the more I believed that Oliver's days were numbered in rugby, and in the All Blacks in particular. In some ways Oliver was old before his time, was perceived as being a bit like a pioneer farmer holding out while all around him agribusiness laid waste to the territory. As Peter Sloane told Oliver in the days before Otago's last NPC game in October 2004, 'You know what you stand for. You know what's important to you in and outside the game. You know what you'd like to restore. It won't happen. It's too late; it's gone. Now's the time to go.'

Most of those who knew Oliver best thought Sloane was right. We were wrong.

Personally, I'd come to see Oliver as one who passionately believed that the best of the values that are found in rugby are values worth retaining and promoting — selflessness, devotion to the team's cause, mutual respect, fair play, loyalty, and so on — and that he had fallen foul of those who say they believe in the importance of those values but whose actions, to him, have in some cases appeared to be contradictory.

I wondered: could it be that Oliver is not selfish enough to sit comfortably alongside those who seek the optimum financial return from the game? Is he becoming more and more an odd man out in a world where, with some players, fashion statements and celebrity appearances sometimes appear to take precedence over on-field performance and plain hard graft? You see, Oliver is the type of forward who believes in the need to do what the tighties especially call 'the shit work', for if they don't, who will? And how can you win tight test matches if you haven't got forwards like Oliver to do it? Not that he wasn't equipped to flit about looking for opportunities to shine and run with the ball in hand; he simply felt guilty about doing it.

I'd seen Oliver as one unwilling to go along with the orchestrated farewells that some leading figures have enjoyed or sought; as one who preferred to go about his business unobtrusively wherever possible. I'd found him the sort of man who makes and has made many friends and who loses very few. His history is ample testimony of that.

Once I asked Oliver where he kept his All Black blazers and jerseys and socks and . . . He looked at me querulously and said he had given away most of them, not because they were unimportant, but because collecting just wasn't his thing. In 2002 he told me he had bundled up a whole heap of clothing that he had acquired while with the All Blacks and taken it down to the local office of the Salvation Army.

That's just Oliver's way. By contrast, by the end of 2003 his mate Carl Hoeft still had most of his 20 test jerseys hanging in a wardrobe along with scores of others, international and provincial. As it happens, Hoeft and Oliver have a strong amount of respect for each other, and one would be hard put to deduce from this that playing for the All Blacks is of more, or less, importance to either of them. They are just different people who share a liking for big-time rugby.

In Oliver's case, he got hold of his father Frank's first test jersey, then had that and his own one framed, and sent them to Frank as a gift. Frank's first test was against South Africa at Johannesburg on 18 September 1976; Anton's was against Fiji at Albany on 14 June 1997.

When yarning to Oliver one night in 2003, I remember him musing, 'For years and years I kept my head down. I did exactly what I was told. I hardly ever took issue openly with what we were asked to do. I may not have liked some things all that much, and I sometimes felt we could have done things differently, but many players are like that. I just wanted to play rugby at the highest level and to the best of my ability. No one could have said I was a troublemaker, or the so-called "ringleader" in anything.

'When I came home from my first tour, to South Africa in 1996, I was raring to play some rugby. I'd had hardly any for weeks. Ken Hodge, the coach of the Varsity A side in Dunedin, remembers me "jumping out of my skin" and turning up at a club practice at Logan Park the day after I got back to Dunedin. It was a Wednesday. I grabbed my gear, went to the ground, got changed and ran over to Ken and said I was keen to play on the Saturday.

'Hodge told me that the side had lost to Southern the previous Saturday, that the forwards hadn't played well, and that they really "needed to redeem themselves" as a pack "without" me. He didn't think it would be good to use me as a sort of saviour.

'I said I understood that, then said, "Well, would the Bs have room for me?" He said we'd find out, and he took me across to their coach. The upshot was on the Saturday I went out to Waikouaiti, 30 km north of Dunedin, and the Eastern senior side got a bit of a shock, so I'm told, when I ran out of the shed.

'Hodge's Varsity As had some good players in it, including my friends Duncan and John Blaikie. Duncan was a brilliant openside flanker whose career was ruined by a succession of leg injuries, and John was a quality lock who played for Otago for many seasons.'

I asked Hodge about Oliver and the Blaikies when he coached them. He said, 'If you had a team of the likes of Oliver and the Blaikie boys, coaching would be the easiest job in the world.' He said 'they trained hard and did what they were asked'.

Brian Turner
Oturehua, Central Otago
May 2005

Chapter 1

Back in Black

Rome, November 2004, on what will be one of the most emotional days of my life. The All Black team for the test that evening against Italy files into the team room and sits down in a semicircle, starting from one and finishing at 22. The management file in behind us, stand, and observe the jersey presentation in silence. Sitting down I notice that my hands are getting very clammy, and I feel the build-up that one gets inside the chest cavity when emotion starts to churn. It's a bit like the feeling that wells up inside you when you return to a place you have grown to love. My bottom lip starts to quiver and I realise that I am a goner.

Gilbert Enoka has been given the honour of handing out the jerseys, but I am no longer listening to his words; all my focus is on trying not to dissolve, trying not to bawl my eyes out in front of some old friends and some new ones, in a small room half a world away from home. I fix my eyes on the carpet, every so often stealing a glance at the pile of jerseys on the table behind Gilbert. Next thing the new prop Saimone Taumoepeau is presented with his jersey and sits down. Now it's my turn to stand. I shake Gilbert's hand, receive his perennial warm smile and, with both hands, I cling to my prize and return to my seat.

Then it starts and I can't — and quickly realise I don't wish to — stop it. I start to cry. I drape the jersey over my head, and find myself leaning forward, holding my head in my hands with the jersey catching the falling tears.

The sobs are uncontrollable; I'm not sure entirely why I am crying. I just am. There's an overwhelming deep need to let it all happen, to let defences down. It seems like I have no real choice in the matter, and couldn't care less how All Blacks are supposed to behave or, more poignantly, how they are not supposed to.

I am 29 years old, the second oldest in the team, first called into the All Blacks in 1995 as a mere 19-year-old kid. How different a person I was then compared with the wreck now hiding my emotions under my test jersey. It was the first time I had openly cried in front of a group of grown men. At 29 some might argue that such an outpouring was well overdue, especially in light of my experiences over the previous few years. The pressure that I had imposed upon myself subconsciously for over a decade now couldn't hold any longer — that of being the proverbial 'hard-man' front-rower, and clichéd Southern Man, where one had to be stoical and impenetrable, suppressing emotions rather than releasing them.

Nevertheless, I draped the jersey over my head like a black veil. I'm not sure why. I wasn't worried about people knowing I was crying — hell, everybody could hear me — so perhaps I was just trying to keep my face private: a feeble attempt to keep some dignity.

Now, months afterwards, I think that emotional release had much to do with the sudden, powerful realisation that, jersey in hand, I had returned from parts unknown. That despite all the upheavals I had experienced in my recent life, here was the evidence that I had preserved enough self-belief to have made it back. For the last few years I had battled a cynicism about the authenticity and ability of rugby organisations, administrators and media, and felt the pressure of unrealistic public expectation to the point where I wondered if there was any point going on. Very public and hurtful comments describing me as a petulant, controlling, self-centred troublemaker combined with insufficient success with Highlander and Otago teams, had gnawed at me to the point where I was tempted to say bugger it, it's time to give up. My rugby life had influenced my personal life to the point where day-to-day existence simply wasn't enjoyable. But in Rome I cried and it felt good. I'd stuck it out, I'd played well, and here was my reward: I was an All Black again.

When I finally took the jersey off my head to face the boys I had snot and tears all over my face and so, with nothing else handy, I blew my nose into the hallowed jersey and wiped the tears away as well. Bloody handy, the All Black jersey.

By now Gilbert was presenting the last of the jerseys and we all stood up and shook hands. Maxey — Norm Maxwell — was only two down the line from me (No. 4) and he'd been bawling too. The tears were still streaming down his face as we hugged each other and muttered a few words, none of which I can remember now. Tana Umaga was nearby and I hugged him too.

Here we were, Norm and I, arguably the most senior players in the side, and probably the most contentious selections on this tour, the 'hard men' showing just how much it meant to us to be All Blacks again.

How good it felt.

A week or two earlier, flying to Auckland for a camp in preparation for this All Black tour to Italy, Wales and France, I felt as if I was en route to my first ever All Black assembly, nervous of what was to come, and excited by the prospect of wearing the black jumper once again. My reselection had been a total shock: Graham Henry's phone call and the ensuing two weeks had been nothing less than surreal, and I found myself reflecting on the plane about my rugby past and the personal changes that I had undergone over the previous 10 years.

In 1995, I was flying back from a successful New Zealand Colts trip in Argentina thinking about my first All Black assembly, full of idealism and naivety. I wanted to prove that I was good enough, to earn the respect from the senior players, some of whose images had been pinned to my boyhood bedroom walls. Apprehension, uncertainty and general fear were also prevalent — one foot on the first rung of the long All Black ladder.

Now, flying north, I knew that there was plenty to prove again. However, this time it was different. I wasn't desperately trying to make a name for myself, to gain respect from those who had been my idols as a kid. Neither was I asking myself, 'Who are the senior players?', those battle-scarred veterans around whom a young chap kept his mouth shut while trying hard not to upset them.

In reality, I was one of those senior players now. I had been a reserve in a test as a 19-year-old kid, had gone on to play for the team the following year and in every year since, apart from 2002 when I ruptured my Achilles tendon. I knew myself better, and in that pivotal phone call with Graham Henry he had told me to 'be myself' — even though I had a few ideas of what that might mean. 'Being myself' had got me into a few tight spots over the previous four years, but here I was being told it was okay to be me, and the management had selected me, playing abilities aside, because of the person that I was.

I had much to prove, this time 'in from the cold' and that cold had been a gloomy, fraught and bone-chilling period for me.

This time I was only interested in proving things to myself and no one else. I had enough peace of mind and self-assuredness to let myself be my own judge of success and failure, a quantum leap from 10 years before when I was out to show everybody how good I thought I could be.

Camp is always a manic time, with lots of on- and off-field matters to sort out. There are old mates to catch up with again and fresh faces less well known but played against in the Super 12 and National Provincial Championship (NPC) competitions. Now no longer rivals but team-mates, touring companions and roommates perhaps in the weeks ahead, all of us excited by the future challenges, all hoping for the best both personally and as a team.

During our first two or three training sessions I felt I was being keenly observed. The scrum coach Mike Cron especially seemed to be staring straight at me whenever we broke for a huddle and a comment on the last set of scrums. I mentioned this to Greg Somerville when warming down after training; he laughed and said he had noticed it too but not to worry about it. It was well into the tour before Mike stopped eyeing me at every scrum session. I knew what was happening: apart from Wayne Smith, whom I knew well, I had not been coached by any of the other members of the coaching staff, and they didn't know me at all. Cron's approach to me was understandable, for while I didn't have a 'record', I did have some history.

A week before camp in a Christchurch café, assistant coach Steve Hansen had effectively done the same thing.

Hansen had asked me to meet with him prior to the Auckland assembly and later told me he thought at the start we were like 'two old cagey bulls' skirting around each other. I also learned later that when Graham Henry, Wayne Smith and Steve had first been appointed, Henry and Hansen had been inclined to the

The New Zealand coaching triumvirate of Graham Henry, Wayne Smith and Steve Hansen. Along with fellow selector, Sir Brian Lochore, they threw me the 'black' lifeline in 2004.

view that I was 'past it', playing (as Sir Brian Lochore had put it) 'old man's rugby'. But as the NPC had progressed they noticed a distinct change, that I was outplaying my main rivals. They thought that my scrummaging was strong, my mobility around the track was good, and my lineout throwing was reasonable but could be worked on. Plus the Oliver package came with a fair amount of experience for just the sort of situations the All Blacks were heading for, and that mattered a great deal to the new coaches. The Highlanders' difficulties, and all of the media babble surrounding it, were of no interest to the new trio.

So the two old cagey bulls sat at the café table and Steve outlined his thoughts on the lineouts the All Blacks were going to use on tour, how they worked and why, and explained the system of calling — all of it information perfectly normal in my professional life and hardly any news to me. I kept thinking: is this it? Surely there has to be more? Of course, beneath this superficial conversation there was, so I decided to end the charade and take the initiative with the intention of allaying some fears. I told him that I wanted no part in the lineout organisation, that I had enough on my plate trying to get the ball where it was supposed to be, and that was all I wanted to focus on. If he wanted me to, I would be happy to work on helping improve our scrum and other aspects of forward play generally, but as for lineouts, I just wanted to be told where to throw the ball and do it well.

I think this was what Hansen wanted to hear. Whatever reputations may have been pinned to my lapel, this Oliver was not going to be difficult; and I did like what I was seeing of Steve Hansen.

In Auckland the following week, I was told in the third training run that I was going to get the start for the first test. I was elated and ecstatic to hear that I would be running out with the number two on my back. It meant that I had a chance to get involved early in the tour and feel like I was making a contribution towards the team effort. As there were three hookers in the touring squad I wasn't sure how much game time was going to come my way and, for that matter, when, so the early selection stopped me thinking and worrying about the future and forced me to focus on a test match in under 10 days' time. Outside of training I had noticed that the team had a positive, relaxed, focused feeling and, above all, a feeling of equanimity, which hasn't always been my experience in All Black camps.

It turned out there were some obvious reasons for this harmonious team feeling.

As an outsider watching the All Blacks' performances earlier in the year, it was clear to me that they were getting worse as the season progressed. The commitment and teamwork had been magnificent against England. Everybody — pundits and 'experts' alike — agreed with that. But slowly, inexorably, their play became less assured, less clinical and less energetic. The players were clearly disconsolate after losing the last two games in the Tri-nations and there was more than a little criticism and disquiet in the air. The defeat by South Africa and some of the after-hours nonsense following that game were to be a watershed for Henry and his manager Darren Shand. It was plain that the team could not continue like this. Some swift and decisive action needed to be taken.

Henry met with captain Tana Umaga and deputy Richie McCaw. After discussion they promoted the idea of selecting a group of players with leadership qualities who looked as if they had a long-term future in the All Blacks, and agreed that this group would meet often during the NPC competition and prepare the way ahead for the All Blacks' end-of-year tour and beyond. Player empowerment? Absolutely.

I should make it clear that I was not part of that group, but during our many long bus trips on tour, the guys down the back of the bus told me about the process they went through. The group was 11 strong in the end and met half a dozen times on Sundays during the NPC. At these meetings the players told Henry, Hansen and Smith exactly what they thought of the previous campaign and what the All Blacks meant to them. The coaches were told that the players felt they had over-trained, that the team was flat and needed more time off, and that they felt too much time was spent emphasising the history, tradition and mana associated with the All Blacks, and that the weight this gave to the jersey was, contrary to the accepted wisdom, a massive impediment to winning games. In short, many felt inhibited by the expectations to the point whereby the constant references to the All Blacks' past glory days were affecting our ability to perform: the intensity was such that a fear of failure was at times crippling the players.

I'm told that, initially, the coaches had trouble understanding this attitude. They felt that the past could be used as a great motivator and should not be neglected. But the players were saying they had a deep respect for the past, but did not wish to revere it. They thought it should not be used in such a way that it intimidates and, ultimately, inhibits confidence.

The players wanted to assert that they were the All Blacks of today. This is our time, they said. The jersey may change and the people who wear it may change, but what hasn't changed over the years is the blackness of the jersey and the silver fern. Their concept of what it is to be an All Black today was bound to that. And that was the basis for the way in which they wanted to stride forth and create their identity for the future.

Henry, to his credit, listened. And in doing so he, along with the players, set the foundations for a very successful tour.

As I said, I was not included in these discussions, but I am told that the leadership group also felt that there needed to be more emphasis on the haka; education was needed about its meaning and what role it played.

For it to be truly meaningful to them, the players themselves wanted to decide when and where the haka should be performed, not have that dictated to them by sponsors or the New Zealand Rugby Union Board.

By the time we left Auckland for the northern hemisphere, after three days together, we had an established and effective working group of players who had met regularly during the NPC. This leadership group had the blessing and trust of the management and had assumed real responsibilities in setting team standards — how the players were going to be led both on and off the field.

For my part I was thrilled to be involved again in one of the most privileged and exciting things that a New Zealand rugby player can do — touring as an All Black.

We arrived in Rome on a Saturday morning and as our first training run wasn't until the Monday, I vowed to make the most of any free time to explore the city.

When I was last in Rome in 2000, I found it the most extraordinary, captivating city I had seen. History literally seemed present under every step. New and millennium-old buildings meld in ways that seem natural. It is a magical place, rich in culture and art, and I was delighted to be able to gaze upon sculptures and paintings by some of the world's great masters.

I love history and find art history the most fascinating, colourful, intriguing and informative way to study the past. I was not brought up with a strong background in the arts, and it was only in my mid to late twenties that I discovered a latent passion for art and art history. Now, not only am I learning about art, the artists and the artistic movements they were involved in and what they represented, but also about myself.

Anyhow, I managed to visit the main attractions, and as in 2000 was most taken with the sheer presence of the Pantheon and the magnificence of the Vatican and Sistine Chapel. During the week the team was escorted into the Vatican for a private tour, which culminated in a 15-minute stay in the Sistine Chapel — and we were allowed to take photographs! That was an extraordinary situation, just the team and a few guards in the midst of one of the most celebrated artistic creations ever. That experience will always stay with me.

Training on Monday was the first chance to get the cobwebs out of the system and have a good run around. We trained well that day and all week, so by the time the captain's run on Friday was completed we were ready to play.

The hotel was starting to feel claustrophobic, so as I often do the day before a big game, I went for a wander by myself and used that time for quiet contemplation. The Villa Borghese gallery is a museum full of Bernini sculpture and Caravaggio works and it was there that I spent the afternoon. Bernini's works were fabulous; I was taken with the unbelievable level of detail, and his ability to encapsulate movement and drama so graphically in stone with such palpable realism, and on such a large scale.

The Caravaggio paintings that I saw, for the first time, truly showed me chiaroscuro, a technique where extreme contrasts of light and dark are used for dramatic effect. More than with any other painter I felt a realism and deep brooding in his work, and I decided I wanted to learn more about him.

Unusually for me, prior to the test I had no nerves at all; I felt relaxed and at ease with everything around me. It was a peaceful state, not emotional in any way. We bussed to the ground, walked around for a bit, then started warming up and finally ran out onto the field focused and ready.

Just after we ran on the field Norm came up to me and said, 'Bro, let it all go, we got nothing to fear anymore,' and I understood exactly what he meant. The game was an easy victory for us,

Stadio Flaminio, Rome, November 13 2004. I'm ninth from left and Norm Maxwell is next to me. 'Maxey' was right when he said we had nothing to fear anymore.

as the Italians didn't really turn up to play and our backs played well. I got subbed with 10 to go and Corey Flynn came on as my replacement.

It was a happy mood in the shed; we had won and played well in patches with several of the boys playing their first test. Once we had showered and changed into our suits, the new test inductees were presented with their first and only test tie, usually by someone of significance to them: be it a close mate or an old hand in their position. The tie is presented with a speech and then accepted with some words where the new test player has the floor and greets the rest of his comrades for the first time as a true All Black. This is a time-honoured tradition and an integral thread of the cultural tapestry that makes up the All Blacks.

Touring life never stops and we were up early the next day on the bus off to the airport en route to Cardiff where we were to play Wales.

We had a meeting on arrival at our hotel in Cardiff and I was to be a reserve in the next test. As a bench player you have a different mindset from those starting. You still have to know all of the moves but you are not on edge mentally to anywhere near the same degree.

A reserve can waste too much energy being tight as a drum and having no game as an outlet. On the bench, a player needs to be able to assess the game and observe, then once on the field reverse the process and become closely involved in the game. This is impossible to do if your focus is too narrow and arousal levels too high, so you practise the ability all week of switching on then off, as most of the training time goes to the starting 15.

So I found myself more relaxed leading into the game but also found that there wasn't much to explore in the city. Quite frankly, Cardiff was the antithesis to Rome, so with little very stimulating outdoors I stayed indoors, read a book and played my guitar for most of the week.

While we were in Cardiff, Wayne Smith suggested we visit the Angel Hotel and have a beer there for Keith Murdoch, in an effort to bury ghosts of the past and right wrongs. Murdoch, a prop on tour with the All Blacks in 1972, was involved in a late-night scuffle with a security guard and within 24 hours had been ushered onto a plane and sent home. The consensus is that Murdoch was treated very badly, shamed and humiliated. He got off the plane in Australia and disappeared into the outback for years.

We were fortunate to have veteran photographer Peter Bush with us on tour. 'Bushy' was able to give us an account of how he saw it, and he also took his camera along to document our visit. It was a cathartic experience, the first official visit to the pub by an All Black team since that tour. Too many years had been allowed to slip by. We felt like we had gone back to restore the mana of one of us.

I shared the occasion, and a pint of Guinness, with Sir Brian Lochore. Sir Brian is a quite remarkable fellow. As large as a Massey Ferguson, with tons of humility and wisdom, he was hugely respected by young and old in the touring party. Lochore was able to honestly appraise the new and accept much of it without allowing his views to be clouded by rose-tinted comparisons with his heyday. Unlike some of his peers, he wasn't keen to remind us how little players of his era had to come and go on. I have never told him this, but I always tried to sit near him at meal times. He usually had some interesting anecdotes to tell if you asked him the right questions.

In memory of Murdoch . . . sharing a pint with Sir Brian Lochore at the Angel Hotel in Cardiff.

We won the test on the Saturday night in a tight game; the Welsh had improved immeasurably over the previous five years but we showed enough composure to close the game out when it looked like it could have gone either way.

On the Monday, when I was named in the team for the test against France, to say I was shocked is an understatement. I had heard a whisper that I might be starting but didn't believe it. Keven Mealamu had played very well against the Welsh, particularly when the game freed up and he got to use his great running game. So when my name was read out I was utterly surprised and felt as though I didn't really deserve to be playing. Keven was clearly unlucky not to be named in the starting 15. After the team was announced I went over, shook his hand and told him so, and he being the decent, humble man he is said something along the lines of, 'Mate, you deserve to be there. You have had an awesome year — go hard.' Selfless and generous, yet those familiar with Keven know that is the only way he can be.

We didn't leave for Paris until Tuesday afternoon, which I was privately miffed about; I would rather spend days in Paris than Cardiff. The main training focus for the forwards that week was on scrums. The French had an impressive scrum and we all knew that they gained immense confidence from dominating the opposition in the tight. To prepare for this we did plenty of live scrum work against each other: with such a large touring party we had the numbers to do this. Live scrums at training are fine if both packs comply with the training objectives; they are an abomination if the test team hasn't been picked and men are trying to prove their worth. Look out, for the fists can fly.

Fortunately, there was none of that. The sessions were very constructive thanks to good planning by Cron and Hansen and the forwards' understanding of what was trying to be achieved: we managed to simulate what we thought the French would do to us and how we would counter them.

However, on Thursday I had had enough of practising how we would cope with the French and let forth a bit of a tirade halfway through either Hansen's or Cron's speech. The gist of my outburst was that we had done enough thinking and worrying about the French, put that in the bank and bury it. Now it was time for us to focus 100 per cent on what we were going to do to them, at every physical contact situation. They can worry about us, I said.

From then on our attitude was that of the hunter, not the hunted.

I'm not sure how that went down with the coaches. Nothing ever got said to me but a few of the boys approached me and said, 'Good on you; that was needed.'

On the Wednesday I went to the Musée d'Orsay, a building brilliantly transformed from its original role as a railway station to a gallery for French Impressionist art. Light poured in and, unlike most museums, its voluminous interior didn't feel claustrophobic. I was like a little kid trying to find his hidden Easter eggs, for I wanted to make the Impressionists' works a priority and then, if I had time, look elsewhere.

Eventually after wandering in and out of many alcoves and side alleys, I found my way to the fifth floor where most of the 'good stuff' was on show. Armed with my skeletal knowledge about Impressionism I soon enhanced my appreciation of works by artists such as Monet, Renoir, Pissaro, Cézanne, Sisley, Manet and Van Gogh. It was quite a different experience from the great Renaissance works that I had been viewing in Rome a week before but no less exciting or interesting.

Prior to the test in Wales Graham Henry had asked me to prepare a speech to be delivered to the team in the build-up to the French test. I didn't think much of the request initially; unbeknown to me Smith had suggested to Henry that I talk to the team about the greater significance of the game, as I had done the same for him in 2000 when the All Blacks had toured France.

I had no real brief, but it was suggested I talk about Dave Gallaher, the first All Black captain, the man after whom the trophy we were playing for on Saturday was named.

I had actually forgotten about the talk until Henry asked me at lunch, 'Can you do your speech tomorrow?'

So that night when I started to think about Gallaher and the man he was, it soon became apparent to me that in order to describe him, I had to paint a picture of the times he and other New Zealanders were living in some 90 years ago. That meant talking about the war and why Gallaher found himself in France, and what New Zealand's involvement in the war meant.

I sat up most of the night sourcing material off the Internet, cutting and pasting, and weaving in my own narrative. I got our analyst Wayne Richards, a whiz with computers, and Marc Weakley from allblacks.com to help me with some images that I had selected for showing on a projected screen at specific times during my speech. I practised it once in the morning and went down to the team room where everyone was waiting for me.

This is some of what I said, using both sourced material and my own words.

Initially known as The Originals, Gallaher's 1905 team toured the UK, losing only once, 0–3 to Wales, in the test featuring the infamous disallowed try to Bob Deans. The significance of the French connection to Gallaher's team was that it was France's first rugby test, a game the All Blacks won 38–6. Ernest Booth, a team-mate, said of Gallaher: 'Dave was a man of sterling worth . . . girded by great self-determination and self-control, he was a valuable friend and could be, I think, a remorseless foe. To us All Blacks his words would often be, "Give nothing away, take no chances".'

In 1916 Gallaher was 43, married, with an eight-year-old daughter — who said she remembered him 'as a jolly man' — and had already served in the Boer War as a sergeant-major in the 10th NZ Mounted Rifles and seen a lot of war. He had no need to volunteer and would have been exempt from conscription but he enlisted in July 1916. His younger brother had been killed in France so he lied about his age, left his wife and child and marched into camp. He left New Zealand for the last time in February 1917.

After a few months Gallaher was promoted to sergeant and sent to France to join the 2nd Auckland Battalion.

After passing through Ypres (in Belgium, near the border with France) the soldiers found their way in the dark to their trenches. This was across planks laid over a swamp with stray bullets and shells falling around them. It took hours to get there and their new home was a line of holes scraped into the mud. They settled down to wait.

They were to be sent in on 5 October to attack towards the village of Passchendaele. This stands on the ridge above Ypres, just 10 minutes' drive away. It took the allies from July to November 1917 to reach it and over a million men died in the process. The Kiwis were just one small part of this huge battle. They were to attack under cover of a heavy artillery barrage. One wave would go in and establish a line. Then a second wave would leapfrog through them and push on to the final objectives. Then they would dig in and wait for reinforcements.

I told of the lethal artillery barrages and of how up to five per cent of our casualties were caused by so-called 'friendly fire' from our own forces. When David Gallaher climbed from the trench and began walking across no-man's-land, he would have been carrying about 60 pounds of equipment. The ground was torn up and treacherous.

They walked into heavy machine-gun fire. All their officers were hit. The men tried out the drills they had practised so often and one by one wiped out the machine-gun posts. They had taken their final objectives by 11 a.m. They started digging in and getting ready for the inevitable German counterattacks. These came at regular intervals until darkness and were all shattered by artillery. The Kiwis held the ground they took.

David Gallaher wasn't there. He had been shot in the face as they walked from the trenches. He was taken to an Australian first aid post and died there of his wounds.

The New Zealand Division suffered 1200 casualties in this one attack. Of these, 390 were fatalities. The attack was called a great success. A week later they attacked again and this time it was a debacle. With no support and in thigh-deep mud they flung themselves at uncut barbed wire while German machine-gunners scythed them away. In just two hours over 1000 men died and another 2000 were wounded. It is one of the worst man-made disasters in New Zealand's history. And it achieved nothing.

At this point, for reasons that I explained at the end of my presentation, 13 players were asked to stand. I said, 'Carl Hayman, Dan Carter, Ali Williams, Ma'a Nonu, Reuben Thorne, Piri Weepu, Jerry Collins, Casey Laulala, Mils Muliaina, Rico Gear, Richie McCaw, Jimmy Cowan, Marty Holah, stand please.'

I then pointed out that about 18,000 New Zealanders died during the Great War, a higher percentage per capita than any other Allied nation. The population of New Zealand at the time was about one million, so 18,000 killed is a huge proportion for such a small country. The dead still lie in Turkey, France, Egypt and Palestine. The war affected everyone: Maori, Pakeha, rich, poor, trade unionist or Tory, virtually no one escaped the effects of the war in some way. Men came home blind, mutilated, shell-shocked. People grieved for the loss of a son or a brother or a husband. We still live with the effects.

Many New Zealanders went into the war as 'sons and daughters of the Empire' but they came out as Kiwis. They knew they were different from the Australians, the Canadians, the English and all the rest. They had their own ways of doing things and their own ways of thinking. New Zealand's sense of nationhood emerged from the war. New rituals such as Anzac Day came from it and a new sense of what it meant to be a New Zealander. We are still working out what this means at the start of a new century but everyone agrees that it means something important. That's why thousands of young Kiwis stand at Anzac Cove a long way from home on 25 April.

Then I said, 'Thirteen All Blacks were killed in the First World War, guys mostly the same age as us, mates. And probably not too dissimilar either in our goals and aspirations as people, to love and be loved, enjoy life and be happy.'
The 13 were then told to sit down. It was a quiet room.

As I filed out of the room with the rest of the boys to go to training, Sir Brian gave me a nod and a handshake and said, 'Well done, lad.'

A shirt with a message we didn't 'forget' — 45-6 is as good as it gets against the French on their soil.

We went along to the Stade de France for our captain's run early on Friday afternoon. I had good memories of the ground and immediately took a shine to it again: we had won here in 2000, the first time the All Blacks had beaten the French on Armistice Day and the first time we had played for the Dave Gallaher Trophy. As with the other captain's runs we did a haka on the field after the training. It was eerie, an empty stadium and us going full on.

I kicked a ball around and had a bit of fun while the kickers were practising shots at goal, and generally switched off mentally. All the work had been done, now it was just a matter of waiting.

I had planned to go to the Rodin museum but we trained late in the afternoon and so I had run out of time due to our late arrival back at the hotel. I was rooming by myself and so was left to my own thoughts. I like it. I'm used to my own company, having lived alone for a couple of years now. As my rugby career has unfolded my tendency to seek my own company has become more obvious to me. The issue for me now is not to become too isolated from others. I have learnt to read the signs when I am becoming too introverted and all that it requires is a trip to the team room where I come out of my cocoon. The main bonus of having your own room is there are no snorers!

The night before the French test I went to the team room and watched a movie with Byron Kelleher and Carl Hayman, then headed off to bed for a good sleep.

The game was a late one so we had the whole day to deal with; other than reading and watching a movie I can't remember anything of any real significance that I did. That is often the way before night rugby, just killing time.

I packed my bag and listened to some relaxing music then headed down to a quick meeting and onto the bus. The traffic was heavy and we had a long trip ahead so I curled up and went to sleep. That doesn't always happen, but on this night I seemed to be relaxed and found resisting sleep an impossibility.

Once we were at the ground we went through the same preparation that the team does for every test and before I knew it the 15 were alone in a huddle, arms linked in a surprisingly quiet room, before a knock on the door disturbed the silence and we were told: 'Time to go.'

Waves of emotion broke over me as we were running out from under the stands. I felt terribly proud. It was as if the tunnel wasn't big enough for me to get through, such was the effect of being back in black. We sung the anthems and I fixed my gaze on a small group of men dressed in black suits singing along with me. They were the rest of our touring party and management sitting in the stand. At that stage, to me the only Kiwis that existed were them and the boys to the left and right of me. It was us against the rest.

The haka was a goodie, and we threw ourselves into the opening moments of the game. Fast, furious, almost frantic. Then came the first scrum. They got a good hit on us and we folded a bit. The same thing happened in the next scrum, but we managed to regroup and go right over the top of them. And when the mass imploded my knee ended up smack in the face of one of the opposition. From then on we had both the psychological and physical edge, and they were spent.

Initially their front row engaged in lots of sideways glances and not much talk, but as their uneasiness intensified they started unloading on each other. I sat back and kept pushing. Before the game it was agreed that I would play 40 minutes then Keven would come on for the other 40, but I found myself walking out of the tunnel at the start of the second half.

Ten minutes later, during a stoppage, I saw Tana and Richie McCaw arguing with the referee. So I stuck my big beak in to try to figure out what all the commotion was about. 'Golden oldies,' said Richie, in reference to the referee deciding to revert to a no-push scrum at France's request. A great deal has been made of the look this elicited from me, and many and varied are

Preparing to engage the French front row at Stade de France. From the second scrum of the match we gained both the physical and psychological advantage.

the interpretations of just what I was thinking. Well, it was this: You must be joking! We have been working on these buggers for the last 50 minutes and are just starting to get some real ascendancy, and now they are pulling the plug!

But I also felt a sense of satisfaction at having outmuscled our opposition and I know Hayman and Woodcock did too. It turned out to be the death knell for Norm Maxwell and me, though, for without the scrummaging and physical aspect we were no longer needed; we were both subbed at the same time. As we walked off, Norm started cursing the fact that we were being subbed as he was just starting to feel really good and wanted to keep playing.

I sat in the stand and couldn't believe how quiet it was. The place was full — possibly around 80,000 people — so the silence was surreal. And as is always the case when golden oldies scrums are decreed, the game became a scrappy affair, principally because suddenly there are 10 tight forwards with more energy than they know what to do with, and therefore they get in everyone's way.

We won by a big margin, 45–6, and the reserves went down to join the rest of the team on the field where lots of hugs, handshakes, high fives and many other handshake derivations were being exchanged. It was such a fantastic feeling to know that we had won the match and in such an emphatic manner. Spontaneously the team decided to thank our supporters in the crowd, for there were many Kiwis cheering us on, and we went around the field, Dave Gallaher Trophy in tow, waving and thanking them for their support.

The euphoria intensified in the shed as it was just the team and management again and I sat with my front-row mates having a beer, utterly consumed by the feeling of that moment. I had a smile from ear to ear. A lot of New Zealanders were happy because they saw our victory as a return to so-called good old-fashioned, traditional-style forward play backed up with

Fulltime at Stade de France. Byron Kelleher has his hand on my shoulder. I have my hand on the Dave Gallaher Trophy. How sweet it was.

resolute tackling and, when the opportunities were there, exciting, attacking back play. We had played 15-man rugby all right, but only after we had got 'control up front'. This was a victory for those who said rugby was, first, fury and strength up front, not froth from the outset. We had played like a team truly unified and had given all-round unpretentious effort, where we had done the basics well and the boys had played with passion. We'd done a demolition job and our supporters loved it.

Maybe, too, talk of Dave Gallaher and what he represented might have steeled us and driven us to a fine performance. Who knows, but I'd like to think that my Gallaher presentation had a positive effect.

I was asked to go outside and do an interview with one of the New Zealand television networks that were covering the game. It had been a fantastic day and had meant a great deal to me and I know that came through in the interviews that I and others gave in the post-match media melee.

Interview over, back inside the shed, we decided to shut the door of our changing room and do a haka just for us, so we faced the management and let one rip, a very private moment for the team. This, I thought, is what we play for. For me that one game erased all of the bad memories and, again, I was graphically reminded of how few such satisfying times I'd had in the previous couple of years.

I showered and changed and then had to make a speech for Tane Norton who was stepping down as president of the NZRU, and was also off home as his mum was ailing. I missed most of the test dinner as I had a drugs test to perform; then it was onto the bus for a boisterous trip home. We got to the hotel, unpacked and had a meal together before dispersing into the Paris night.

Later, after meeting friends in a pub off the Champs Elysées, and then having a couple with a few of the guys in our hotel house bar, I ducked downstairs to the toilet which was next to our team room. There I stumbled across Joe Rokocoko and about 30 Fijians who had come out of the woodwork for a kava session. I accepted their invitation to come in — well, I didn't have an option, really — and sat down.

This was my first kava session so I wasn't sure what was required. Luckily Ma'a Nonu turned up and sat next to me and every now and then gave me a nudge on what to do. I was the only white guy, or Palagi as the Islanders call us, there. It was fun. I sang songs that I didn't know the words to and clapped away and sipped kava. My lips started going numb; it wasn't the most palatable of drinks.

It was about 6 a.m. by the time we finished and I went straight in for breakfast with Carl Hayman. I told him I was off to get a couple of hours' sleep before we left, which, from memory, was to be about 9.30 a.m. I was stuffed. He asked whether he should come and wake me and I said I would be fine.

The next thing I knew I was being violently shaken by Steve Hansen and Ma'a Nonu, my buddy for time checks, saying I was late and that everybody was on the bus and waiting for me. Bloody hell! I was sitting bolt upright with my gear on and there was a huge flurry to pack my bags before we left.

I felt like an idiot, a senior player letting the side down by committing the ultimate sin, being late. It was odd and disappointing that, after everything I had learned in all the years that had passed since my debut in a test — where I was also late the morning after — I was still capable of making the same fundamental error.

All I can say, lamely, is who needs sleeping pills when you have a skinful of kava?

From the bus to the train station and two hours later we are in London, once again on the move. At this point I knew I had not been picked to play in our final game on tour, against the Barbarians at Twickenham. I had already started in two of the first three tests and was a reserve in the other so it was no surprise to me that Corey Flynn was to start with Mealamu on the bench.

Of course, I would have liked to play but wasn't concerned about the prospect of missing it: the important games were over. Then Flynn damaged a hamstring muscle on the Monday, which put me on stand-by for the whole week. A tricky position to be in: neither in the team nor out of it, so I had to prepare both physically and mentally as if I was going to play. Flynn failed a fitness test the day before the game so with 20 minutes to go the coaches put me on. We won the game 47–19.

During the week the reserves and the boys who weren't playing on the weekend were required to travel to central London most days for various promotional activities. As we were based on the outskirts of London this made the journey a two-and-a-half-hour round trip. I did that trip six times in six days.

Norm, Byron Kelleher and I sat at the back of the bus, in the 'back seat'. This was recognition of our time in the jersey and also a sign of respect from the leadership group who had selected the role for us. The further a player makes his way down in seating order to the back of the bus, the more time and seniority he has attained in the team. This is a hierarchy of players whose function has historically varied from basically running the team to, as is the case presently, being figureheads only.

On one of these trips in the back seat, Norm and I had a long talk about test matches and what they really meant to us. As has often been the case in our friendship we broached topics that usually are considered sacrosanct among the team because they require a need for absolute honesty. We talked about the myths of what the All Blacks are said to play for.

Our view was that a high proportion of New Zealand rugby supporters believe that playing for one's country is the main thing that drives an All Black to give his best. Of course, that is highly significant, and I commented to Norm that it was something I was far more aware of when I was younger, but neither of us thought it was the main driver. We both agreed that when we're on the field listening to the New Zealand anthem, we're not thinking of family and friends and other New Zealanders and vowing to play well for them.

I said to Norm that I thought a great many people see the All Blacks and the code we are said to live by as part of our country's mythology. That mythology takes the form of people believing that a love of one's country drives All Blacks to play with the utmost passion, and that All Blacks will be stoical and show no pain. Also, more tellingly, people appear to want me as an All Black to think and act like this because they believe that if they had their chance to wear the black jersey, if they could stand and sing the anthem and perform the haka, that is what they would and should be feeling. As a consequence expectations of us are weighty.

Norm and I agreed that a test match wasn't really about preparing ourselves physically for the battle, but instead it was about meeting one's fears and deep-seated anxieties head-on, for there is nowhere to hide. Every player has such anxieties, be it worrying about catching kick-offs, or getting lineouts right, or not missing tackles, or catching and dropping the ball, kicking well and kicking goals. These are all skill-based fears. But there are plenty of other worries about performance.

All players ask such questions, have such fears. However, not all rugby players play major tests in front of tens of thousands of people, a great many of whom are craving a victory.

In our opinion, the essence of the pressures surrounding the build-up to a test was facing a week of fine-tuning and controlling both body and soul. That means managing negative thoughts, self-doubt and public or private expectations to the point where, come the match, you function properly and play well.

I said to Norm that I doubted many people quite know what it is like to have to deal with such an array of pressures, where private battles are subject to intense, regular scrutiny — regionally, nationally, internationally. People seem to assess your character and attributes as a person on the basis of their observations of how you perform on-field.

This is what separates our job from others: its public nature and the scrutiny that All Blacks receive. I've often found it emotionally draining being a professional sportsperson, not that I've made a point of whingeing about it, for the rewards in all sorts of ways are wonderful. To be any good you have to put yourself out there every week and ask questions that often seem to have no firm answers. I have found — and I'm sure many players feel similarly — it is extremely taxing emotionally lifting oneself to perform for a big game every week. Afterwards, one day off, then you start the whole thing all over again. When I've been playing well it's been an easy process, and when I haven't been it's become a real mental quagmire, but mostly over the course of a season it is utterly draining. Player burnout is often associated with the physical, but I always associate it with the mental.

Norm said that prior to the French test he was really looking forward to the game, for how often in the course of a life do such chances present themselves? He wanted to see how far he had come in his absence from the All Blacks, not as a player but as a person: that was his real test.

My major realisation on tour was that while I really respected the jersey, and felt incredibly lucky and thankful to be an All Black again, what I got teary-eyed and chest-puffy about was an intense feeling of nationalism. Given my background and abilities, playing a test for the All Blacks provided the ultimate stage on which I was able to express my passion at being a New Zealander. I wasn't playing *for* my country, I was running out *as* a Kiwi and pretty damned proud of that. I think being on tour away from home has always brought that out of me, especially having our war history brought to my attention when overseas.

After the Barbarians game we had dinner and came home to our hotel and had a team drink together where everybody got the opportunity to stand up and say their piece regarding the tour. I was taken by some of the guys' thoughts, and particularly how they expressed them, especially with Mils Muliaina. Afterwards Mils and I had a chat and I commented on his words. For his part, he said that seeing me cry before the Italian game really affected him and many of the other boys he had talked to, because it showed how much it meant to me and, even more than that, how much it still meant to me after having been an All Black for 10 years.

Once an All Black, always an All Black. How often has a top rugby player heard that said? But, if ever I was sceptical about that cliché, or how proud and lucky one is to call oneself a New Zealander, I'm not now.

Chapter 2

A Big Little Guy

When it came to naming their third son on the ninth of September 1975, Frank and Marilyn Oliver, my parents, both agreed that my first name would be Anton. Dad was playing rugby for the Marist Club in Invercargill where he locked the scrum with a large red-headed man whose name was Father Anton McLean.

Dad liked McLean, thought he was a good man, and liked his name — Anton. Dad also said that when I was born my name was further cemented as I was a chubby kid and I looked like a big teddy bear, much the same as Father McLean was off the field.

As for Mum, she had been a nurse working in the local hospital where she had met a doctor named Anton de Croos. Dr de Croos was of Sri Lankan descent and Mum said that she admired him as he was such a 'gentle, polite person' and she also liked the name Anton.

Dad was one of nine children. His father, also called Frank, was wounded in the Second World War and was captured by the Germans. After the war, he was foreman cooper at Speight's brewery in Dunedin, then ran his own business making concrete posts and other things in Lawrence, about 80 km west of Dunedin. Dad's mother, Evelyn, when she wasn't looking after her large family, cooked at the local hotel to help put the kids through high school.

My mother was brought up in Tokanui, a windswept, rigorous settlement on the south coast about 60 km east of Invercargill in Southland. Mum, who trained as a nurse at Kew Hospital, was one of five children. When her father, Lester Briggs, returned from four years' fighting in the Second World War, he and his wife, Edith, went farming.

Mum and Dad met in unusual circumstances and at rather a late hour — at four in the morning in Invercargill. She was in an ambulance attending an accident; he was a policeman. They started seeing each other. Before long my brother Mark was conceived, they were married, and in succession after Mark came Brent then me. Mark is five years older than me, and Brent two years. In 1976, Dad left the police and we moved to Tuatapere where he became a fisherman. At the time Dad was playing as a lock for Southland. We then moved to Milton in South Otago where Dad got a job in forestry and started playing for Otago. This would have been late 1977 or early 1978.

Mum says I was a big kid, over 10 pounds at birth and a 'terror'. She'd dress me for school but I'd arrive there having discarded long pants, shoes and socks, and would be spotted running around in shorts and bare feet in the most appalling weather, frosts, rain, the lot. Teachers complained to Mum, implying she wasn't dressing me properly. I always seemed to have stubbed toes and blood and nicks here and there.

There was a big backyard at home and as kids we played everything: cricket and rugby especially. Being younger than Mark and Brent, I was a bit off the pace, but I loved participating and playing, as it was all fun to me. We nearly drove Mum crazy. She recalls we broke 15 windows so, as we got older, at every opportunity she sent us along to the nearby rugby grounds beside State Highway 1.

Mum slaved to support us, working night shift because that paid best. She was always there in the morning before we went to school, and she was awake and up when we got home in the afternoon. For three years Mum made do with five to six hours of sleep a day until her health

started to deteriorate. She had a few boarders and her three boys managed to drive most of them away. (By this time Dad was living in Palmerston North; my parents divorced in 1979, and I have no memories of Dad being with us in Milton.)

I can't remember ever going without essentials like good food or clothing. We got Christmas and birthday presents, and new footwear. Mum refused to allow us to wear second-hand shoes or boots. So we weren't poor, but there weren't any frills. Three hungry, sometimes destructive, growing boys are expensive to

Below: The Oliver clan before my parents Frank and Marilyn divorced. I'm second from left. Next to me is Mark and opposite is Brent. Left: Aged about two with my puppy Smoke. Below left: Mark, me and Brent.

keep, especially in a solo-parent home. I've always seen my mother as brave and dependable, qualities that count for a lot in people. They are among the things I look for most in others and I hope they are imbued in me. If they are, it's because they originate in my mother's example to me and my brothers.

Footie loomed large. I pestered Mum, wanted to play in teams with my older brothers. Because I was too young to take part, she dressed me in rugby gear and boots and I ran up and down the sideline happily while the others were on the field playing. Then when I began playing all I can remember are the bus trips, the tries I scored — I was bigger than other boys my age — and the lollies we were given afterwards. How I loved those lollies.

Mum recalls that, from the first, teachers told her: 'Anton is always looking after the underdog', which in part may be why at school my best friend was a boy named Devon Shanks who lived close by, and who had spina bifida. We must have made a strange-looking pair. I recall getting into a fight in the playground with bigger kids who had been picking on him. Devon took off the plastic mouldings he wore to help him walk and bashed the other kids with them. Devon has since represented New Zealand at skiing.

Once, aged about five, and throwing a childhood tantrum, I threatened to run away from home. That flight for freedom took me as far as the garden shed — I didn't have the courage to even leave the property.

Mum says I was a cuddly kid who used to suck his thumb, a kid who was less aggressive than his brothers. All that thumb sucking gave me an odd bite-pattern, a legacy evident in my mirror every day.

Occasionally Mum took us down to Toko Mouth for outings by the sea, and I'll never forget my first trip to Dunedin, about 55 km away. We went to see the film *Rocky* in the Octagon, in the middle of Dunedin. I couldn't believe how big the city was, and whenever I heard anyone talk about 'the world' I thought they meant Dunedin.

Mum thought it important that her three boys had at least some contact with our father, and Dad wanted to see us as well. Our first plane flight to Palmerston North was traumatic; we all cried our eyes out. The emotion of leaving Mum for the first time was overwhelming, we were all scared by the plane and the noise it made, and going to a faraway place was very unsettling. The hostesses must have wondered what was going on. We were all air sick and, embarrassed, left the sick bags under our seats.

The decision was made to leave Milton. Mum was feeling the pressure and needed some additional support, so her parents drove down from Blenheim and helped us pack up. It wasn't hard to leave Milton. When you are young there's not a lot to look back on. I sat in the front seat of Grandad's old Zephyr the whole interminable way north to Blenheim. Once there Brent and I enrolled at Springlands School and Mark started at Marlborough Boys' College. Our grandparents' house was conveniently situated only two doors away from Springlands School, so Brent and I stayed there after school had finished and waited until Mum was home from work.

I was becoming an even bigger little guy, so much so that a special desk had to be made for me. When I managed to worm my big pins under the one I was originally given, the legs of the desk floated two or three inches off the floor.

I had no difficulty making new friends at Springlands. Making friends has never been a problem for me, although so far I have had very few really close friends. One of my new mates played rugby for the Opawa Club so I joined him. At training we generally played bullrush instead of proper rugby and that was even more fun. Blenheim suited me in other ways too: I could go everywhere on a bike.

I got pocket money by doing odd jobs for Grandma and Grandad. He was a stickler; things had to be right, and like many old diggers his toolshed was immaculate. Every time I cleaned the car or mowed the lawns he inspected my work and he always found something that needed rectifying; until I fixed it I didn't get paid.

Grandad Briggs became a kind of surrogate father for me. As I got older, he occasionally shouted me a glass of beer when I had done a good job. He had grown up on a farm and he taught me about plants, how to look after a garden and to make good compost. Before the war he'd worked in a family butchery and he showed me how to skin and cut up a sheep. Now and then he took me along to the Returned Servicemen's Association (RSA) and we played snooker on the big tables there. At the RSA, he sometimes shouted me a drink and had a few himself. I won a few games of snooker but can't recall ever winning a series against him. He'd grin and come out with the old one about his snooker ability being evidence of a 'misspent youth'.

In my last year at school it was clear, when he was drinking beer with his mates at the RSA, that he was proud of showing off a grandson who was head boy at the local high school, and was captain of this and that sports team. I owe him plenty, not least for all the repair jobs he did on tyres and other parts of my bikes! He had some rather harsh things to say about other peoples — wartime hangovers one could say — but given his experiences, I decided it was better not to challenge him on certain issues. When he'd had a few, bad memories from the war surfaced unexpectedly, and on one occasion he mistook Mum for a Nazi and said he was going to hurt her.

But I have got a little ahead of myself. At the age of nine or ten I was the fastest kid in my class and won all the sprints, and when I took part in the long jump, the pit wasn't long enough. Mum wanted me to wear footwear but I wouldn't; I insisted on bare feet.

My best friend was William Nelson. It was another odd match. William was a tiny, fair-skinned kid, the son of recent immigrants from England whose mum (also a nurse) worked with my mother. The Nelsons lived in a massive house on four to five acres. To William and me it was like having a jungle to play in and often it was just on dark before I got home. Both William and his father were keen on soccer and we played it all the time. In hindsight I can see that I learnt a lot from the Nelsons: they seemed like a happy nuclear family and strike me now as having had a passive, liberal outlook on life. For instance, in summer they got rid of their TV and during the daylight-saving months they spent a lot of time on family-oriented activities, reading or playing games together. Their example was good for me, coming as I did from a very competitive, aggressive environment where rugby was becoming utterly dominant. It was my first insight into a more rounded family environment.

By midway through the first form, I was on the other side of puberty. Before that I'd often been ridiculed for being a fatty. While I didn't tell anybody, those comments really hurt, and as a consequence I started to defend others who were mocked or derided because of their physique; kids can say the cruellest of things without knowing the ramifications of such ridicule.

In the second form I was miles bigger than any of my classmates, and Brent couldn't call me his little brother. It was quite difficult for him to handle. Brent, who now towers over me, had a bigger brother for a younger brother, which could be awkward to explain. With clothing he was getting hand-me-ups from his younger sibling. At 12 years of age I was 12 stone (about 76 kg) and wore size 12 shoes. I was far too heavy to play representative rugby, about 24 kg over the weight. Kids of my age, and their parents, acted as if I was a latter-day mastodon. So for a couple of years I donned my square-toed Rugby King Leos with metal sprigs and played soccer as a goalie. Most kids seemed afraid of coming anywhere near me and my boots and sprigs. And in other sports I continued to be competitive and enjoyed the likes of athletics and swimming.

For a few years we moved from one rented house to another in Blenheim until, when I was in the fourth form, Mum decided it was time we had a home of our own. Having a family home made me feel more settled, and I was also very proud of that humble little three-bedroom home; finally we had a place that was *ours*.

Being an early developer has its problems. I started sprouting body hair in my last two years of primary school. I dreaded swimming, so much so that I went and changed in the toilet, not wanting to show that I had hair everywhere. It was the same sort of dread that late developers have, but for the opposite reason. The upshot was that I was forced to consider others' feelings because being different — in any capacity — in your early teens brings about negative comments. I didn't like it when my peers said nasty things about me because I was different, so I refused to treat people in the same fashion. Growing up in these circumstances taught me to place a greater importance on being fair and on behaving properly towards others.

I started playing Nelson-Marlborough Seddon Shield age-group rugby. On one occasion we were asked to play three games in a day. I just wasn't fit enough, but it was a year or two before I took action to rectify that. I still scored far more tries for my club team than anyone else — over 50 of them — and sometimes looked to hand the ball on to boys whose parents had promised them, say, five dollars if they scored. Mum says I was told I was allowed four tries only in a game and thereafter, when a few metres from the line, had to look for someone who hadn't scored that day, and give it to him. Some parents were heard to mutter that 'someone ought to ask to see that big bugger's birth certificate'.

At 14 I started to play in the Under 17 grade. Poor Mum, she worried about me being too young. On the other hand, she'd grown weary of parents complaining that I was too rough. Reflecting on those times, Mum has since said that I was 'a big softie who several times won the fairest player award'.

In the Under 17s I began hanging out with older guys. Brent resented that for a time. They were his friends, not mine. He likely felt I was stripping him of his own identity. Very quickly he'd gone from being son of Frank to brother of Anton. He mellowed, eventually, and the fact that initially I played at centre and not with him in the forwards may have helped.

A defining moment occurred at the South Island Under 16 tournament where I, barely 15, and playing at number eight, was told that I had the ability to make the tournament team but my work rate was too low. Now, for the first time in my life, I had hit a road block. In the bus home I sat there feeling devastated. I decided there was only one solution: training and more training. By chance, Mum had a book on training for rugby that she had got when she attended a coaching course in Balclutha, and it got read from front to back. From that moment on, not only did I train properly, I trained hard. It is a work ethic that has never left me: if I missed selection in a team it wasn't going to be because I hadn't worked hard enough.

Next year, as captain of the Marlborough Under 16s, I played at number eight and scored two tries in our first game against Otago. Their captain, Duncan Blaikie, subsequently became one of my very best mates. And it was at such under-age tournaments that the fact that I was the son of the tough former All Black, Frank Oliver, kept hitting home. Everyone — so I thought — looked at me, marked me. Everything I did or said was noticed. At first I was thrown. Why, I asked, couldn't I be treated the same as everybody else? It was unnerving to have so much attention for something that wasn't really an indication of me and my play. It was unsettling initially, but within the next year I decided that it had to be turned around to become a positive experience. I decided that I would say to myself, 'Great. That means everyone is looking at me already.' In other words, 'I already have the selectors' attention; all I have to do now is play.'

In 1992 I was in the South team that lost to North in a curtain-raiser at Lancaster Park, now

Jade Stadium. For the first time I had to play against some guys as big as me; Andrew Blowers, for instance, whom I marked, and Isitolo Maka. Later I heard that the North had left a really big guy behind, even bigger than Blowers. 'Couldn't be,' I said. But it was true — his name was Lomu.

After the game a really neat thing happened that has occurred countless times since, something that I have never forgotten: a young boy asked me for my autograph. I was stunned: 'Mate,' I said, 'I'm not in the Canterbury team. I was only in the curtain-raiser.' He said, 'I know, that is why I want it.' I had to decide how to do something that had not been required of me before: how to write my own signature.

The tournament team wasn't to be announced until several weeks later, so I fretted and wondered if I'd be deemed good enough. In between I had a dreadful time with injuries and pulled both hamstrings twice. I have no idea why. At the time our coach at Marlborough Boys', Kieran Keane, who got close to making the Otago team when at Otago University, and who subsequently played for Canterbury and New Zealand as an inside back, goaded me and said he was sick of hearing about my hamstrings. He said I was a 'pussy'. So I thought, 'Stuff you,' joined in the training session and pulled another hamstring. I railed at him and said, 'Are you happy now?' What saved me from the recurring injury problems was reading where stiff-legged dead lifts helped strengthen hamstrings. I tried it and they healed.

When the New Zealand Under 17 team was announced and my name was there, I was thrilled but couldn't believe it was true until I actually pulled on the jersey. We played a Waikato Under 19 side in Hamilton. I was number eight and the already-famous Lomu and Blowers were the locks. I wore new boots and got the worst blisters imaginable.

Until I made this team I had never thought that one day I might be an All Black. Previously, being selected as an All Black was purely a dream, a dream more likely to become a glorious reality for those exceptionally good players you heard about that were bred in the powerhouses of New Zealand rugby: Auckland, Christchurch and Dunedin. Surely not from Blenheim, anyway. But now, with my mates coming round home to see my jersey, and to put it on and feel it, I persuaded myself that maybe I was the best young number eight in the country. From then on, locally, I was a marked man, and every time my name was mentioned in the paper, 'New Zealand Under 17 rep' was tacked on. I soon tired of that, and it was clear that, because of the focus on me, some of my mates weren't being given the credit their performances deserved, and that upset me, but solving this problem appeared impossible.

In the fourth and fifth form, in the end-of-year holidays, I worked on Glazebrook, a high-country station at the head of the Waihopai Valley. We had power by generator, no phone or TV. I think the property may have backed on to the fabled Molesworth Station. At Glazebrook I learnt a hell of a lot about putting your head down and getting on with the job no matter how unpleasant it was. For example, I dug holes for a hayshed about 200 m from the river. The ground was a shambles of massive boulders. The job took ages and I lost a lot of skin in the process. Contract scrub cutting, working in a gully in the searing heat of a Marlborough summer, was pretty rugged. Another time I spent a few days laying out 7-ft-long waratahs for fencers. Tar from the waratahs stuck to my back for days.

One of the most memorable experiences was rising at four in the morning and climbing out onto the tops in time to watch the sun come up before starting the muster. It's not simply the sweat cooling that sends shivers down your spine. I often made that liberating climb in the mornings and I never tired of it. Each time there were new sights, new sounds.

I learned how to work with sheep and cattle in the yards, to drench sheep and wean calves from cows. I'll never forget the day I was given a dog that would listen to and work for me while we drove a mob of cattle down the Waihopai River to the yards. It took all day and it was a game of chaotic chess figuring out where and how to drive the mob without pressing the cattle too hard. Some of the heifers with calves would turn and charge at me. More than once I had to hit one on the nose with a large stick while slipping away into flimsy cover. Then when each day's work was over I headed off for a training run. I did some growing up on that station.

In my last two years at school I worked as a builder's labourer during holidays. By the end I could almost have passed as a hammer hand. I learnt from my time at Glazebrook to do all of the thankless jobs that labourers have to do without complaint.

I was still playing at number eight for Marlborough Boys' First XV when we beat St Bede's of Christchurch for the first time in 30 years or more. Our coach, Kieran Keane, had a big, and beneficial, influence on me. For instance, when, as a seventh former, I started playing senior club rugby in Blenheim, he came and watched me play. On the Monday he came up to me at school and said, 'What were you trying to do out there? That wasn't your natural game.' Keane felt I had been too respectful, possibly deferential, to the older men on the paddock. He told me, bluntly, that I was as good, possibly better, than anyone I was playing against. 'Back yourself and get stuck in,' he said.

It was very good advice and the results in 1993, when I captained the New Zealand Under 19s and the New Zealand Secondary Schools teams, reflected that. What Keane had pointed

We may look like a rabble here, but the 1993 NZ Secondary Schools team was a hell of a good unit, scoring big wins over both our English and Australian equivalents. Back row: James Kerr, Royce Willis, Chresten Davis, Jonah Lomu, Paul Thomson (bending forward), Daniel Harper. Third row: Nash Jack, Christian Cullen, Brad Fleming, Henry Peita, George Leaupepe, Trevor Leota (bending forward), Brendan Haami. Second row: Neil Familton (physio), Eugene Morgan, Isitolo Maka, Andrew Blowers, Duncan Blaikie, Karl Te Nana, Graeme Syms (assistant manager). Front row: Des Smith (manager), Scott Hansen, Anton Oliver (captain), Rex Kerr (Chairman NZSC), Carlos Spencer (vice-captain), Pita Alatini, Evan Crawford (coach). Absent: Daniel Godbold, Matthew Carrington.

to was something that had held me back, particularly until late 2000: a tendency to be a bit too humble; a habit of suppressing the need to be more assertive.

If anything, though, I was overcommitted. Just about everything I did I was 100 per cent committed to, except for my school work. Academically I was classed as an 'A' student when I started at Marlborough Boys', which meant I was required to study French, for instance, but I didn't apply myself well. Sport, the physical side of living, generally, was the only life I had really known. Mum tried hard to get me to do my homework. She says that every night she reminded me of the importance of doing it, and doing it well, or there would be no TV watching. Alas, as a 14-year-old who associated with lots of 16- and 17-year-olds, peer pressure prevailed. The low point came in the fourth form when I was kicked out of an English class. Sitting outside, humiliation shook me. I thought, 'What am I doing here? This isn't me; I'm really letting myself down here.'

It still took a while to climb out of this trough, and it was not until my seventh form year that I accepted that working hard academically was truly beneficial, not for anyone else but for myself.

Being made head boy of such a large school was both a help and a hindrance when it came to setting a good example all round. The principal, John Rodgers, and Kieran Keane, among others, provided invaluable support. Keane says that I 'was so much in demand as a rugby player, was so saturated in rugby, that we devised a special educational programme for him. I think I may have tutored him in maths, English and Phys Ed.' I put more emphasis on my studies and worked hard. Once my mind is made up about the importance of something, I try to do that task to the best of my ability. Without the extra tutoring at school I would not have got the A Bursary needed to get accepted at Otago University.

Rodgers was a big fan of mine. He recalls speaking to the local Rotary club and saying that he thought I 'would one day be All Black captain'. I wasn't aware of this at the time, and the thought of being an All Black captain had never entered my head. Rodgers also told the Rotary group that he'd 'never seen a young man more capable of getting guys to follow him'. All very flattering.

Marlborough Boys' College deputy head boy Campbell Algie and I (head boy) pose for the local paper.

> ## 'He had the ideal approach to sport'– John Rodgers
>
> John Rodgers, principal of Marlborough Boys' College, found Oliver 'an immensely polite, nice young man. An excellent runner, cricketer and rugby player. He had the ideal approach to sport: competitive on the field, relaxed and restrained off it. Anton was always very good with other kids, was interested in them as individuals. He was never a nuisance, an all-round impressive leader for his age. We made him Head Prefect.'
>
> As with most people, Rodgers found Oliver 'always spoke his mind, but he wasn't given to boasting. He was honest, and hard on himself, too.'
>
> Rodgers thinks that rugby today, at the professional level, while it might like to espouse the values traditionally associated with amateur rugby, 'doesn't really live up to them'. He sees that as, probably, one reason why, at times, Oliver would have found it hard to fit easily into the world of professional rugby and its politics.

Rugby was taking over my life. I'd made the cricket First XI in the fourth form as an all-rounder but I gave that away when cricket overlapped with rugby. And my milk run, which I'd been doing to earn some money, was getting in the way of training, so it had to go too. When my 17- and 18-year-old mates and my brother Brent were refused alcohol in a bottle store, at 15 I went in and bought three bottles of the cheapest, nastiest vodka going. I had a crew cut and figured that I looked like a young bloke from the Woodbourne air base near Renwick a few kilometres outside Blenheim. Mark had left home by this stage and gone to live in Palmerston North to work as a carpenter. I was still playing with Brent in both our club team and for Marlborough Boys' College and we socialised together as all of our friends intermingled.

For six months I was training in the gym before and after school; I went to two club and two school rugby training practices a week, and I also fitted in three runs on my own. When I played in the South Island Under 19 tournament I was billeted in, of all places, the Criterion Hotel in Westport. I was the Marlborough number eight, but for the tournament team that played against the Otago Under 21s I jumped at number two in the lineout and scrummed at tight head. This was the first sign that number eight was no longer going to be my position. At school, though, in order to strengthen our forward effort, I had sometimes scrummed at lock and jumped at the front of the lineout. After our match against the Otago Under 21s in Dunedin, the majority of the South Island Under 19s watched Otago play Waikato from the Carisbrook terraces. It was the first game I had ever watched at the historic ground that, in time, was to become the home of my rugby life.

In the summer of 1992 Dad, who was coach of the New Zealand Under 19s, told me that in his view my best chance of making that side in 1993 would be at hooker, not number eight. Over the summer I had talked to some experienced front-rowers who had played plenty of club rugby in Blenheim and gleaned as much as they had to teach about scrummaging. I also bought a rugby ball and used to walk over to a nearby school and practise my lineout throwing against a wall. I wasn't really sure what I was doing; basically I just watched some video footage of Sean Fitzpatrick and tried to replicate what he did.

At 17 I began playing senior rugby in Blenheim as a hooker. Mum, still a worrier, tried to dissuade me but I had my eye on the big prize — being an All Black — and carried on. In my seventh form, some private schools in Christchurch were pressuring me to join them. I deflected two easily enough but St Andrews persisted. Initially, the school offered to pay for my tuition;

I would have to meet accommodation costs. When I didn't bite the offer was tuition fees plus half of the accommodation costs. Finally, the school offered to pay the lot. I still didn't budge from Blenheim; it was where all my friends were, it was where my mum was and it was home.

'A natural leader, mature beyond his years' – Kieran Keane

Kieran Keane, teacher and coach at Marlborough Boys' College, says Oliver was 'a natural leader, mature beyond his years; he could be single-minded but was not full of himself. He was not belligerent. He was a genuine, extremely caring guy. People warmed to him.

'But he has always been an independent thinker. Forthright and quite deep. He challenges others and himself, and that discomforts some people who construe his attitude as a threat to their authority.' Keane is another who sees Oliver as being disturbing to those who, privately, doubt their own abilities.

When Oliver asked for extra work so that he could catch up, Keane says, 'Unlike many students, Anton actually did the work. He really was incredibly diligent all round. I gave Anton the code number for entry to the school gymnasium. He'd go in there and practise shooting baskets for hour upon hour.'

The only reason I thought about going to the Christchurch private schools was to make the New Zealand Secondary Schools rugby team. At the time the view from the provinces was that my chances of making New Zealand Secondary School teams were much greater if I attended certain so-called 'good' schools. Christchurch Boys' and St Andrews, for example, came into that category. But some friends said that when it came to being noticed, there was a case to be made for believing that it was better to be a big fish in a small pond than a little fish in a big one. They were right: I ended up captaining the 1993 New Zealand Secondary Schools side and we played a 'test' against our English equivalents — and beat them easily — at Carisbrook in Dunedin. My mother was determined to be there but because of her recent ailments she couldn't drive her old Ford Cortina station wagon. A friend came to the rescue and arranged for her to ride south from Blenheim to Christchurch, then on to Dunedin, with a couple of truckies. I was unaware she was coming. She arrived just a few hours before kick-off. When she learned that there was an after-match dinner to which parents were invited, she borrowed some decent clothes from a friend and sat with me.

In 1993, my last year at Marlborough Boys', there was just Mum and me at home. Brent had gone off to Otago University and Mark had been in Palmerston North for five years. About this time, and to my dismay, Mum was stricken with rheumatoid arthritis. It all happened so quickly that, initially, she was deeply shaken. Within a few weeks she couldn't hold things safely, couldn't walk properly, and needed special care from physiotherapists at the swimming pool in order to maintain mobility. Her nursing training helped. She knew she had to fight the pain and remain active or she would seize up and risk losing her mobility forever. It upset me to see how she had to fit her hands and feet into specially-made plastic casts to prevent serious deformity. The casts also helped reduce the pain at night. It was heartbreaking for me to watch my mum suffering such pain, but she refused to give in to it. She was tough, stoical, brave. Her hope, and her sons', was that in time she would go into remission. I felt aggrieved, thought that she deserved more than having to rely on a son to help her up and make her breakfast, then come home from school at lunchtime to see that she was okay.

But there were a few lighter moments: one Saturday I pulled a hamstring — again — and that night I was lying on the floor and Mum was on the couch when the phone rang. Neither of us had a hope in hell of getting to it before it stopped ringing, so we both lay there laughing.

A friend drove Mum to Nelson where specialists decided to put her on medication that gradually gave her relief and alleviated the worst of the symptoms. Nevertheless, there she was, almost free of the boys, with independence and more variety to life beckoning, when crippling arthritis hit, along with all its associated uncertainties. It was a terrible blow.

When I was appointed captain of the national Under 19 side in 1993 I felt a bit uncomfortable; after all, my father was the coach. But I was assured that he hadn't chosen the captain. When we lost to Australia in Brisbane — a last-minute penalty was the difference — I took the defeat hard. Afterwards, the sound of the Australians singing their national anthem in the shed next to us stung me. Typically, I blamed myself for the loss, thought I should have made different and better calls on the field, should have contributed more to our preparation the week before. As captain I thought it had been my responsibility and I vowed that we would not lose the next year. It took a long time to get over that loss. In these earlier years, without the perspective that

Cuddling up to Mum before one of her routine inspections of my student flat in Dunedin.

age brings, the Australia defeat hung over me for too long, its effects were disproportionate to reality . . . it was, after all, only a game.

Around this time I was included in the Marlborough sevens side. In Christchurch we stayed in the Russley, along with the Otago squad. Early one morning, at breakfast, I set eyes on Gordon Hunter for the first time, sitting by himself. He had a large intimidating moustache and an eye that didn't appear normal. He looked at me and in a booming voice said, 'Morning, lad.' He scared the hell out of me.

It was all happening for me now. I played for the Marlborough senior side against Nelson, but because of my commitments to the Under 19 team, and the New Zealand Secondary Schools side, I wasn't able to play for Marlborough again.

Life was all rugby, invasive and sometimes upsetting: I had to phone my partner for the school formal and apologise for pulling out because I'd been picked to play rugby in Australia. And there were many times when the deputy head boy had to fill in for me during the school year. When I got invited to attend the Marlborough Sportsperson of the Year dinner, I told Mum such occasions weren't my thing and I wasn't going to bother to attend. But she said it would look bad if I failed to turn up so she dragged me along. To my great surprise, I was presented with the award.

To say that 1993 had been a full and eventful year would be an understatement. The year had been one of great excitement; I felt I was building confidence in some areas, which also served to highlight the awareness of my own uncertainties. I wasn't complacent — the Australian defeat and many bumbling head boy speeches had seen to that — and the hard work that was required for me to achieve academically had been a lesson well and truly learnt. It had been quite an astonishing year for the chubby, barefoot kid from Milton.

Flanked by former running great John Walker and former New Zealand Silver Ferns netball skipper Julie Carter after receiving the Marlborough Sportsperson of the Year award in 1993.

Balls in the Air

When I left school at the end of 1993 I was proud of myself. I'd managed to get an A Bursary which, considering all my extra-curricular activities, took some doing. Then, early in 1994, I set out on the next stage of my life: I enrolled to study for a health science degree at Otago University.

I'd been hoping to get into the physiotherapy school but the criteria for selection were based on school sixth form results and mine hadn't been good enough. Health science, however, gave me a fair amount of freedom; there is a broad range of choices once you've got through the first year, allowing plenty of flexibility for career options.

I packed up all my stuff, crammed it into Mum's little white Honda Integra and we headed south. It took all day to get to Dunedin. When we arrived at the Unicol hostel the place was swarming with activity. Families and first-year students were everywhere and their gear was clogging up the foyer and elevators. I was a bit shy so registered quietly, grabbed my key and walked up the stairs rather than join the queue for the elevator. My room was number 512 in the south tower on the fifth floor, and I didn't really think of Mum having to lug stuff up that far. I settled in and kissed Mum goodbye. Her boys were all gone from home now and it was time for her to live her own life again. I was happy at the prospect of her having the freedom she so richly deserved.

Those first few weeks in Dunedin were a whirl, meeting people, forgetting their names just as quickly, going to lectures and finding my way around the university.

I still vividly remember the first time I met Simon Maling. It was lunchtime and I arrived late and sat at the back of the hall by myself. During lunch Simon came up to me and said, 'There is a bit of a piss-up on in south three; come up and have a few.' That was the nicest thing anyone had done and it captures some of the essence of Maling. Friendly, open, and very social — at least in those days!

I had been asked to take part in training for the Otago sevens team and so, being the serious chap that I was, I didn't go to many Orientation activities because of training commitments. Actually, I was far too serious and I missed out on some good student fun.

My studies took a back seat again. Like so many other first-year students I was a bit slack when it came to exams and assignments; where I differed from several was that I didn't drink a great deal. I didn't do many random midweek booze-ups because rugby still had a strong grip on me. Although I did enough to pass all of my exams bar one, I underachieved academically. Basically rugby had taken over again. It meant I was away from Dunedin for large chunks of the year and I realised I had taken on far too great a workload. By the time I woke up to this it was too late to pull out of a paper without the university officially registering that I had enrolled in the course for the year so I simply turned up to the exam with a book and read it until the examiners signalled I could leave if I wished. I had to cut at least one paper otherwise I would have failed some of the other papers that I was sitting. I got an E, and was told that that was better than having an Absent written on my academic record. In hindsight, I would rather have had an Absent; at least that leaves room for explanation — not many places to go explaining a triple pronger.

'Right into it from the whistle' – Simon Maling

Maling first met Oliver when they lived in the Unicol hostel in Dunedin in 1994. He sees Anton as a hard-nosed, confrontational player. 'The thing I noticed about him was that he was right into it from the whistle. Some guys take a few minutes to warm to it, not Anton. He was ready to go.

'He is a fine defender and was always a really good ball carrier. If he hasn't stood out quite so much in that area recently it's because there are more players around who will take the ball up than there used to be. And, under Mains, us tighties weren't encouraged to do much of that.

'Providing all those in lineouts were doing their jobs properly, there was nothing wrong with Anton's throwing.'

I played rugby for the University Colts, a team called the Blues. A few people had advised me to play colts rugby and not rush into senior football, even though I had played against men in Blenheim the year before and knew I could make the step up. I actually played my first game for Otago a few months later without having taken part in a single game of senior-grade football in Dunedin, so I guess it was the right call.

I captained the University Blues side that was chock-full of excellent players, my brother Brent, Simon Maling, Duncan Blaikie, Jason Bird, Richard Kinnear and Bill Tapealava among them. We were all the same age, had similar interests and were playing for the same reason: to have fun on and off the field. We did just that and ended up winning the competition. Unfortunately, I missed the final, having been dragged away to play a representative game, so Duncan stood in as captain.

I could hardly have had a fuller year of rugby, what with reselection as captain of the NZ Under 19 side, coached by my father again, and then being picked for the New Zealand Colts Under 21

Packing down for New Zealand Under 19 against our Australian counterparts in Wellington in 1994. The 55–6 victory was sweet revenge for the loss we suffered in Brisbane the previous year. My props are Michael Nui and Greg Feek.

team. Both Dad and I were still smarting about having lost the Under 19 match against Australia the previous year. During the lead-up I incurred a grade-one tear to the medial ligaments in my knee so I was in doubt right up till a few hours before the game. It was a curtain-raiser to an All Black test and I remember getting a ball to throw into a lineout and being aware that all of the ABs were right there on the sideline looking at me. We won the game and scored about 50 points.

After that it was straight to Sydney, Australia, to play for the New Zealand Colts where we beat the Australian Colts 41–31. In that game my opposing hooker was Brendan Cannon and we had an on-field scuffle. It was to be a strange start to a good friendship. The New Zealand Colts included future All Blacks Tana Umaga, Justin Marshall, Kees Meeuws, Andrew Mehrtens, Jonah Lomu, Carlos Spencer and Taine Randell. Brendan Laney was in the side too.

When I got back to Unicol after two months away with the New Zealand Under 19s then Colts I was incredibly busy, well behind in all of my academic work and so spent a fair amount of time at the library. On every floor at Unicol there is a communal phone. And while I was away studying Gordon Hunter, then Otago coach and the man I had been terrified by a year previously, had been ringing often and he also left messages at reception, none of which got to me. Eventually I learned that I was to ring him. I knew who he was, of course, and was excited and apprehensive about what the phone call would mean. I rang and a gruff, deep voice boomed down the line: 'Gordon Hunter here.'

'Hi, it's Anton Oliver here. I have a message to call you.'

'Where have you been lad, out shagging?'

Well, I didn't know how to respond to that. He asked me to come to training that day and I said, 'Great,' then added, 'I have been getting strapping on my knee. Will I be able to get that done there or should I get it strapped before I get there?' And without really answering the question he said, 'Don't worry about that lad, just get there.'

My first training was after the team had a humiliating loss to North Harbour, which I was obviously not a part of. So Gordon ran the team into the ground, and it was a very early night for me, as I crawled into bed absolutely spent, having never experienced a training session like that before. I was simply not conditioned physically to cope with that kind of workload. We did plenty of rucks and scrum-machine work, down-and-ups and shuttles.

I didn't enjoy that first year for Otago. I was right back down on the bottom rung again and I was made to know it. Newcomers were made to feel uncomfortable, and at times felt like second-class citizens.

David Latta was captain and the number-one hooker. After my first game as a reserve the team had a few drinks and everyone was asked to stand up, drink a seven-ounce glass of Speight's and make a comment. I have always found this practice to be very valuable. Everyone in the whole squad from coach to baggage man has to get up in the same forum and speak his mind. For me it's a practice that harks back to the Greeks and the birth of democracy. You can say whatever you like and it will be received. Often quiet people who are normally hard to read will say the most perceptive of things, offer opinions that carry real weight. I said just three words: 'Looking, listening, learning.'

I was in awe of Gordon Hunter; I think the whole team was, though possibly for different reasons. I hung on to every word he said. Gordon was incredibly magnetic, and although I rarely spoke to him I tried desperately to train and do everything I could to gain his approval. The essence of the team, its spirit, had its source in Gordon. Sure, we had a bunch of fun-loving free spirits, such as Marc Ellis, and a general youthful undercurrent that had its origins in the many past or present students in our team, but Gordon was the reason everything got expressed. His sheer passion for winning, for giving it a go and never giving up, drove us to believe we could perform at a level way above what we thought possible.

I got my first game for Otago — a 5- to 10-minute cameo — when David Latta, the quintessential Otago man, came off for some attention during a game against Wellington on Carisbrook. After the game, John Leslie, who had been giving me the hardest time of anyone in the team, stood up and said he thought I 'went like a rabid dog, went hard, so good on you'. It was then that I realised the key to not being the young bugger that everyone picked on was to gain the respect of the older guys, and that that respect was gained either through time in the team or time on the field. Time in the team would have taken too long; I wanted time on the pitch.

My first starting game was against Southland in Invercargill. I scored a try from 40 m out and played with plenty of vigour, so it was a good day.

David Latta — the quintessential Otago man.

I hadn't been in Dunedin long before I realised that my horizons had broadened markedly. For me, Dunedin was an amazing place. Compared to small-town Blenheim, where anything slightly different was seen as strange, or attention grabbing, not simply an expression of how you genuinely felt, Dunedin gave you the right to express yourself freely. You could wear what you liked, say what you liked, behave differently and not feel peculiar or likely to be reined in.

But what I did resent was the way some people, students and others, tended to assume that all rugby players ('rugby heads' was the pejorative term) were thickos who thought about and did little else but play rugby and drink piss. It still seems as if there's never been a time when people haven't made erroneous assumptions about me — assumptions about my intellectual interests, morality and values — because I am known as a rugby player, and rugby players are presumed to be rather limited, crude creatures.

Initially, that brassed me off and I got very angry. Then I went through a phase of trying to show and prove to people that I wasn't a rugby head, that I had more to offer. Then, slowly but surely (and it took five years or more) I became comfortable with not having to do that and decided to be myself, and that anyone who came my way could make up their own mind about who I was and what I stood for. The fact that some were inclined to see others as stereotypes warned me against prejudging people, for I was starting to realise how upsetting it was to be typecast, so the last thing I wanted to do was to make assumptions about others based on such superficial, primitive thought.

When I look back, I see that 1994 was a year of immense personal change and growth. That first year at university was great. During 1994 I managed to open up more to people, and I became better at making close friends. I became less insular, began to trust people more by revealing more of myself to them. For the first time, at the age of 18, I was beginning to understand myself. That is the beauty of university and, in particular, of the initial year. Till then I had always done things by myself, had trusted myself and not sought help from others all that often. That wasn't a conscious policy; it was just the way I was.

So it was with renewed optimism that, with the university year over, two friends and I packed our gear into an old Holden HQ, left Unicol and headed home. We cruised through the Mackenzie Country, drove over Arthur's Pass to the West Coast and back home to Blenheim, taking a few days on the journey. To read that year's Unicol magazine now is to reawaken memories of interesting people, and of times good and bad. Rugby was disruptive of university life, though, there's no doubt about that. There is not one photo of me in the 1994 Unicol magazine (I missed many social and formal events), but I had gained plenty from that year and didn't need photos to make those times more real to me.

From the time I arrived in Dunedin in 1994, and for the next few years, rugby and university life as a student were inextricably linked. I coped, but it was extremely taxing and I never found it easy.

That first year in Unicol spoiled me: all meals were provided, my cleaning was done . . . all that changes when you go flatting. My first flat in 1995 was on Castle Street with two other young men. In the Castle Street all-male abode, cooking and cleaning were a low priority. Some mates flatted in the house behind us. They had an outside loo so during the colder times, which is all year round in Dunedin, our little inside toilet was going overtime, with not much cleaning going on. Those were the days when toilet paper would run out occasionally and the *Otago Daily Times* was called upon to serve a welcomed but unintended purpose. You know you have hit rock bottom when: (1) the *ODT* is used as toilet paper; (2) you have a plague of mice in your house; (3) the three flatmates have only one meal each in their repertoire and cook it all year; (4) your toilet is getting used by eight guys; (5) the house has no Pink Batts insulation, only wood scrim and paint for warmth; (6) when you shower you have to leave your socks on; and (7) when your grandma comes to visit, you meet her at the front door and quickly escort her to a café.

Luckily, I managed to meet my first serious girlfriend that year and stayed at her place more often than not. As a result of that, and my rugby commitments that took me out of Dunedin for over three months of that year, I didn't spend much time in the Castle Street Grand Hilton.

My university life stalled. I didn't know what I wanted to study, except that it wasn't physiotherapy, so I took more science papers. I thought I would major in chemistry.

It soon became apparent that the time rugby took up would kill any thoughts of attempting a chemistry degree. I couldn't get to the compulsory labs that are a fundamental part of a science degree and while I passed the papers the content was starting to get pretty tough.

I still hadn't worked out what I wanted to do. I had passed several science papers and accrued a handy number of points. The trouble was, if I were to carry on with science I would have to find the time for labs, and no other department wanted all of those science points. So at the end of 1995 I had little choice but to switch departments and enrol in physical education.

It was becoming increasingly difficult to find the time to study for exams or to complete assignments by the due date. So I worked hard to optimise the time available. Recently, I was sent this amusing tale, which points up the stereotypical view that some people, students included, had of rugby players. The correspondent said I might like to see it in 'the context of [me] not being a quintessential rugby front-rower with a cauliflower for a head and two poached eggs for ears:

'Jess [his son] liked to get through exams at university with the least work possible, and his pre-exam study technique involved going to the library and picking someone to sit beside. When that person stopped working and left, Jess would stop working and leave also. Naturally, he sought out people who looked like they would only last there about five minutes. One day he saw Anton working away and he thought, well, a rugby front-rower, he'll be outa there in 10 minutes tops, but after 10 minutes, Anton was still there.

'Jess checked to see if he was asleep but, no, he was actually working like buggery. And he worked on for *hours* and poor Jess was stuck there having to work all that time as well. He was totally shagged when he got home, eyes hanging out like dogs' balls.'

The Otago rugby side was in the Super 10 competition and, at the start of 1995, I made the team and we went to Cape Town, which was an amazing experience for a Young Turk like me. I had been to Australia a few times but that was it, so to find myself at the bottom of the African continent in a country with so much history in comparison to New Zealand was a real thrill. Anyone who has been to Cape Town will understand the beauty of the city, nestled under Table Mountain and perched between the Indian and Atlantic Oceans, a quite remarkable place.

All concentration for Otago in my first full season for the union in 1995.

We won the game but my temper got the better of me when I saw one of the opposition stand on one of our boys so I punched him and got sent off. That was extremely upsetting. I felt I had almost cost the team its chances of winning and was very sensitive about it for a good couple of months.

It was quite a dizzying time. I made various New Zealand A teams and also played in the North-South game. This was the big time for me. About six days out from the game, Arran Pene came round to my place and said some of the guys were having an impromptu drink and 'we are on it'. Well, I had exams and was focused on the game too, but you don't say no to Arran. So I got pretty boozed then snuck out early and went for a run when drunk. I wanted to get the booze out of my system quickly, but was probably taking that to the extreme considering I was still well and truly merry!

The North-South game was a major event. The North was basically the All Blacks and I had never played against Sean Fitzpatrick before. The first scrum I got popped rather easily, but after that I was okay. I remember the scrum going down on Olo Brown's side and Sean said to Olo in a very calm voice, 'Get it up, Olo,' and sure enough up the scrum went. Other than that the game was a blur, I was just concentrating on my own job. Later, when I made the All Blacks, Robin Brooke suggested I get a tape of the game; he said it was the best he had seen me play. I haven't gotten around to acquiring the tape — probably never will.

I also went to the All Black trials in Whangarei where the World Cup team was to be picked, and was on the bench in the shadow test team — another great experience. After that I was in the New Zealand Colts team that went to Argentina and won the first southern hemisphere tournament where Australia, South Africa and Argentina also competed. On the last day, travel day, I was duty boy and had to go to see our manager, Mike Banks, and ask him what needed doing. He said, 'Well, actually, I have some pretty good news for you. Norm Hewitt is down with a crook knee and you have been selected to go and be reserve for the All Blacks in the centenary test in Aussie.' WOW, I hadn't even started in an NPC game, had only made the transition from number eight to hooker in 1993, two-and-a-half years ago, and now was going to be an AB. I was stunned. The rest of the boys had a boozy flight home but I stayed away from alcohol, my mind racing with thoughts of what I was going to confront when I got into camp. I didn't have high hopes about that. More of the young kid on the block being treated like shit was what I figured would be in store.

I was met at the airport and taken to the Poenamo Hotel on the North Shore where I roomed with Richard Loe. He was fantastic in his own gruff way, couldn't have been better; I felt comfortable around him. Loe had lived in Blenheim for a while and was from a rural background so we had plenty to talk about.

I didn't have any gear as I had swapped it with

Apart from the fact I marked Sean Fitzpatrick — and got popped in the first scrum — the 1995 North-South game at Carisbrook was a blur.

Jonah Lomu and I admire a V12 Lamborghini Diablo at Coogee Beach in Sydney prior to the 1995 Bledisloe Cup match against Australia.

players from other national Under 21 teams. When Mike Brewer, who was working for the Canterbury Clothing Company at the time, heard about this, he got me a bag of CCC gear, so I could at least look like I was fitting in.

Jonah Lomu, a superstar through his deeds at the 1995 World Cup, went out of his way to sit beside me. I remember looking at his thighs and thinking they were as big as kauri logs hauled out of a swamp. All in all, this was a pretty tight team, having been together through all the World Cup training camps in the previous year before losing the World Cup final.

There was also far more going on than I realised. I was completely unaware of the World Rugby Corporation (WRC). Indeed, the concept blew my mind and was very hard to understand. We arrived in Australia and it was clear players were apprehensive when any board members were around. I still didn't know what was going on. We went for a walk as a team and I heard one of the boys say, 'There's Lochore. He has been brought over the ditch to try to talk to us. Don't get isolated.'

I roomed with Michael Jones, who was a delight. He had been a player whose picture I had had on my wall for many years as a kid and now I was rooming with him — very surreal!

He had a quiet way about him — very gentle — and I found rooming with him easy as he asked me questions and seemed genuine in his desire to learn more about me.

In the captain's talk the night before, Fitzpatrick said that if we didn't win the test we would have nothing to show for all the hard work and effort that had gone into preparation for the World Cup. His comments were met with a collective steely determination; the team had been through too much not to have any silverware to show for it.

We won the test the next day and retained the Bledisloe Cup. After the game while still in their kit in the changing shed, Frank Bunce and Walter Little tried to explain to me what the WRC thing was all about. I understood some of what they were saying, but had plenty of questions that needed answers, like, 'What do you mean, no All Blacks?'

We jumped on a bus and went to a house in the swanky Sydney suburb, Vaucluse. At the time

I had no idea where we were or what we were doing. This was my first time on an AB bus so I was going with the flow. We ended up in a large room and when some finger food came out I dived into it heartily. Then I got a tap on the shoulder. It was Fitzy and he said they were having a meeting and I had to leave. So I did. I had no idea at the time why I wasn't invited in and I felt utterly excluded and isolated. The reason I wasn't inside was that I hadn't been involved in any of the negotiations up to that point and so was effectively not part of the All Blacks, even though I had worn number 21 on my back a few hours earlier. I roamed around this massive empty house for a while and found the homeowner's son, so we shot some hoops outside and talked. He was about 10 I think, just a kid. I waited for what seemed ages and got sick of this and went looking for the bus. It had gone some distance to find a spot to turn around. When I sat down at the front of the bus all I could hear was the manager, Colin Meads. He was livid: 'Why the hell is this team here when we have all of the greats waiting for us at the centenary dinner? What have I done?'

Eventually the team emerged and Marc Ellis sat beside me on the bus and showed me the contract that they had earlier that day received from the NZRU to counter the WRC bid. It was their final offer. Marc was saying that the NZRU were crazy, that the figures they came up with were nowhere near what the WRC had offered.

At the Bledisloe test centennial dinner later that evening the room was abuzz with talk, animated meetings at tables all round the place, lots of clandestine goings-on. Thankfully my father was there, and he was a huge emotional shoulder for me to lean on. I suddenly felt less isolated, less alone. I had someone to talk to who could help me understand a little about what was happening. He got former All Black manager John Sturgeon to come over and talk to me as well and that helped fill in a few more blanks.

That night had a profound effect on me and my impression of All Black rugby. Here I was a newcomer among a group of men, members of the All Blacks team that I had wanted to be a part of since I was a little kid, who with more greed it seemed than care or compunction were intent on abandoning all that the All Blacks stood for. And also, in the process, possibly destroying so much that was good about the game in New Zealand . . . all in a chase after money.

For a whole week, culminating in the captain asking me to leave a team meeting, I'd been kept in the dark about something as momentous as this.

I felt like shit, disillusioned. My whole perception of what the All Blacks were was shattered and it left me in a daze. It has affected me ever since. That night my innocence was stolen.

I was so glad to get back home away from rugby, and I arrived pleased to see my girlfriend again after about eight weeks away; she felt real to me.

In Otago we had WRC meetings in the boardroom of the legal firm Gallaway Cook Allan. There were about 10 of us and we had phone hook-ups with other provinces which lasted well into the night. There were speaker phones, but no one wanted to declare their intentions. Some were for the WRC, some against. I remember waiting for what was to be the pivotal phone hook-up with other unions, the most important rugby conversation of our lives, and what did we do? We had a quiz. JL (John Leslie) made up a quiz with lots of strange but funny questions. It made the whole event seem very comical.

It turned out the Otago guys wanted to stick with the NZRU. This was the real turning point in the WRC struggle, because once we decided to stay, and over half the number of New Zealand domestic players concurred, the WRC's pool was greatly reduced. Next day the Otago players, including key All Blacks Josh Kronfeld and Jeff Wilson, were at Dunedin Airport when we signed to stay with the NZRU. When we got to Wellington Kronfeld and Wilson were whisked off to a televised media signing. This was a key moment that set off a domino effect around the country that laid waste to the WRC. I trust the NZRU will ever be grateful to Otago.

Auckland and All Black prop Craig Dowd receives attention from the medics after having a few teeth dislodged in the 1995 NPC final. I was penalised and later suspended for one match for throwing the punch that did the damage.

Our last game of the season was the NPC final against Auckland, and the last game that Arran Pene and Jamie Joseph were to play for Otago. It was also the hundredth game that Stu Forster and Paul Cooke had played for the province, a big day. We controlled much of the game, trying to avoid the forward strength of Auckland, which was where they finally won the game in a dubious pushover-try refereeing decision. It was also the game where I got clipped around the head, turned around and threw a reactionary right-hand jab at the first player I saw, Craig Dowd. I got penalised for that on the field and thought that would be the end of it, but the next day was told by our manager that I had to face a disciplinary committee as I had dislodged a few of Dowd's teeth, which made the incident more serious. I thought it was ridiculous that the incident had been seen by the touch judge and referee and dealt with, then reopened via video footage. So the next week I had to go to Auckland and receive my punishment of a one-week stand-down, which would rule me out of the first game in the brand new Super 12 competition the next year.

The Auckland final was also my blazer game for Otago so I slept in it all night. That blazer meant so much to me: 15 games for the province. Finally, I had the recognition I had been craving for. Essentially that is what the blazer means: you have served your apprenticeship. I was no longer the young guy; there were new players who didn't have blazers and so it was their turn to be the new boys.

Halfway through my Phys Ed degree I thought it would be a good idea if I knew more about the money I was earning and where I could invest it. So I started another degree, this time in Finance. That was to take me a long time to complete as rugby began to take up more and more time. Super 12, All Black Tri-nations, NPC, then end-of-year tours — where do you fit papers in? In hindsight I wish I had done different degrees; neither Finance nor Phys Ed hold much attraction to me now and have been a mistake in terms of a career path. But at 18 how do you know what you want to do? And what really interests you?

Chapter 4

Gung-ho and Wide-eyed

When I was selected to tour South Africa with the All Blacks in 1996 I realise now that I was extremely naive. A reporter asked me if I aspired to play in the tests. What, with Sean Fitzpatrick as the 80-odd test veteran, hooker and captain? It was clear the intention was to 'blood' me and in large part I was there to soak up the ambience, learn 'the culture'. But, in response to the reporter's question, I stupidly said that I would try to put pressure on Fitzy and his test spot. I'd read plenty of references through my childhood about the All Blacks culture, about never taking your spot for granted. So I was just parroting, really. Much of what is said and gets reported by media outlets has no depth and the flow is unceasing. At 19 years of age, gung-ho and wide-eyed, artless but not fully aware of it, I had just added my bit.

I wasn't nearly as much in awe of the All Blacks as I had been in 1995 when I'd been called to Australia as a back-up to Fitzy in the 100th Bledisloe Cup game. It was there that I first encountered the All Black lock Ian Jones, the 'Kamo Kid' from North Auckland. That shattered a few illusions. At practice he was deliberately throwing ill-directed passes, either at my feet or out in front of me. Four in a row were like that. He meant me to drop them; that was the only conclusion I could draw. I thought, 'What a wanker!' Kamo had a reputation then for being a bit of a bully boy towards the younger players in All Black sides, and I was the youngest there in 1995, so he directed his aim at me.

Quite quickly the gloss got taken off some All Blacks and the 'culture' as a result of this kind of treatment by the senior players. Mind you, Kamo was the worst at making it difficult for the newcomers. Most of the rest were pretty harmless. Thankfully, there were others, like Michael Jones, who showed some humility.

I had breakfast with Michael in Cape Town. He told me that when he first made the All Blacks, the Auckland guys— Gary Whetton and others — set the tone, and then there was

53

'the rest'. He thought it terrible the way some of the senior Auckland-based players tended to ignore anyone outside their immediate circle. In 1995 Ian Jones was a senior All Black. Only guys of his standing, as it were, would have been able to challenge someone like him. It harks back to schooldays when treating newcomers abominably was said to be part of the process of 'making a man' of a boy. As a young player, my predominant thought was: keep your head down and don't make mistakes. Or, as my father was apt to say, 'Keep your powder dry.'

There was a hierarchy in the All Blacks back then and there still is now. I approve of that, if by hierarchy one means the young are required to be aware of and respectful of the senior players and what they have gone through and achieved. There's nothing wrong with insisting a player earns his strip.

Before I became an All Black, I saw the team as cloaked in a shining aura. All Blacks were people who, individually and collectively, performed great deeds. I was imbued with a sense that the All Blacks owned and subscribed to a noble tradition. I thought that noble tradition was built upon courage, commitment and formidable, sometimes heroic, acts on the field, and I wanted to be part of that. I thought every All Black would be living and espousing my definition of what the All Blacks stood for. However, once I got inside, the reality dispelled some illusions. As a young All Black I had to work hard to gain the respect of those further up the pecking order. While I agree with that entirely, it is the manner in which it is achieved that is contentious. Having experienced a torrid induction, I can't see much benefit in discouraging the new or young players from talking to or sitting with more senior players. I am not advocating getting into an argument with a veteran on your first tour — now that wouldn't be a good idea. But I am suggesting that social interaction — as simple as sharing conversation over breakfast — would be beneficial for both parties.

One of the good effects of professional rugby has been to get rid of much of that 'class system'. On the playing side, when I started it wasn't legal to take off fit players and replace them with substitutes, 'impact players'. I felt sorry for players like Mark 'Bull' Allen and Norm Hewitt, because tight forwards are far more constrained than young backs are. Backs have a different culture within the team, they are extremely laid back and less serious than forwards, and young backs are included straight away and given far more leeway. Forwards are the polar opposite, and made to know that, especially a tight forward. So perhaps I received a concentrated 'do your time' dose as I was a young hooker and had to be put in my place.

In 1996 I was captain of the New Zealand Colts, the national Under 21 side. We were involved in a southern hemisphere colts tournament in New Zealand with Australia, Argentina and South Africa. Before our game against Argentina in Palmerston North, Andrew Blowers, Chresten Davis and I were approached to see whether, should we be selected to go to South Africa with the All Blacks, we would sign NZRU 'development' contracts. These were worth $15,000, well short of the other players' payments.

At that time I knew little or nothing about what monetary offers were fair and what were not. My gut feeling was to say, 'Stuff the money.' I just wanted to go on tour as an All Black. Dad put me onto a financial adviser in an effort to give me some impartial advice. Now I was getting very confused. The adviser talked about looking 'at the big picture', which to him meant that Fitzy was getting to the end of his reign as hooker, and Hewitt didn't look as if he fitted into John Hart's idea of the classic All Black mould. But was that a true reflection of Hart's view? Only Hart could tell us that. The adviser was saying that I was playing well, and had plenty of 'bargaining power'. Quite quickly my level of discomfort grew to the point where I said I'd take what I was offered, and get on with it.

After beating Argentina and South Africa we had to beat Australia in a winner-takes-all final at North Harbour's Onewa Domain. We played poorly but were still leading when, with time up on the clock, the Australians got an intercept try to win the match and the tournament. I was angry and frustrated. After the game I did my first ever live post-match interview, steam still billowing and emotions still raw. My speech was poor; in effect, I apologised to the nation for my team's lacklustre performance. Stupid, inappropriate talk. Later on I learned that some of the All Blacks, watching from their hotel, were singularly unimpressed. A few of them may have decided that I was a bit of an upstart and decided there and then not to give me much rope on the forthcoming tour. I'd never done a live interview straight after a game before. I didn't have the skills to put the on-field emotions aside and give a dignified, diplomatic, sporting response. But that was me at 19. I set myself high standards on the field, hated pretence on and off it, and if others didn't have, and meet, similarly high standards, exasperation took over. It would be some years before I learned to be a bit less harsh on both others and myself.

Apart from the poor result, and my silly remarks, the game is memorable for my getting my first nasty cauliflower ear. I had it drained after the game and it was extremely painful. A doctor shoved in a needle, sucked out blood and squeezed the ear as well. Next day the whole process was repeated and was going to be repeated for some time until I told the doctors that their efforts were wasted on me, accepted the loss of my contoured ear, and resigned myself to a life with rugby 'dog tags'.

Blowers and Davis and I, and a number of other All Blacks — those who weren't in the test team or the reserves to play Australia at Suncorp Stadium, Brisbane — assembled in Auckland. We were outfitted — an exciting time for me back then — and we had to do a signing session, also a novelty. We signed over 500 items and were paid one dollar a signature. I thought it was great; not yet 20, here I was with all those big 'red ones' in my pocket. Having performed hard manual labour to earn my pennies both on the farm and as a labourer, sitting on my behind for three hours earning a fortnight's wages in three hours was the easiest money I had ever made in my life.

I was starting my All Black career in one of the last long All Black tours of modern times. While not like the three-month tours of yesteryear, this was still a six-week tour, with plenty of midweek games for the second-tier All Blacks to play and push for a spot in the test team. Such tours gave everyone an opportunity to contribute significantly on the field as well as the time to enjoy the surroundings of the countries visited. It's not like that now. Tours are all about revenue, which in basic terms means televised tests. A template for a modern rugby tour would be a three- to four-week excursion with three or four tests on the Saturdays and no midweek rugby. I would have liked to have been playing when the longer tours were still 'financially viable'. Touring, in my opinion, is the best experience a rugby player can have: different cultures, different styles of rugby. You grow as a person and as a player when exposed to a rugby life outside New Zealand shores.

The players not involved in the weekend's test flew to Australia, went straight to the ground and watched the All Blacks win 32–25. As we hadn't met the rest of the team we sat in the stand with the public with our black suits and ties on but still like fans really. For me that set the tone for the tour — mostly just watching other guys play. On the team bus after the game, Fitzy stood up at the front and said that all the Under 21s would be 'duty boys' while we were in Australia because, he said, you never lose to Australia as we had done. I thought, 'Some might think that a bit hypocritical, Fitzy. I think you've lost to Australia.' Of course, I may have taken his jibe a bit more seriously than others did, as I'd been the losing captain of the Under 21s.

There were 45 in the All Blacks party — 36 players plus all the rest from masseur through to manager. Frank Bunce and I, along with Chresten Davis and Andrew Blowers, were told to load the mountain of gear into the massive bus hired to take us all to the airport. We were wearing our number ones: blazers, ties, dress pants. But it was so hot we soon disrobed and worked without our tops on. By the time I'd finished and got on the bus I couldn't see a spare seat. Hot and sweaty, I didn't stop to think about protocol, to remember my place and realise the situation. So I kept walking down the bus, getting further and further towards the back, where I categorically shouldn't have been until I got to the very back and motioned to sit down. Everyone was watching me, but pretending not to watch: the older hands no doubt waiting for the proverbial to hit the fan. Immediately, I got a bollocking from Kamo and rightly so. I was told to piss off and sit down the front with the new boys. But there weren't any seats there, so I stood in the aisle until Todd Blackadder, halfway down the bus, got up and went and sat further back, making room for me.

For the rest of the tour our buses had few if any spare seats, so the younger players, whenever we heard the cry 'Bus-o', would scramble to get on first. Some of us even made sure we were there five minutes before the bus arrived. We wanted a 'safe seat' in order to avoid the demeaning and scary ridicule that went with having to stand up.

Ah, the words 'back seat' . . . they conjure up images of fearsome old guys, gnarled, grumpy, hard-headed All Blacks. On the bus I never had the courage to turn and look at the back seat to see what 'they' were up to. None of us at the front did; it wasn't the done thing. My mistake first-up on the bus was compounded when, on arrival at our destination, I had to room with Kamo. I wish I'd said straight away, 'Look mate, I wasn't thinking on that bus. I didn't mean to do that,' but I didn't, and I think that was held against me for the rest of the tour. He and others may have thought I was deliberately being a pushy young bastard. Soon after, Norm Hewitt came up and said, 'Don't worry, it's okay.' I replied, 'I should have known better,' and he muttered, 'Yeah, you're right, you should have.' I'll never forget that incident on the bus. I remember nearly peeing my pants.

We arrived in Jo'burg, South Africa, with much fanfare and media attention. I had never seen such passion and fervour, some screaming, 'We hate you, we are going to kill you.' That kind of talk was certainly off-putting. We then relocated and settled in at Plettenberg Bay on the southern coast. The week involved a mix of training, rugby practice and socialising. I pigged out at the first barbecue, ate till I could no longer move. A classic example of a young man, on his first tour, unable to make the right decisions; in this case, controlling dietary habits.

The first game was a midweeker against a Boland Invitation XV, in the wops, at Worcester, where the population was predominantly black. Our bus barged through the crowd into an area surrounded by barbed wire and patrolled by white policemen. The blacks adored us, especially Jonah Lomu, who was in the side for the game. It felt like we were playing at home with the massive crowd support that we received.

The blacks were kept behind a wire fence. They screamed and yelled and tossed stuff into the air and stamped their feet on the ground. We won the game easily. I was a reserve and sat back and watched with horror the pressure and expectation that the black population, in particular, put on Jonah. The previous year he was stellar, a god, partly because of his efforts in the World Cup and in South Africa especially, partly because of his colour. From the moment we got off the plane, the cheers went up. There were cries, 'We love you Jonah. You must win for us.' Jonah was swamped. He wanted to play but was troubled by a knee injury and who knows what else. As a result he became part of the 'dirty dirties' (DDs) most of the time. In some ways he didn't do himself many favours because he had friends in Africa and occasionally socialised with them rather than us. It wasn't an easy juggling act for him. At times, instead of

Testing out the bars in Nelson Mandela's old prison cell on Robben Island.

coming with us on the bus, he'd go off in a flash Merc. He was the rugby equivalent of a big Hollywood movie star, whereas many of us were not much more than bit-part boys in a B-grade picture. A few of the DDs, Eric Rush in particular, worried about Jonah's peripheral behaviour brought about by his fame. We all felt a bit sorry for him in many ways. There is no way I would have coped with what he had to.

Off to Cape Town and the build-up to the first test. During the week the non-test players were taken in army helicopters out to Robben Island, infamous as the prison in which Nelson Mandela was held for the best part of 30 years. At one point I actually jumped into his cell. I spent the day with my Otago coach, Gordon Hunter, one of Hart's assistants; Gordon kept his eye on me throughout the tour.

On the way back, we flew low over the light blue of the Atlantic Ocean before climbing above Table Mountain; looking below into the clear blue waters, I spotted a massive whale. It was breathtaking, a sight straight out of a Wilbur Smith novel. But, as with so much in South Africa, the contrasts were unsettling. The sameness of the architecture was a reflection of the apartheid era; away from whites-only areas the place was dirty, with evidence everywhere of poverty, people fighting to survive. As international rugby players we were taken to wealthy vineyards and entertained in opulent surroundings wherever we went, but that life we were shown was not the real story of South Africa.

It was almost impossible not to lose items of clothing. Gear sent to the laundry often disappeared, stolen. Worse was the fact that some senior players stole gear. It was common practice to write your name on the outside of your clothing, otherwise it could get pinched. I thought, 'They've been on plenty of tours, have heaps of gear, why do they want more?' I saw these acts as selfish and petty, and wasn't the only one hacked off by it. It was utterly contradictory to the ethic of 'team first'.

In order to feel safe, I mixed with the likes of Tabai Matson, Taine Randell, Scott McLeod, Justin Marshall and Mehrts, guys of my age whom I'd played with. We had a board game called 'Risk', which we played at all hours of the day. Each player had an army with which he set out to conquer other parts of the world through aggression and cunning. We played that board game the whole tour and all became firm friends.

I was one of the DDs, thus not required to strip for the Cape Town test. Traditionally, the DDs went out on the booze the night before a test. I didn't because I was way behind with my university work, so stayed in and did some anatomy and physiology study. When I went and asked our medical staff a few questions some of the test players raised their eyebrows and wanted to know why I wasn't out 'on the piss'. After explaining my situation I wandered back to my room, pleased I'd stood my ground and buried my head in textbooks for the night.

I didn't know John Hart beforehand. From what I'd seen and heard of him, he struck me as intelligent. As a new and young All Black I had no basis for comparison. It was just great to be an All Black. Initially, I thought some of his team talks were great. But after a while they were predictable. Andrew Mehrtens was a master at mimicking Harty's talks, both the content and the varying levels of intonation, going quiet then rising to a crescendo. Mehrts had the voice, the gestures — the way John would flick off his watch, take his glasses off and put them on again. Mehrts did the whole lot and had us in stitches doing it. 'Ah,' flick and slap, 'critical,' slap, 'we want to go wide.' Hart was not noted for brevity and this was the source of both amusement and irritation. When we were at Plettenberg Bay I was intrigued, and surprised, to overhear some of the players betting on how long Harty would speak for, and to find that the doctor and the physio were also in on the bet. Until then I had thought that there was a clear split between players and management. If Harty had known that was going on, I assume he would have been angry to find that members of his management team were having bets like that with the players.

The following year, 1997, it got to the stage where players were dreading Harty's talks. There was a scramble not to sit at the front where you would be forced to make eye contact with him. Hart was a brilliant speaker and I was not contemptuous of him, but at times he simply went on too long.

If Gordon Hunter and Ross Cooper, Harty's assistants, were concerned about the lengthy talks, I wasn't aware of it. Gordon always kept such thoughts to himself, was always careful to show no dissent publicly or privately. Gordon was unmoveable in his loyalty. There was a view that Ross was being groomed as an All Black forward coach. My impression was that the 'big boys' in the pack didn't see him as having enough mana for that, so it looked as if he was given the job of looking after us, the DDs. There had never been three coaches on a tour before. Having 36 players meant that there were essentially two teams and they needed to be trained and coached as such. More recently, the name DDs got dropped and was replaced with the more pally, politically correct 'The Crew'. So what? They're still treated the same.

During the first test at Newlands, I felt like a fan. I didn't feel like an All Black at all. As a DD I was in my number ones and, being the youngest in the squad, tradition demanded that I go down and get food at halftime. I got given all the money and had to thread my way through the crowd, buy 16 pottles of chips, and 16 hot dogs. This required two trips back and forth and I missed a fair bit of the second half.

South Africa was ahead 15–6 at halftime and it wasn't until Glen Osborne scored with 13 minutes left that the All Blacks led 19–18. A try to Dowd seven minutes later, then a conversion and a penalty to Mehrts clinched it: 29–18.

The game and the whole occasion were unbelievably intense. That's South Africa, on and off the field. At the time I wasn't able to see myself being out there playing; I still felt as if I was on the outside looking in. This is not to say I felt as if I was being neglected, or deliberately ostracised, it was simply that that was the way it was in the All Blacks in 1996. And, probably, it was also a reflection of my state of mind at the time.

I knew I was up to the standard required at that level, for I had played against Fitzy and Norm, and wasn't intimidated by either of them. But selection for tests still seemed only a distant possibility. Hart's view was that the likes of me were there to learn off the field as much as on. Yes, but what were we learning? For me, a lot of my boyhood All Black myths were shattered. The feeling of disconnection grew and grew to the point where, when we got home, I was relieved to escape from the vaunted 'All Black environment'.

This is not to say that the Otago environment was all that comfortable when I first played for the blue and golds. Initially, some of the senior players — John Leslie, for instance — could be a bit like Kamo: 'earn your stripes'. When I got back I just wanted to play rugby with my mates, feel good about myself again, have some fun. In the All Blacks you had, basically, been stripped, made to feel like an accessory.

From Cape Town we flew to Port Elizabeth for a game against Eastern Province at Boet Erasmus stadium. This would be the first game in which I actually started for the All Blacks and, coincidentally, it was 20 years almost to the day since my father had played his first game for

My first haka in an All Black jersey . . . against Eastern Province at Port Elizabeth in 1996. On my right is Scott McLeod and on my left is Carlos Spencer.

New Zealand on the same ground and against the same team. Strangely, I wasn't overly emotional about the game until, with five minutes to go before kick-off, I took off my T-shirt and grabbed my black jersey off a clothes' hook. I sat there with the jersey on my lap staring at the silver fern and occasionally passing my thumb over the embroidery to make sure that it was real. This was it, I was going to realise a dream, walk out the tunnel with 14 other men and represent my country. I was going to be an All Black. I stood up and slipped the jersey on, and looked around the room where other first-time All Blacks were thinking similar thoughts to me. Suddenly there was no more time for contemplation and we filed out of the changing rooms. It was touch and go on the field: 26–23 to us until Matthew Cooper scored a try close to fulltime. Afterwards, Norm Hewitt came up to me and said, 'Mate, you don't have to do that. You don't have to go to every ruck.' I'd been filled with so much energy and enthusiasm that I'd gone into everything. I remember little about the game itself; it seemed as if I had played only 20 minutes.

Next stop Durban, and easily the hottest place I'd been to. The sea was warm but dirty. We were told not to go to various parts of the city because of the number of muggings and killings. Much of South Africa was lawless and desperate and I simply didn't feel safe most of the time.

The DDs had a huge night out on the eve of the test at King's Park. Richard Fry, the assistant manager, escorted us: 13 or 14 players. We drank a great deal and feasted. I wasn't going to go because I'd vowed to train hard, keep myself very fit. But then I thought, well, it wouldn't look good to stand apart, so why not go out and have fun. I needed a break from my studies, which were becoming mentally draining.

Next day we were put through a massive training session: scrum after scrum after scrum, and lots of running. I had eaten half the ocean the night before, and while scrummaging I stopped and gritted my teeth. Oh my God, I thought, I am going to crap myself. Halfway through training I scurried off to the changing sheds and told our doctor that I was vomiting and might have a viral flu. In fact, just staving off disaster, I went in and sat on the throne. Oh, the relief.

If I refer a lot to the drinking that went on in the All Blacks, it is because it was such a large part of life on tour. This is something that characterised the All Black scene for years, something that, in my later years, I and others, including Doc John Mayhew, and Andrew Martin, our manager in 2000 and 2001, were concerned about. Unless you were able to duck it on religious grounds, it was hard to avoid and to be honest no one wanted to avoid it. Excessive drinking was accepted but in time this attitude had to change.

The Durban test was close, 23–19. Our boys held on for the last 20 minutes and most of the 52,000 crowd went away with a sense of foreboding. The All Blacks had won the last two tests, the first in Cape Town as part of the Tri-nations competition, and now led 1–0 in the test series with the Durban victory. A first ever series win in South Africa was a serious possibility.

Our next destination was Pretoria, to prepare for the second test in the series at Loftus Versfeld stadium. The midweek team bussed from Pretoria to Potchefstroom on the morning of our match against Western Transvaal. We had brunch in the worst hotel anyone had experienced, and we were served the worst food imaginable. Doc Mayhew is still blamed for that to this day. Mouldy big broad beans, greasy bacon, eggs as hard and tough as old boot leather, a curry that made you fart with sufficient force to blow holes in upholstery. The bread was rock hard, stale. Harty gave Doc a bollocking. Potchefstroom seemed like a ghost town, like a scene out of the film *Deliverance*. No one in the town could remember when they'd last had rain. Then, 20 minutes before play was due to start, it came down in sheets. All our gear in the changing rooms got soaked and there was a foot of water in the sheds. Hail bounced up off the ground, lightning flashed, thunder cracked and the pitch was flooded. I got just 20 minutes on the park and was disappointed. I knew the test team, back in Pretoria, would be watching and I had decided that the only way to get their respect was by performing well on the field. I just wasn't getting enough of a chance to impress.

None of the pre-match shambles — a pantomime really — upset me. I think that was because, back in New Zealand during the tour with the New Zealand Under 21s, I decided that I needed to be flexible when it came to pre-match routines so that, if there was a hitch, I could alter things without much bother. This certainly helped me in Potchefstroom. I had never experienced water above my boots when running out of a tunnel to start a match.

Unbeknown to us, TV commentators Keith Quinn and Wayne Graham went along to the Western Transvaal dressing room to 'put names to faces' before the match. In a side room they saw four or five players getting injections in their backsides. Western Transvaal sent on two replacement props at halftime and one of their substituted props was later found to have failed the post-match drug test.

The test series-decider at Pretoria was stunning. I don't think I have ever seen, or played in, a more intense, dramatic game. All Blacks ahead 21–11 at halftime: two tries to Jeff Wilson. With 15 minutes to go, Culhane left the field with a broken wrist, the score was 24–23, and on came Jon Preston. His first touch was to be handed the ball 38 m out and told to kick for goal. It went over: 27–23 became 27–26 a little later. Preston then kicked another penalty, this time from 50 m, and the mercurial Zinzan Brooke dropped a goal from their 10 m mark to make the final score 33–26.

It was clear that this win meant the world to the older players like Brooke and Fitzy, and to Hart. On that day history was made; a dream had come true. The South Africans were crestfallen, but not without dignity in defeat.

I'd have seen all the game if it had not been for my usual excursion to the food stalls at halftime to buy the fatty stuff for the rest of the DDs. After the game a group of cameramen came over to us and the DDs stood up and did a haka in their white shirts and ties. All except me; I slipped away. I saw the haka as a bit of grandstanding, as a bit contrived and didn't feel as if we had truly been a part of the victory. There was no resentment on my part; it was simply

I made myself scarce when the Dirty Dirties stood up and did a haka after the All Blacks' 33–26 win over South Africa at Pretoria. I didn't feel I deserved any credit for the victory.

that I didn't feel I had done enough on tour to have earned any credit for the victory. It may seem a bit overly sensitive now, but at the time I didn't see justification in my doing that haka. I went off to look for another hot dog. No one noticed I was missing.

Most of the DDs were in bed early that night, partly because of the previous evening's activities, and partly because we had our biggest game of the tour coming up, against Griqualand West at Kimberley. I stayed up and hung about quietly, recognising the significance of the series win, wanting to be a part of All Black history, away from the cameras and reporters. Ian Jones had a knee ligament injury so he sent me to look for Doc Mayhew. He was nowhere to be found. Jones then sent me off to find some Voltaren, anti-inflammatory tablets. I wasn't successful, so he sent me looking for the liaison officer, wanted me to ask him to find some. That typified Ian for me on that tour; so I left.

It wouldn't surprise me if, nowadays, he regrets aspects of his behaviour in those days. He has since become one of our best-informed and more pleasant TV presenters and commentators. Jones is one of the few former All Blacks who doesn't bag current players and I respect him for that. I have no time for ex-All Blacks who publicly slate today's players.

I had a deep respect for the efforts All Blacks had put in over the years of trying to win a test series in South Africa. Dad had toured South Africa in 1976 and come home empty-handed. So the significance of this win was not lost on me. Others had convinced me that shady things had gone on in the past, and the refereeing hadn't always been kind to the All Blacks.

In Kimberley I shared a room with Chresten Davis. He was idiosyncratic; his sense of humour and way of doing things struck many of the team as strange. I think many misconstrued some of his remarks, and his behaviour. He didn't behave like an archetypal All Black and he was definitely not a macho man. Some saw him as a bit soft and because he wasn't a very confrontational guy, a few guys took him on. He appeared confident, failed to read certain situations correctly, and that invited trouble from some. I had some sympathy for Davis. He and I were pretty raw, but I wasn't copping it like he was. I think the fact that my father had been coaching Bull Allen and Norm Hewitt at the Hurricanes meant they looked after me a bit. Chresten was in the Hurricanes too, but I got a better deal than he did.

Norm had another reason for protecting me. He said that Fitzy had treated him like a piece of you know what when he first made the team, and he hated it, and didn't want anyone else to go through what he had suffered. He never agreed with the view that said he had failed to show Fitzy sufficient respect.

It wasn't that easy for Bull and Norm and the other test reserves. They weren't a concrete part of either the test team or the DDs and as such were left in a kind of no-man's-land. At least we had a sense of identity in the DDs.

Griqualand is unforgiving country populated by tough Boers. Touring sides have never found it easy to win there. We were behind 10–18 with 20 minutes to go. Then Jon Preston kicked a penalty and Glen Osborne scored right on time to tie the scores. Preston had to use the opposition's kicking tee when attempting to convert the try, as one of the touch judges had Jon's behind his back and wouldn't hand it over.

While the test squad prepared for the final test at Ellis Park in Johannesburg, the DDs were sent off to Sun City, our tour virtually over. I studied, played some golf, and was stunned by the luxury, the opulence. This just heightened the extreme contrast between wealth and poverty that characterised South Africa.

There were concerns before the final test that many of the test All Blacks were emotionally and physically tired. Those concerns proved to be accurate when we were well beaten by the

Boks, who played as if they wanted a victory more than the All Blacks did. In retrospect, said those in charge, we should have had more 'fresh legs'. The South Africans made five changes to their team; we made one.

One of the All Black traditions is that, after the last game of a tour, the new boys take on the back seat of the bus. Harty had made it clear he didn't want that to happen. There had been some unpleasant moments in the past, including the time when Justin Marshall got strangled by his tie and things got fairly desperate for him before somebody cut him free. I decided to try my luck, possibly because the attitude of some of the senior players had annoyed me. I took off my tie, watch and blazer and undid the buttons on my shirt. For a while I, and one or two others — Chresten Davis being one of them — couldn't make up our minds whether to go for it or not. When we got close to our hotel, I said, 'Stuff it,' got up and sprinted towards the back seat. I was out to get at Ian Jones and thump him. I'm not sure who was behind me as the blinkers were on and I didn't have time to look back. I ran into Bull Allen, who was getting up to go to the toilet, and we both fell to the floor. He sat on me and I heard him whisper in my ear, 'Just stay there and keep your head down.' He was protecting me. A few players took off their shoes and smacked me over the back of the head. They drew a little blood but not much. Chresten had followed me

Right: Filming at Sun City. I was stunned by the opulence of the place.
Below: Honing my shooting skills at the Police College in Pretoria.

and got punched several times — he fared a lot worse than me. Back at the hotel we had the mandatory court session to end the tour. I was required to scull a fair bit of grog because of my alleged poor service as a member of the laundry slaves; the laundry committee always gets flak no matter who is on it.

'An inspirational player' – Jeff Wilson

Jeff Wilson said that from the very first time he played with Oliver it was evident that Oliver held nothing back. Oliver has 'never been one to do things by half measures. He has the right core values. You can trust him to do what he says he'll do. His bottom line was always, do the best for the team.

'I think he's been as good an athlete as we've had. Just an inspirational player.'

When Oliver first made the All Blacks, Wilson says he wasn't pushy. 'He behaved like a guy willing to do his time.' But after a few seasons he was willing 'to stick his neck out. He would challenge you, but he also challenged himself. And he'd listen. If you made a good case, he'd go along with it.'

The other thing about Oliver that Wilson noted was that he was protective of his team-mates. 'Anton takes exception to other guys being hammered, being publicly humiliated in front of others.'

He says he sometimes thinks 'Anton cares too much about some things.'

On tour, apart from my friendship with my Otago team-mates Josh Kronfeld and Jeff Wilson, breakfasting with Michael Jones when he talked about Samoa and his cultural heritage was the only time I recall talking to a senior player as such.

But I took my hat off to John Hart. A party of 36 players had never gone on tour before. The main reason there were 36 was so that the test players wouldn't have to back up as reserves in the midweek games. One result was that, logistically, it was a nightmare. However, I think Hart was the right person at the right time. And if some of the younger players, and some of the DDs, felt a bit left out, that was always going to be the likelihood. We don't live in a perfect world; life as an All Black is not all about bouquets and lovely times in swell places. Some things about being an All Black are unpleasant, and being a member of the DDs was one of them. It's still a bit like that when there are over 30 players in a touring party, but much has changed in general team harmony today, and players are friendlier towards each other. There is more interaction between the old and the new.

In Auckland we took part in a ticker-tape parade down Queen Street. Don Cameron of the *New Zealand Herald* termed us 'The Incomparables'. I felt anything but that; I still felt like an appendage. This was really an occasion for Harty, Fitzy and Zinny and the other test heroes. We were taken to a function at Eden Park where the speeches and plaudits continued. After speaking to our manager I slipped quietly away, rang my girlfriend who was in Auckland for the Otago University holidays, and she came down and picked me up. As we drove away from the park, rather than disillusionment, I felt a sense of relief. And when I thought about it later, I was confident that I could hold my head up and say that, in the circumstances, I couldn't have been expected to have done much more.

Chapter 5

Fitz and Starts

It takes a lot to impress a quick-witted, sharp-tongued guy like Andrew Mehrtens, but when I roomed with him at an All Black camp in Taupo early in 1997, he told all and sundry that I was scary. He said I had muscles bulging out everywhere.

While at home in Blenheim over the summer of '97 I had trained really hard, and when I arrived back in Dunedin several weeks before the start of the academic year, I was fitter and stronger and leaner than I had ever been. I'd been taught Olympic power lifting and in Dunedin I had done lots of strenuous gym sessions for up to two hours at a time.

In Dunedin I lived with Olly Sundstrum, Simon Maling and Duncan Blaikie. We shared a flat at the northern end of Cumberland Street, just off the end of the motorway. A friend who stayed for a while named the flat The Depot. On his first night there it rained hard and the engine brakes of the trucks coming down the hill into the city screeched and growled so much that he couldn't sleep. He said it was like sleeping in a truck depot. The flat's since been demolished to make way for a hostel.

I fitted in a two-week swimming module and a week-long camp at the head of Lake Wakatipu. Our group stayed in Glenorchy and spent some time up the Greenstone Valley. All this was part of the requirement to complete my degree in physical education. Wonderful country to roam in. Being in the outdoors has a settling effect on me. I always come away with a more realistic idea of my own significance, or insignificance more accurately, and I always feel the better for it.

The Highlanders squad was on tour in the British Isles. Simon and Duncan were in the touring party (I had stayed behind, having been given a dispensation to do the mandatory swimming module and the outdoor camp). They played as many as nine games in the middle of the northern winter. One game was called off because of snow. Hardly the sort of preparation for a Super 12 competition in the southern hemisphere's late summer, especially when our first game was in Durban in South Africa. And, ah, yes, that game was played at 3 p.m. when the temperature was 45 degrees Celsius. At halftime, sitting in our changing shed, the black dots that often appear in one's vision during a hard scrum session wouldn't go away.

Prior to the game in Durban, we had played a trial match against a Crusaders side at Rugby Park in Christchurch. I felt fit and dynamic. That match was a disaster for us, as most of our key players got injured: Josh Kronfeld, Jeff Wilson, Simon Culhane and Stu Forster.

It was a bad year for both the Highlanders and Otago sides — eight losses and three wins for the former, four wins and four losses for the latter. The Highlanders grasped the wooden spoon. I played well enough: all 11 games for the Highlanders and nine of the 10 for the Otago NPC. We were coached in both campaigns by Glenn Ross, who had had some previous success with Waikato. Ross spoke well in public, didn't engage in petty power games, worked diligently, but not enough people retained or developed faith in him and his methods. Glenn could become very emotional, uncertain, and on some occasions he said we were to do one thing and then changed his mind soon after.

My main memories of that year were that Glenn made us do a great deal of hard contact work. He seemed to think that we were too soft. It may be that he had been told that we were a youngish forward pack and that he was needed to toughen us up, mould us into a replica of the legendary Otago forward packs of old. We simply bashed ourselves to bits at training, ran out of puff and had too little left for the games. Our last Highlanders game was against the

Putting a fend on Blues halfback Ofisa Tonu'u during the Highlanders' 28–45 loss at Carisbrook. We lost eight of our eleven Super 12 matches in 1997.

Chiefs in Taupo. Our scrum, which included Meeuws, Hoeft, John Blaikie, Timmins, Randell, Maka and Kronfeld, went well. Richard Loe started against us and we pushed him all over the place. After he was subbed off we learned why: his neck was shot and he could have got himself killed. Doug Howlett was playing for us and scored three tries, which helped us win and end the competition on an upbeat note.

But it was the end of the line for Glenn Ross after only three campaigns — two for Otago and one for the Highlanders. He went the way of so many Otago coaches — more on that elsewhere.

After the Super 12 competition an All Black trial match was played in Rotorua. The shadow test side was called the New Zealand Barbarians; the aspirants, which included me and captain Todd Blackadder, were called New Zealand A. As is often the case with the underdogs, the A team came together well. We were feeling stroppy; our attitude was, we'll show the so-called stars, for what have we got to lose? The fact that the second team always gets the poorer hotel, the worst bus, the inferior training field, and average food acts as an incentive.

We damned near won. Mark 'Bull' Allen scored an easy try for the Barbarians close to fulltime to make the score 29–22. We had pushed them hard and shaded them in some areas and this was reflected in the team chosen for the first test of the season, against Fiji, six days later on 14 June 1997. I was picked as the reserve hooker behind Fitzpatrick. I hadn't expected that. I thought Norm Hewitt would still be preferred to me, but even then there was the view that Hart, the All Black coach, wasn't sold on Norm. He went off and played for New Zealand Maori against the Pumas.

My dream was to displace Fitzy and become number one. For the first time I began to think that I might be seen as Fitzy's heir. I thought I was the equal of Fitzy in most departments, and better in some, but I accepted the view of those who believe that experienced, hardened incumbents should not be replaced by younger contenders until the younger ones have shown that they are very clearly better. He was battle-hardened and proven and I was not.

I sat on the bench at Albany delighted that, for the second time ever — the first time had been in 1995 — if there was an injury to our hooker, I would be on. It was rare for Fitzy to come off so I was not expecting to get on. But then play stopped, Fitzy got up with some claret on his face and the medicos were saying he had to leave the field and be stitched up. A cry went up: 'Anton, you're on.' I can still remember the feeling: Is this actually happening? I did a couple of quick stretches and ran out onto the pitch, rather startled.

We had just scored so I ran into position ready to receive the kick-off. The ball floated down between me and Robin Brooke. I was expecting him to call for it; he was thinking I was going to take it. So the ball hit the ground between us. That was my first lesson in test football: you snooze, you lose. Don't expect anyone else to do the work; you do it. We had a scrum soon after and I remember pushing with all my might. I was on the field for 10 to 15 minutes and it was the best few minutes of my rugby life to that point. At last, I felt like a true All Black; I had played in a test for New Zealand, and no one could take that away from me. It was, truly, the realisation of a dream that I had long cherished.

The games I had played in South Africa in 1996 didn't really count because, as every rugby player knows, until you have played in a test match, you're something of a spare part.

Afterwards, when everyone had showered and put on their number ones — our formal All Black suit and tie — there was a time-honoured important All Black tradition, the test tie presentation. Sean Fitzpatrick gave me my tie. I can't recall what he said nor what I said, but I can say I was very nervous. And it was an odd feeling, too, to find that some of the older players began to speak to me as if they acknowledged I now had a credibility that hadn't been evident before. It wasn't that they welcomed me as if I'd become a fully fledged, paid-up member, but it was something that hadn't been present before.

I went out to a private party that night with Josh Kronfeld and Goldie Wilson. A lot of the senior players encouraged me to go and get sloshed. I did. I was rooming with Charles Riechelmann. He woke me and told me that the team meeting was to start soon, but still badly sedated by alcohol, I went straight back to sleep. The next thing I knew Charlie was shaking me and saying I was late for the meeting, one of the worst All Black sins, especially if alcohol was a contributing factor. When I got downstairs everyone was sitting there waiting. John Hart scowled at me periodically. I'm sure I looked terrible. A few of the boys caught my eye and gave me a few smiles and winks. Afterwards Frank Bunce came over and joked. He said I had to learn a few of the tricks, like how to look sober. Frank said, 'It's no big deal. Don't worry about it. Everyone has been there.'

Nevertheless it took a bit of the gloss off my first test cap. I had often had to get team-mates out of bed, making sure they showered and dressed while I packed their bags, so I was annoyed with Charlie for leaving me in the room. But in saying that, it was still my fault. Encouraging guys to get pissed and work it out for themselves was part of the All Black ethos that was hard to eradicate, and in retrospect I was unhappy to realise that I had bought into it as well.

The following week in the first team meeting before the test against the Pumas in Wellington, Hart ticked a number of us off: me for being late and drinking too much after the game in

My first appearance for the All Blacks in a test match was in jersey No. 23 — a temporary sub for Sean Fitzpatrick — against Fiji at Albany in 1997.

Albany; Taine Randell for not packing up his room-mate Michael Jones' gear and removing it after Jones had ended up in hospital.

I decided it was time for me to keep my head down and my bum up. On the Thursday, when practising at Athletic Park, Harty was angry when the Pumas arrived halfway through our run. In fact it may have done us good. We saw how big many of them were and that dispelled any sense of complacency by reminding the boys that unless they got stuck in an upset was possible. When the whole squad was stretching and warming down, I was chatting to Bull Allen. We shared a joke and Fitzy snapped at us for laughing. Bull was a very relaxed man and I took note of Fitzy's bite. I didn't want to get offside with the captain. You occasionally noted that Bull and Norm Hewitt, who were quite chummy, who went for runs together, and who were always affable with me, didn't fit into that group of Auckland forwards that was a prominent and strong part of the All Black team. The Aucklanders were tight, and justifiably quite proud of their achievements, but there was a definite attitude of non-inclusion for the reserves, and we didn't get much of a go in many trainings.

On the morning of the match, when the forwards were running through lineout drills down on the wharf near Lambton Quay, Bull and I stood together. He said, 'The boys are going to have a good one today.'

'How do you know that?'

'Whenever they get shitty with each other before a match, like this, they play well.'

The Pumas were given a hiding, 93–8.

During the test dinner that night something unexpected and marvellous happened. One of their props got up and sang an operatic aria, and I was quite taken aback with his skill and ability. On the bus back to our hotel, I sat in my usual place near the front with Taine, Mehrts and Justin Marshall. Justin had overindulged and had an unexpected accident in the bus, a hiccup gone wrong! We were only a few seats behind Hart and he wasn't impressed. Many of the boys found it hard to suppress their mirth — that was obvious.

In the morning Hart told me that I was out of the team for the next test and that Norm Hewitt was back in. That was incredibly disillusioning for me. Because I hadn't actually played I couldn't see what I had done to warrant being dropped and it hit me how gutting this sort of thing must have been for Norm over the years. When I got back to Dunedin I subconsciously became quite aggressive in the sense that, with others, I was prone to turn everything into a competition. This was a change from my normal attitude, and this change was especially prevalent if I'd had a couple of drinks where I became overtly competitive and rather aggressive with it. For a few weeks I failed to realise what an unpleasant creature I'd become. Then one day I caught myself telling one of my mates that I was 'better than you'. It shook me. 'Who the hell is saying these things?' I asked myself. 'Where is this crap coming from?' I realised that being dropped had caused it, and it wasn't pretty. Fortunately, I stopped it and went back to simply trying to do my best and not engage in comparisons.

I played a lot of club rugby — University Club — in 1997. It would be another six years, 2003, before I was to play club footie again, this time for Toko, a country club. Club rugby brought me back to earth. Much of what is good about rugby (its true heart and soul, perhaps) is found in the clubs: no money, media or over-inflated egos; just friends having some fun on Saturday afternoons.

While I was playing for University, Fitzy had injured his knee during the Tri-nations campaign in South Africa. Yet again I got a call to come across to Australia as a back-up for Norm Hewitt and Fitzy. There were lots of golf putting 'tests' in hallways in the hotel. A lot of the team had bought Mizuno golf clubs on the cheap, and some had grabbed diving gear as well. Fitzy had mixed feelings about all this, and, in his captain's talk before the test at the MCG, he said that if you looked at the All Blacks from the outside, it might give cause for alarm. For once, due to his injury, Fitzy had been on the outside looking in and that had given him a fresh perspective, one that didn't impress him. All those flash toys, he said: it looked as if we got everything on a plate. He said he hoped no one was in holiday mode and that they had better front up for the game the next day.

I was merely a spare part, again. But it was Norm that I felt for. Fitzy was given until the end of the pre-match warm-up to declare if he was fit to play. He was dead keen to play. Frankly, Norm was in a prick of a position. In the final lineout session, I had a couple of throws and that was it. If I'd got on I wouldn't have had much confidence to put the ball in the right spot.

It looked certain to me, and others, that Fitzy wouldn't be right to play, so I took my gear along and prepared as if I would be back-up for Norm and there was a chance I would get on. But Fitzy astounded us by playing. Management had delayed the decision on whether Fitzy would play until five minutes before the game. Both Norm, especially, and I were on tenterhooks for ages. When the decision was made that Fitzy would start I didn't have time to shower and put on my number ones, so I pulled on my tracksuit and sat and watched the game with the reserves.

Mehrts was required to engage in subterfuge during the test. He went down and was sprayed with some blood collected a few hours before the game, so he could be subbed off for Carlos Spencer. I wasn't privy to the decision making behind that, but I was privy to the anger of one A. Mehrtens who sat next to me on the bench after he was substituted. The All Blacks won the match 33–18.

Early in August, about a fortnight later, I was preparing to captain Otago in a pre-season fixture when our manager, Des Smith, came over to the scrum session we were having and said that Norm Hewitt had been injured and I was to join the All Black camp as soon as possible. This was for the test against Australia at Carisbrook on 16 August. It was my first involvement in a test for the All Blacks on Carisbrook, my home ground, and I was very excited. It helped immeasurably that I had already been involved in the team that year, not just for on-field moves and calls but more especially in a social setting. I was not as apprehensive as I might have been, and there was an air of familiarity about the team that made my reintroduction smoother.

During a team talk about an hour prior to the test, many of the boys were astounded when Harty gave Josh Kronfeld what amounted to a confidence-destroying ultimatum. Kronfeld was shocked; I was too. Unsurprisingly, he played like a headless chicken. He gives a disarming account of this episode in his book *On the Loose*.

The All Blacks were all over the Wallabies in the first 40 minutes. I was ready and expecting to be brought on during the second half. But when the wheels fell off our game, and the Australians found a supercharger, Fitzy stayed on; I remained polishing the bench. The All Blacks stayed in front to win 36–24.

I was one of 36 players picked for the end-of-year tour to England, Ireland and Wales. Three hookers: Fitzy, Norm and me. At 22 I believed that my time would come, but I tried not to think of when. The captain still had all of my respect. He was a great player, an All Black living legend. But, although I didn't say as much to others, I thought I was as good as he was. I think that was a sign of the confidence every athlete with aspirations needs to have in his or her ability. It was clear, though, that Fitzy wasn't going to step aside for me or Norm, which was fair enough. I don't know what Fitzy thought of me, but I never had a problem with him on or off the field. Whenever I played against him he didn't yap at me — as everyone knows, he was renowned for having a lot to say to opposition players and referees especially.

When we assembled in Auckland and prepared for the tour, the rugby world was aware that John Hart had said that he wouldn't take along unfit or injured players.

'Always gave a bit extra' – Kees Meeuws

Meeuws was one of Oliver's front-row brothers-in-arms. He and Oliver were in the 1993 New Zealand Under 19 side that toured Australia and was coached by Oliver's father, Frank.

Meeuws' opinion of Oliver is almost wholly favourable. 'Focused, determined. He grew as a leader, is astute and greatly respected. He always did it on the field and worked hard off it; he always gave a bit extra. I knew I could rely on Anton in the front row. He helped me out many times. He's very strong. So strong he puts pressure on the opposition props.

'I've never had any doubts about Anton in any sense . . . He says what he thinks. You know where you stand with him. He attacks the problem not the person.'

Prior to departure we stayed at the Waipuna Hotel in Mt Wellington, Auckland. We were put through some rigorous fitness sessions, including runs around the inlet close to the hotel. Fitzy didn't train with us much; it was apparent that he wasn't 100 per cent. The knee injury he had suffered in the Tri-nations was still causing him trouble. Some of the boys saw this as one rule for Fitzy, another rule for the rest. This highlights the problem with exceptions: where, and for whom, do you draw the line?

Personally, I didn't mind Fitzy being given some slack. He was our tour captain and in the light of his past efforts had earned some leeway. But John had made sweeping statements about not taking unfit players, and some of the older players from parts outside of Auckland saw it as another example of northern favouritism. I kept my head down and my mouth shut.

The first match was against Llanelli. I watched from the reserve bench while Norm Hewitt and others thrashed them 81–3. Then I played the next match, against Wales A, which was another easy win, 51–8.

We flew to Ireland to prepare for a test at Landsdowne Road in Dublin. After training on the Wednesday we went out to a bar for a meal and a sampling of the local hospitality. The food was good, the live music had tremendous vitality, and I was very taken with the Guinness. I'd never tried it before. It was a novel experience to be able to count how many gulps you'd had from a pint by counting the froth lines on the glass. Most of us were half-cut when we clambered onto the bus to go back to our hotel, and the test was only three days away.

This was the game around which there was a lot of noise about the dropping of Josh Kronfeld. Josh was by now something of a fixture at open-side flanker. He was also a kind of cult, somewhat hip, figure to many outside of rugby's inner circles. (He read a few books, drew comic book characters, played a mouth organ and was a surfer . . .) I recall Josh sitting down beside me just before the test team was announced — Hewitt was hooker, me the reserve. Josh looked extremely disconsolate. Nobody in rugby could look more crestfallen than Josh.

I asked him, 'Are you all right?'

He said, 'Mate, I've just been dropped.'

When I quizzed him Josh said Hart had told him that he and the other selectors felt that his form wasn't good and that at the time Andrew Blowers seemed a better choice. I guess the thing that interested me was seeing what a devastating effect being dropped could have on an incumbent test player. It can be a cruel game. As for Kronfeld's form, I hadn't noticed that he'd been playing poorly. We all have good and not-so-good days. Sometimes play runs for you, sometimes not. What I was absolutely certain of was, irrespective of what anyone who knew him may have thought about Josh's demeanour and idiosyncratic approach off the field, no one questioned the intensity and commitment of his efforts for the team on the field.

'Hatch hates to lose' – Carl Hoeft

Hoeft first played with Oliver in the 1993 New Zealand Under 19 side. He was impressed by Oliver's aggression and all-round ability. Hoeft saw Oliver as the most hard-nosed forward he had ever played with. 'I thought he was the best hooker around back then and I still think he's the best. I thought he would get back in the All Blacks when Graham Henry took over.

'None of us like to lose, but Hatch hates to lose. He has always been his own harshest critic. He can be hard on others but he's just as hard on himself. Maybe too hard at times.

'His honesty brings out the best in other blokes. He is valued by other players for his frankness. In many ways he and Tana Umaga are similar in those respects: both are direct, lead by example, are straight shooters.

'Anton's one of the best ball carriers and tacklers I've played with or against. I can't think of anyone better. He's also the hardest trainer I've ever met.'

I was still very much a member of the second-string component in the All Black touring troupe — the likes of myself and Blackadder, Surridge and Hopa, for instance. We second-stringers played in games like the one against Emerging England in Huddersfield, and England A at Leicester. In Leeds — I hope I'm right here, for my memories of specific games are often hazy, to say the least — I went out mindful of Hart's edict: no foul play would be condoned. Early on, my opposite kneed me in the head after a scrum collapsed. I did nothing. Later on, after another scrum collapse, he stood on my hands. Again, I did nothing. Then, a bit later still, he did something else that pissed me off: he started abusing me. At that my restraint finally collapsed: I had had enough and I donged him a couple. I was penalised but felt pretty good not to have taken any more shit. Bull Allen, beside me, said, 'Good on you, mate.'

After the game my opponent and I were having a beer and he said he was astonished when 'I got you twice and you didn't do anything about it.' I told him that Hart was vehemently opposed to any sort of action that might cost the team points.

Later, John Hart said I'd played very well, 'But watch your discipline.' I told him what had been going on. He said he understood but, nevertheless, asked me to consider what might have happened if it had been a test. It could have meant a sin-binning or a sending off. I could see his point but I'm not sure he saw mine. Regardless, I would have to work on trying to curb my inclination to react angrily.

At the time All Black hookers attracted more than their fair share of attention in the media. In the test against Wales in London — at Wembley Stadium, of all places — there was a celebrated, rather peculiar, incident featuring Norm Hewitt and Fitzy. Norm started in the match.

Plenty of elevation here during this standing jumps exercise with the All Blacks on the 1997 end-of-year tour of Britain.

The 1997 midweek front row of Con Barrell, me and Bull Allen take on the scrum machine at Bracknell Rugby Club in 1997.

At lineout time, after 55 minutes, Fitzy was sent on to replace him. According to some, but not others, Norm's reaction to Fitzy's advent was disrespectful — he appeared unwilling to give up the ball. This was the prelude to his after-match bollocking — some would say shaming — by the coach. Most of the senior players, including a number of the Auckland group, felt that Hart's treatment of Norm was unnecessary and unjustified. To me, Norm's alleged 'insult' was blown out of proportion.

Over time, my impression — and it was one that was shared by several players — was that John Hart may have been a bit too deferential, and possibly reverential, towards Fitzy. A lot of the boys were stunned and confused by the to-do surrounding Norm's subbing by Fitzy.

For Norm, his position was still unsettling. He and I went away wondering whether we were actually going to continue to be Fitzy's back-up men, or not. The question ever uppermost was: will he or won't he be fit to play? And: who will play if he can't? Norm actually started in five games. I started in the other four. It became obvious that Hart was keen for Sean to play the final test against England so that he could end his All Black career in style. Only a few are given the chance to exit with dignity, with the whole blaring fanfare, and Fitzy, for all that he had achieved, deserved that chance.

In one of the midweek games I started and Sean was the reserve. That put Norm in a unique position, the first time he had ever been a DD. So Zinzan Brooke took Norm out for a few quiets, as some put it. The word was that Zinny was having a very good time of it after hours, as

The end is nigh . . . Sean Fitzpatrick (centre) has just replaced Norm Hewitt in the test against Wales in 1997. It would be Fitzy's last game for the All Blacks.

it was his swan song and he had recently clocked up 100 games for the All Blacks, a magnificent achievement.

I hadn't noticed the extent to which Zinny had been living it up; I was still too junior to witness anything first-hand, but on tour the word gets around eventually. In hindsight, in order to get the most — or more — out of Zinny, it might have been better to have given him the tour captaincy. I think that he would have been keen to rise to the challenge of having been appointed captain, and would almost certainly have been less enthusiastic in other respects. Tour captaincy was one of the few honours not to have been bestowed on Zinzan. I think he would have done well at it. That would have left Sean free to float about in such a large party and provide input here and there.

In the game I had played the week before our lineout had not functioned smoothly and I took that anxiety through to the following game, our last midweek one for the tour, against England A in Leicester. I worried and worried and for much of the night before the match I was awake, sometimes out of bed. If there had been a ball in the room I swear I would have been down the stairs and outside throwing a few up against a wall. Call me paranoid, call me nuts, but I was thinking that my whole career might depend on how well our lineouts went the next day. This sort of pressure is something I have put myself under too often in the course of my career, and it has been greatly to my detriment. We won the game and the lineout went okay so I put those thoughts away for the meantime, although not too far away.

Fitzy's knee was shot. He couldn't play in the finale, the test against England at Twickenham where most of the crowd of 75,000 were baying souls hoping against hope that we would lose.

So Norm got to play, and I was reserve. At halftime England led 23–9. Oh, the triumphant singing, the glee behind a lust to see those colonial, rough-hewn upstarts vanquished; oh, the decibel rating in south-west London. Then, a transformation. It had all been far too premature. With 18 minutes left, the All Blacks led 26–23 and most of the crowd was aghast. Mehrts had scored 21 points himself. Ten minutes were remaining when Grayson kicked another penalty and that was the final score, 26–26. The reaction from the England side was peculiar; you'd have thought they had won by 15 or 20 points. They did a . . . what . . . lap of relief? Victory? Whatever, and leaving aside the psychological speculation, that day it seemed a draw was as good as a win for England.

We were to fly home on the Monday. The Sunday was crazy. Champagne at breakfast, then along to a place called The Church. It was open for about three hours and there was mayhem. Usually, you had to buy drinks in a plastic bag, but we were given VIP access to go backstage where cold Lion Red awaited us. I saw some stuff acted out on stage that was well-nigh unbelievable, too sexually immoral to be recorded. A bit later we all floundered into the Walkabout pub in Shepherd's Bush where Josh Kronfeld and his trusty harmonica put on a cameo performance with Midge Marsden and his troupe. Ah, the good old days! Yes?

There was a great deal of drinking on the flight to Los Angeles and a lot of the guys were casually dressed. It was a rag-tag lot that disembarked. Definitely not a good look for the All Blacks.

I left the team in Los Angeles and flew to Seattle with Mark Robinson, Jeremy Stanley and Mark Carter. We went to the K2 ski factory there then drove to Whistler, north of Vancouver. Jeremy and I had never skied before and we had a lot of laughs trying.

This excursion was both pleasurable and disconcerting for me. My overriding emotion, a fair bit of the time, was to go home to New Zealand. But to what? And yet, I thought, these opportunities don't come very often. Enjoy it. So for eight days we had a great time, and then it really was time to go home. I wanted to see the sun, warm and dazzling. I wanted some clear skies, some hours at the beach; wanted to get home to Blenheim and check to see that Mum was okay.

After that, myself, along with a group of friends from Christchurch, Wellington and Taupo, hired a camper van and we drove to Pauanui on the Coromandel where we welcomed the New Year. A day or so later I dropped the van off in Auckland and . . . what else? Started to think of rugby, of training for 1998. Rugby, rugby . . . it seldom lets up.

Chapter 6

Five Black Eyes

Tony Gilbert had been appointed coach of the Highlanders Super 12 team for 1998. He had been Gordon Hunter's assistant coach in 1994 and 1995. His background included coaching successful University and Kaikorai club sides in Dunedin, not much else deemed significant. So Gilbert had little experience at top level rugby — for many it was a case of 'Tony who?' For a long time Tony had been a school teacher, then school principal. He was measured and firm, not given to histrionics, and he appeared secure enough not to need to engage in pointless controlling behaviour.

Tony also had the good — or the bad — fortune to take on the job after we'd had a disastrous year in 1997. I recall being told the odds on us winning the Super 12 were 100 to 1 against. My personal preparation for the 1998 Super 12 season was sabotaged by my decision to take a product called Creatine over December and January. A lot of my team-mates had told me they had used it with fantastic results, meaning they lifted more weight, and they recovered quicker.

After three weeks I went to Dunedin, then weighed myself. I couldn't believe it; my mates couldn't believe what they were seeing either. My usual playing weight was 110–112 kg. The scales read 121 kg. I looked as if someone had used a bike pump on me — I was big all over. When I went for a 3 km run and recorded my worst time ever I was demoralised.

The next five to six weeks were very painful. I had become a big, heavy, leaden plodder — great in the gym where I lifted more than ever before, but hopeless around the park.

The 1998 Highlanders side was a very harmonious, carefree lot. We had no expectations placed upon us externally, and even we didn't think we would go all that well. As has been the way in Otago rugby over the years, alcohol has been used as a means of bonding and maintaining team spirit, and the new Highlanders team of '98 followed that tradition in fine style. We had a drink together — the notorious 'court sessions' — after every game. Sometimes a lot of fluid went down. In a way this was contrary to much of what professionalism is meant to be about. Paradoxically, perhaps, we played well in 1998. At times extremely well.

Oddly, the after-match court sessions weren't where the worst damage occurred. Most of the players would then go out and hit the top shelf. Unbeknown to me, a few regulars went out on Wednesday nights and got tanked up then as well. So how the hell, you might ask, did we win games? The fact that Tony trained the pants off us acted as a counter. And hard training can be a massive unifying factor. Get the boys working really hard together and this instils a pride that pulls a team together.

Every Tuesday we knew that we were going to get flogged. In those days, fitness sessions were done in conjunction with training, unlike today.

So there we were — a fairly young team in many ways, myself, Hoeft, Meeuws, Maling, Blaikie brothers, Middleton, Kelleher, Brown, Alatini, Stanley, Ropati — behaving like cavaliers and often succeeding. I remain amazed by our successes that year. In the long run I can't see how we could have kept up that level of alcohol intake and continued to win. That side of our behaviour was unprofessional. I think Tony was a bit worried there and knew the whole set-up was on a high wire, tightrope walking. The team really could have gone right over the falls, but it didn't.

At other times I have played under managers who have religiously, and piously, gone to the opposite extreme. What we are talking about here is where you draw the line in the need to find the right perspective and balance.

We beat the Reds at Carisbrook then lost away to the Brumbies and the Blues. The omens were not good. But then in a high-scoring game we beat the Sharks 41–35 at home; then down to Invercargill for a 57–27 romp over the overfed and lethargic Golden Cats. After that we beat the Chiefs and the Hurricanes at home before falling 24–40 to our South Island nemesis, the Crusaders, in Christchurch. A loss (22–23) to the Waratahs in Sydney meant we had to beat both the Stormers and the Bulls in South Africa, and get a bonus point (for four tries) in each game, in order to make the semi-finals.

The guys were remarkably sanguine, even light-hearted to be in the semi-final against Auckland on Eden Park. Our plan was to throw the ball around and attack at every opportunity. If we lost, we lost. We knew, considering all the travelling we'd done in the two weeks before the match, that it would take something very special to win. Well, it was close: 37–31 to the Blues. Josh Kronfeld tells how, 'at a vital time Jonah Lomu ran through and over us to score under the posts'. Kronfeld says he 'thought' he 'had him' but Jonah was 'a lot of muscle and meat to hang onto and stop. All I was left with was a handful of cloth from his shorts.' Josh says, wryly, that he put the missed tackle down to 'the inferior quality of his [Jonah's] shorts'.

In some quarters our loss was seen as yet another example of how Otago and Otago-based sides haven't got what it takes to win the really important games. Subscribers to that view like to describe Otago teams as chokers. I think that is unfair. Wouldn't it be more accurate to say that, given the region's limited financial resources and smaller population-playing base when compared with most other 'major' centres, Otago has actually punched above its weight for decades? Maybe the reason we haven't won more trophies is simply because we haven't had quite enough depth all round. A case can be made for asserting that management infighting has been unsettling and has hampered Otago. Our turnover of coaches has been far too high, and players have often felt extremely insecure. Mind you, especially since the advent of professionalism, that is true of just about every province and franchise. And, it has to be conceded, other unions — Canterbury, Wellington, Auckland, for example — have all had more than their share of squabbling and infighting too. Whether Otago's has been worse than theirs I don't really know.

Steve Surridge tries to halt my progress during the Highlanders' one-point loss to the Crusaders in the 1998 Super 12.

There's also the misty-eyed view, the summoning up of memories of a proud and glorious past. Those victories against touring sides, for instance, are mentioned frequently. In those good old days, so it's said, players had more pride in Otago rugby. It meant more to them than it does to today's players. I can understand where that view comes from, because I started playing for Otago before professionalism arrived. At that time most of us played for enjoyment, and were driven by a desire to emulate the deeds of our predecessors. Among those were the likes of my father and his generation; to them, playing for the love of the game, and subscribing to a certain brand of rough-hewn, not always seemly, camaraderie, was almost all they knew.

To my delight, I was picked to play for the All Blacks against England at Carisbrook on 20 June 1998. In a way it felt as if I was truly beginning my career as an All Black. I had first made the team three years previously, but due to the dislocating experiences I had had, combined with limited playing time, the All Black environment still felt slightly foreign to me. I was excited, once again, at the prospect of playing on Carisbrook in a test for the All Blacks, although this time I was going to get on the pitch for sure.

We prepared for the Dunedin test in Queenstown. I was buzzing, raring to go. When practising a Willie-away move off a short lineout I felt my calf tweak as I was racing around to be in support. It didn't feel good but I thought I could 'run it out', so I kept training. Then it went again, and this time it felt a lot worse. I told our physiotherapist, Dave Abercrombie. He dragged me off immediately and strapped ice on my calf.

I was anxious and annoyed but I tried to remain positive. It was ice and rest for me that week. My mother and father, my brothers, and my aunt too, I think, had all come down to Dunedin to watch the game. The night before the game Doc John Mayhew and Abercrombie got me to jog barefoot down the hallway in our hotel and do a couple of hops on one foot. I knew they had been easy on me and, looking back, I don't think I was fit to play. But it's not hard to see why I chose to ignore the seriousness of the muscle tear. After having sat on the bench for so long I hated the thought of having to pull out at the very moment I'd been accorded the honour of being named first choice for the All Blacks in a test.

For the whole game against the Poms I scrummed on one leg and I made sure that whenever I hit a ruck I drove through with my good leg. And when running with the ball, I never stepped, propped or changed direction off my bad calf. At contact times with or without the ball I really wasn't doing a full job. This was the game where the England lock Danny Grewcock got sent off. A scrum went down after about 10 minutes. I was lying face down in the crucifix position and he booted me in the head. We won easily, 64–22.

There was quite a lot of shabby behaviour in the team around this time and a few All Blacks blotted their copybooks and got away with it. One who didn't was the ill-fated Norm Hewitt. Norm had an altercation at the Bowling Green Hotel. He had words with another feisty, combative individual, the England hooker Richard Cockerill, and one or two blows were then exchanged. The word was that Cockerill had passed a remark to the effect that Norm must have a fair few splinters in his bum by now, given the number of times his posterior had warmed the All Black bench during his career.

It was all a bit shambolic. When we got to Auckland to prepare for the second test against England, John Hart gave us a roasting. He ripped into us for our performance both on and off the field and he had every justification in doing so.

We played very badly in Auckland. There was a lamentable lack of combination and we were flattered by the 40–10 result. About midway through the first half, when trying to support the ball carrier after a kick-off, I felt my calf muscle go again. I tried to play on but eventually

Above: Ofisa Tonu'u, Olo Brown and Robin Brooke are in support as I launch an All Black attack against England in 1998. Right: My troublesome left calf is strapped as I warm up prior to a weights session in Auckland.

I had to go off; I knew I was letting the team down by attempting to play on with the injury. I hopped around with ice on my leg and sat on the bench. But not for all that long. Norm Hewitt badly injured his knee and the call came through for me to go back on. Someone had to throw the ball in to lineouts and the coaches decided I was the only one who could. Off with the ice, off with the jacket, and out I hobbled. If farmers in Central Otago saw an animal walking like that they'd say, 'We've no choice but to put the bastard down.'

I couldn't have been colder. It was hard to join the fray when I couldn't even get up to half pace. At one point I felt my calf tear even more. By the end I was down to a pathetic limping jog.

Norm Hewitt and I spent most of the night in Lipi Sinnott's hotel room. Lipi, our masseur and team baggage man, was good at his job and a top bloke. He was to go on and become a valued

The All Blacks suffered a devastating 16–24 loss to Australia at Melbourne to kick off the 1998 Tri-nations competition. Little did we know this was to be the first of five consecutive test losses in '98. With me here are Olo Brown and Craig Dowd.

member of the All Blacks support staff for the next few seasons until he too was deemed surplus to requirements.

Norm and I were a comical sight. We lay on our backs — Norm the Taniwha, me Hagar the Horrible — legs raised and encased in ice while eating room-service food and whining away about our mutual misfortune. Meanwhile Lipi sat there watching us like a scout by a campfire, sipping from a magnum of Steinlager that we couldn't drink, so he drank it for us. All three of us could see the black humour and irony in the situation. We all shared a few laughs that night; laughter was the only antidote for the depressing situation Norm and I found ourselves in.

There was a fortnight before we were to play a Bledisloe Cup match against Australia in Melbourne. I did all I could to help that calf tear heal, and, thankfully, 24-hour treatment for two weeks saw me back out on the field again. What do they say about things coming in threes? During a game of touch at the MCG on the eve of the test, our team needed to score a try to win the game. A difficult pass was floated my way and I had to dive forward to gather it. Alas, I also collected a hoarding on the edge of the in-goal area, and . . . One of the boys came over to see if I was okay. He bent down and picked a piece of tooth up off the ground: 'Shit, is this yours?' Sure enough, a brief pass of the tongue detected a big space that hurt. Ouch. I had lost half of a front tooth. How come? Because it had been touch rugby I figured I wouldn't need my mouth guard. I had put it down my sock.

Soon after I was off to a dentist who built the tooth up. It has since come off again more than once.

We lost 16–24 and it was devastating. In the shed afterwards most of the boys were sombre. But one who wasn't was Ian Jones, the Kamo Kid. Ian had played well that day and his demeanour in the dressing room certainly reflected that. He didn't seem too bothered to have lost, although it might have been more diplomatic to disguise that. Not all that good a look from one of the most capped All Blacks of all time. On the other hand, was he saying that All Black sides haven't benefited from being, and appearing, so disconsolate in defeat? All Black sides have sometimes been slated for being too sullen and emotionless regardless of results.

Our next test was in Wellington, Athletic Park's last test, and the 50th All Black-Springbok international. It was a close affair until the Boks scored the crucial try from a scrum near our 22. I have since talked about it to their prop Ollie le Roux. He said that Henry Honiball had spotted defensive weaknesses in our set-up and had worked out a move the day before the match. It worked a treat, hence the extent of their collective delight when they scored. It was just so easy, as if the All Blacks had become onlookers rather than participants.

Two losses in a row dent a team's confidence and I sensed that, overall, there was a lack of self-belief, insufficient collective resolve in the team. We knew we had to win the game against Australia at Jade Stadium on 1 August if we were to retain the Bledisloe Cup. For some reason, possibly a psychological need to re-establish the dominance we once exerted over Australian rugby, winning and retaining the Bledisloe seems just as, or more, important to the New Zealand rugby fraternity than winning the World Cup. And how not winning that World Cup since 1987 gnaws at New Zealand rugby's vitals!

The night before the test in our hotel, I was playing cards with Taine Randell, Justin Marshall and Andrew Mehrtens. If you lost a hand you had to scull a glass of water — a stupid way of hydrating. Taine lost several hands in a row and just couldn't drink any more. The rest of us found this funny. The assistant coach, Peter Sloane, didn't. He happened to walk into our room and castigated us for fooling around. It was, he said, a dumb way to prepare for a test the next day. He was right: it was stupid.

When I look back at 1998, I like to see myself as fairly mature and focused. But at 22 I was still just a big kid really, and kids — and not just kids, either — are prone to make errors of judgement. Nevertheless, I was becoming more confident and determined. My play, especially around the field, improved quite a lot with every game. I put that down to the fact that I was starting every test and also to focusing entirely on my job. I was quite selfish in my outlook at this stage of my career. Do my job, play well — that was how I saw my way of making a contribution to the team.

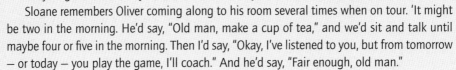

'A team barometer' – Peter Sloane

Peter Sloane is a great fan of Oliver's, whom he describes as 'a thinker, a leader, a team man, a straight-shooter. Direct, but always for the sake of the side. He works hard. And he's a caring guy. I remember him ringing up when on a trip to the Pacific Islands and saying, "Send them a scrum machine," and he'd pay for it.'

Sloane has coached him in Otago, All Black and Barbarians sides. Right from the beginning, Oliver struck Sloane as 'a real athlete, explosive, quick, strong.

'Anton had the complete skill set: good hands, and he could kick with both feet. What else could he have? He could do anything a coach asked.'

'Players go to Oliver,' says Sloane, 'which is why he's a team barometer.'

Sloane remembers Oliver coming along to his room several times when on tour. 'It might be two in the morning. He'd say, "Old man, make a cup of tea," and we'd sit and talk until maybe four or five in the morning. Then I'd say, "Okay, I've listened to you, but from tomorrow — or today — you play the game, I'll coach." And he'd say, "Fair enough, old man."

'I've never doubted his commitment to the team on and off the field.'

He admires Oliver's forthright approach. In Sloane's view, 'If you're not prepared to rattle a cage, you're not adding to the cause.'

The Australians put us under immense pressure and led at halftime. After the break, Carl Hoeft came on and our scrum improved immediately. At just about every lineout, Kamo was calling for the ball on a back lob even with Eales marking him closely. If my throws had been even a fraction short, Eales would have stolen the ball. My back was up against the wall. I had to ensure that those throws were spot on. Unusually, all doubt vanished and I became robot-like. I had a job to do and simply did it — sometimes the more you think about it the worse it gets — but my throws hit the mark that day, not that it mattered much as we lost 23–27.

Three losses in a row was very un-All Black. Everyone was upset about it. Both coach John Hart and our captain Taine Randell were copping fire. That night, after the test, we had a few quiet drinks together. Randell was going off to the toilet when John Hart stopped him and gave him a lashing. I've no idea what was said, but it must have been pretty savage for it left Taine devastated, in tears.

The Boks were waiting for us in Durban for our next game. We stayed at a game park about an hour away. Many of us sat around yarning until late; we wanted to minimise the effects of jet lag. I spent time debating with Wayne Smith. We talked about whether rugby is a simple game made too complex, or a complex game made too simple. Smithy and I had a vigorous, but not heated, discussion, and I can't even remember what conclusions, if any, were reached. But our physio, Dave Abercrombie, decided to butt in. He said I should pull my head in and know my place.

That browned me off. The subject was interesting. Here I was, a young player interested in analysing and discussing matters relevant to the game. We're all entitled to a view and to express it, aren't we? If anything, I felt I was too buttoned up, and that the All Black environment wasn't benefiting from insisting on a kind of 'young people should be seen and not heard' attitude. In 1998 there was a changing of the guard; in particular, Zinny and Fitzy were no longer there, neither was Bunce. All had been leaders. I sensed that some within the camp were hinting that it was time for me to show some leadership. But I continued to be fairly hesitant. I was still very much 'Know your place, Anton', and it wasn't until two years later that I was able to shrug that off. In 2000 I felt it was time to step up and stop being the sort of stolid, compliant individual that some in rugby circles still seem to prefer.

Abercrombie's remarks were indicative of an attitude that annoyed me, so I decided that rather than look to him for treatment I'd manage my own bad knocks, rub them out myself. Some of the players in the team felt that Abercrombie had his priorities, which meant that the older members of the side got treated first. It smacked of favouritism. For the next year I treated myself.

There were some old campaigners in the side. Men in their late twenties seem like old nuts to the young guys. Olo Brown and Craig Dowd had been around a while. In Durban I had a heart-to-heart with Olo and, to my astonishment, he said that, fundamentally, he liked one of his team-mates getting stuck into him verbally on the field. Here was a player I had, and still have, the utmost respect for, who was telling a 22-year-old, five-test wonder, to rip into him. Olo said that Dowdy needed the same treatment.

In essence — and I'm not taking anything away from his playing ability — this was where the team missed Sean Fitzpatrick the most. Fitzy's ability to tell the senior players to pull finger, and for them to listen, really counted. Without this the pack lost its shape. Even his presence and what that implied gave the pack unity.

We approached that test in Durban with a do-or-die attitude. The preparation was good. We sang the national anthem with vigour and had asked for the New Zealand flag to be there in front of us while we sang. At every scrum during the game I talked to Olo, and told him what I required and how he was going. We were in control for most of the game until the final few minutes when the Boks stole it from us and won 24–23. We had been ahead 23–5. Newcomers like Royce Willis and Isi Maka were playing well. The Boks sent three fresh forwards on in the second half — we didn't — and the failure to use the likes of Kamo, Dowd, or Spencer in the backs, was criticised. This was the game in which the Boks scored three tries in the last 12 minutes, including hooker James Dalton's match winner in injury time. Later he admitted he had lost the ball over the line.

Everyone was completely shattered; some were disbelieving. It was our fourth test loss in a row and we had thrown everything into the game. Afterwards we went back to our hotel and crammed into a room and had a few beers together. It was appropriate. We'd tried our hardest and it hadn't worked out. Later that night, in town, Olo couldn't stand up so he sat on the floor beside the bar. Unbeknown to us he had a disc bulge in his back. A great All Black prop had played his last test.

Kees Meeuws and Xavier Rush were called in to replace the injured Brown and Maka for the final test of the series, against Australia at the Sydney Football Stadium a fortnight later. Otago's front row of Kees, Carl Hoeft and myself were, said Taine Randell in a media interview, 'young, squat, hungry and dangerous'. Later, Brendan Cannon, the Waratahs and Wallaby hooker, said that other sides found Carl, Kees and myself 'intimidating, hard to scrum against'.

My only vivid memory of the game in Sydney was that I tackled my heart out and was utterly spent after the game. Australia won 19–14. David McHugh, the Irish referee, dished out 31 penalties, 21 of them to Australia. Eales kicked four goals. It's not easy to win a game when two out of three of the penalties go against you. Afterwards, and not for the first time, Harty told the media we weren't 'mentally tough' enough. Possibly true. The interesting question is: what does that phrase mean? How do you become sufficiently tough mentally?

To me, that Tri-nations series was surreal. I had put my head down, tried my best and, at the end of it, all the All Blacks had to show for it was five losses in a row, their second worst losing streak ever.

I felt so sorry for Taine Randell. There he was, appointed by Hart and his assistants to follow Fitzpatrick, and as far as the rugby fraternity and the media were concerned, he'd been a colossal failure. I don't believe Taine should have been made captain in the first place. And, having observed Taine over many seasons, I don't think he ever really *wanted* the captaincy. Taine was a first-class all-round rugby player. He did what he was asked to do and no more. For Taine, captaincy in the traditional sense of the term seemed to stop when he left the field. If he often seemed a bit phlegmatic, is it any wonder? He got so many mixed messages from coaches and managers, and was made a scapegoat for our losses. I admire him for maintaining his dignity, given his in-favour, then out-of-favour, then in-favour career at All Black level. I know that it can't have been easy for him given the media and public baying that occurred at the time.

Taine Randell and John Hart at the press conference to announce Taine's elevation to the All Blacks captaincy in 1998.

Whenever I have looked back at videos of those five losses, technically it's obvious why we lost. Our defence was awful, inadequate. Individuals made the odd telling tackle but, generally, we were a very leaky boat on defence. Both Australia and South Africa made easy yards and broke the advantage line at will against us. Unless a team has a good defence it will never win big games.

There was also the matter of a team in which the old guard was being replaced by the new. Uncertainty and insufficient faith in our leadership made us vulnerable. Some of the more experienced All Blacks weren't wholehearted in their support of Taine as captain. It was evident that we lacked unified purpose and hunger.

Our Otago NPC campaign in 1998, though, was hugely satisfying. We lost to Waikato and Auckland in pool play but apart from that we won every game. Against Auckland at Eden Park we were ahead by about 20 points and contrived to lose. Our tight five, which played superbly all season, was decimating Auckland's, which included Steve McDowell. He'd been brought back and wasn't up to it. Our backs tried to run everything and, in the end, it was the same old story of Otago in Auckland: we were crucified by turnovers. Against Wellington we ran up a cricket score. The word is that for some time that game was used by coaches and others as an example of the near-perfect performance. True or not it was certainly a spectacular display, as we made hardly any errors and systematically dismantled a very good Wellington team and made them look quite ordinary.

Thirty thousand people turned up on a mild Saturday evening to watch us thrash Taranaki 61–12 in the semi-final at Carisbrook. The crowd and the players and all . . . we were just

Otago have just won the 1998 NPC first division title and it's beer and bubbles all round in the dressing shed. I'm in the front row, third from left.

Under Tony Gilbert, Otago rugby prospered in 1998.

so happy. Oh, halcyon days. Then, a week later, again at Carisbrook, we gave another convincing performance to beat Waikato 49–20 in the final. It was fantastic playing in front of a vibrant, initially anxious, ultimately elated and triumphant full house at Carisbrook. Pain for Waikato, immense pleasure for us. Our pack gained control eventually and the whole team fronted up. For the whole of that season, the Otago pack was the dominant force in the competition with names like Hoeft, Oliver, Meeuws, Timmins, Blaikie, Middleton, Kronfeld and Maka. I can't recall, before or since, having played with a pack that was regularly as efficient, skilled and ruthless all round. And our backs were also skilled and penetrative all year. Go to the rugby almanacks and look at the mix of 'big' and not-so-big names in the Otago squad in 1998: the list is impressive. Crucially important, our reserves were talented, resolute and reliable.

Under Tony Gilbert Otago had played marvellous rugby. The team environment was good; I thought I had made progress as a player and looked forward to improving still more. It was a blessing to end a season on a high after so many lows with the 1998 All Blacks.

Chapter **7**

'The Nation's Eyes Upon Us'

In days gone by, January was very much still the middle of the cricket season. Many wish that were still the case and, to be honest, I feel a bit the same way. But for the modern rugby player, and everyone associated with the game, 1999 was World Cup year, and it was time the All Blacks repeated their triumph in the first ever Cup in 1987.

I was keen to play, naturally, but for me the season still seemed a long way off — I always have mixed feelings about the intensity of my involvement in rugby so early in the year. So I was intrigued rather than entranced by the prospect of the All Black SAS training camp at Whenuapai in January. When we assembled we were split into small groups and then, basically, were given very little food, water or time for sleep for the next three days. We went through a series of arduous physical tasks that involved thought, tenacity, strength and sheer bloody-mindedness. According to the SAS boys, people 'quickly revert to type' in such a situation: your frailties, physical and mental, are exposed. Some of the boys found it hard going in every respect. The whole thing, although extremely taxing, didn't worry me greatly; however, I ended up losing 7 kg in three days.

I have doubts about the value of such physical punishment. In 1998 the All Blacks hadn't been on an end-of-year tour. That was to allow most of the team time to rest and train, recover from injuries and so on. Andrew Mehrtens, for example, had been working in the gym and had put on four or five kilos of muscle. He lost that on the SAS camp and never got it back. It takes skinnier players a long time to put on muscle, and the camp broke a few of them. For all that, John Hart says it was useful for identifying 'leadership, endurance and decision-making' qualities in players. As for Mehrts and his muscle loss, Hart accepts that such camps are very hard on the skinnier men. Nevertheless, he says, 'Mehrts' form was pretty good that year despite the weight loss.'

The SAS 'torture' was a new experience for me. I liked the experience, even though many of the tasks were meaningless, because it taught me a bit more about myself and others. In the end we were reduced to one big, amorphous mass of humans. That's the army way.

According to John Hart, I was one whose performance at the camp was rated highly. He has generously remarked that he 'always saw [me] as a captain from early on' and that the camp 'confirmed that'.

Once back in Dunedin and with the Super 12 series under way, Peter Sloane, one of the All Black selectors, rang saying that he and the other selectors, including coach Hart, were keen for me to accept the job as captain of the All Blacks. I was unsettled by the offer, not because I didn't want to be All Black captain, but because I wasn't at all sure that I was sufficiently rounded and experienced to take it on. I was still only 23, and that is very young to be captain of an international team. There was also the fact that, from discussions with Jeff Wilson, I got the impression that he had been asked if he would accept the captaincy. Hart says, contrary to popular belief, 'Jeff hadn't been asked to be captain.' The selectors knew he didn't see himself as an All Black captain; it is a tribute to Jeff that he either knew his limitations in that regard, or simply believed that unless a player was willing to throw everything into it, he shouldn't accept the job. The selectors did ask Wilson for his opinion on who would be suitable and Hart says Wilson 'endorsed Oliver'.

At the time Robin Brooke was said to be under serious consideration until he was thought to have been a leading figure in player disquiet in Auckland that led to Taranaki coach Jed Rowlands' departure after just one season. John Hart is blunt on this: 'Robin was never approached and offered the captaincy.'

During this period rumours were rife. You could have been forgiven for thinking that instead of men leaping at the chance of becoming All Black captain they were a bit like heading dogs slinking away, hoping the shepherd wouldn't notice. Sloane said he was just doing his job in approaching me — 'no pressure, mate' — and that no one would hold it against me if I turned it down. Then a little later Gordon Hunter arrived at my flat in Dunedin, sat down with me in my room and, in his characteristically quiet, quirkily firm and persuasive manner, said that I should (actually 'must') take the job. The pressure was enormous. Nevertheless, I couldn't afford to let myself cave in. I had to be sure it was the right time for me, and that I believed I was right for the job at that time. My instincts said no.

Then, ah, the pervasive presence of cell phones. Gordon's rang. He answered it and before the person on the other end had time to get started he said, 'Hi, honey. That's right. Sure, I'll be home shortly.' Pull the other one, Gordon. I could hear the voice of the person on the line — it was a male voice, not that of Gordon's wife Jenni — it was John Hart. He was saying, 'Gordon, it's John. What's going on?' I was a bit miffed with Gordon over that. I trusted him and he had never, to my knowledge, deceived me before.

I didn't say no to possibly the biggest honour in New Zealand rugby. I said I needed more time to think about it.

Which begs the question: what does a man need to be All Black captain? First, there has to be no doubt that you are the best in your position. I wasn't sure that I was number one in my position. Being number one is your rock, your base. If it gets eroded, as it did with Reuben Thorne, then your job is so much harder. If many players think there's someone on the bench who is better than you are, your ability to lead is called into question. On the field a captain must have some ability to read a game and have a feel for how his side is faring, and to be able to make the necessary calls in the heat of battle. What is paramount, of course, is that the captain must have the full respect of his peers. So he has to be seen as mature, to have experienced the highs

Andrew Mehrtens (second from left) salutes for the camera during an exercise at the infamous 1998 SAS camp. Mehrts, though, wasn't smiling at the end of the camp. He dropped a lot of weight over the gruelling three days at Whenuapai.

and the lows and faced the pressures of international rugby. He has to know his troops well, be aware of their idiosyncrasies. He has to know when and how to be firm without being unduly harsh, to be principled and unequivocal. In that respect, captains — and coaching staff too, for that matter — can't afford to be seen as individuals who insist on certain standards of behaviour that they then fail to comply with themselves.

I was still thinking about the All Black captaincy when the Highlanders flew to Wellington to play the Hurricanes on 15 May. A win there would give us a home semi-final, most likely against the Stormers. But before the game I felt like a character in a farce. Hart and his co-selectors felt it was time for me to make up my mind one way or the other on whether I would take the All Black captain's job. Our coach Tony Gilbert suggested he and I and my father have a chat about it. The snag was that Dad was coach of the Hurricanes, the opposition later that night. Were we going to shove him in a laundry basket and lug him up the back stairs? Eventually we managed to get him up unseen in an elevator. Neither Frank nor Tony pushed me to take the job, they just asked me to tell them what I was thinking. In the end they said that my reasons for not wanting to accept the captaincy made sense, and Tony agreed to tell Hart and Sloane of my decision. Hart says he 'quite admired' my decision to turn the captaincy down.

I walked down to reception with my dad, said I'd see him at the after-match, then went back up to Tony's room to thank him for his counsel, only to find that Taine Randell was there. I said, 'Sorry, guys,' and shut the door. A while later I knocked on Taine's door and asked him what was up. He said he had been invited to continue as All Black captain. I was more than surprised; actually, I was flabbergasted. After five losses in a row the previous year, and the fact that Taine knew the selectors had been looking to replace him, I asked him straight out: 'Why do you want to do this? You know you're the fourth choice.'(Wilson, Brooke, Oliver then Randell, well that was what I thought was true at the time without accurate information that I have subsequently obtained.) I said to Taine that if I was in his position I'd turn it down, especially after the events of the previous year, and that he shouldn't feel obliged to take it. He really was the backstop.

I had real sympathy for Taine's predicament. He'd been appointed captain when he was still very young. All the senior All Blacks were lukewarm at most about his appointment. Maybe, in 1999, he felt he had something to prove; maybe he desperately wanted to experience the ultimate, of being captain of a winning All Black World Cup team. Maybe he felt he would be wasting his captaincy experience if he didn't carry on. And maybe he felt that by not taking it he would feel, and be seen as, cowardly. A bit of all that, possibly. But I don't know because Taine never confided in me. I doubt that he explained his motives to anyone I know. Taine tended to keep personal matters very close to his chest. Emotionally, and in other ways, Taine and I were greatly different.

It took tremendous courage for Taine to agree to continue in the job. John Hart saw it that way, and so did I. Hart also says that the bottom line for him and the other selectors was that they had to have someone 'who wanted to be captain'. And the reason they had to look elsewhere was because, 'at the end of 1998, Randell said he didn't want to continue as captain'. Hart thinks that in 1998 I may not have been sufficiently supportive of Randell as captain, possibly because, although Taine 'was very intelligent, he sometimes missed a few of the little things that the likes of [me] saw as important to a team'. There was some truth in Hart's point. I have already stated that given my relative inexperience in test football in 1997 I believed I should be focusing on my own performance first and foremost; I didn't feel entirely secure in respect to my own place and influence within the side.

I was still rather naive in many ways. Even though I had lived for a few years in the fishbowl that is All Black rugby, I was unaware of the amount of clandestine political manoeuvring that goes on. When I look back over my All Black career up until the demise of Smith and Gilbert — of which more, later — I was more willing to take people at their word.

As for the game against the Hurricanes that we played that night, their halfback Jason Spice scored a last-second try in the corner in injury time to beat us 21–19. Many of our boys couldn't believe that he had been allowed the try because the TV replay showed Spice to have been in touch before grounding the ball, with a touch judge right on hand.

That meant a hastily arranged flight to South Africa where we beat the Stormers 33–18 in the semi-final in Cape Town. We were motivated; our tactics were good, both backs and forwards played well. We were down 0–11 after 15 minutes. It was one of the very best performances by any Highlanders team that I have played in. Going back and forth to South Africa in the space of a week, especially from Dunedin — getting back to New Zealand is one thing, getting back to Dunedin is another (we always have to stay a night in Christchurch before heading home the next day) — seriously affects an individual's performance. We desperately wanted to win in Cape Town, in order to keep faith with our supporters back home.

We didn't get home until the middle of the week. Then on the Sunday, in the final, the Crusaders beat us 24–19 at Carisbrook. There wasn't a lot in it. We were up 14–6, but a try to Gibson and a couple of kicks from Mehrtens got the Crusaders in front 16–14. Then So'oialo scored a mercurial try, Mehrtens kicked another goal and we were sunk. We did come back strongly, considering we were running low on petrol, but it was a bit too late. Really, it was the Mehrtens factor, again, that did us. His kicking game was better than ours, he organised their backline moves, and they scored a couple of slick tries.

I've talked to Canterbury players about Mehrts. In 1998–2000 he controlled rugby games like no one else in the country. Their players loved the way that, when they were in trouble, Mehrts blew the ball way down field, or kicked another long-range penalty.

In 1999 and 2000 I flatted in a house in Woodhaugh, Dunedin, with team-mates Simon Maling and John and Duncan Blaikie. The loss was disappointing but we still went ahead with an end-of-campaign party after the match. I remember standing with one hand in my pocket having a pee before going to bed when I must have begun to nod off, rocked back and forth and then, startled, stuck out an arm to stop myself falling through the window behind the toilet cistern. I cut my hands and arms and when I woke in the morning there was blood everywhere. I went to see our doctor, Steve Bentley, who stitched me up and applied bandages. It was very embarrassing explaining how such a large cut came to be on my hand.

Later that morning I had to turn up for a photo shoot with Kees Meeuws and Carl Hoeft. It was for that shot of the All Black front row that appeared on Weet-Bix packaging and on the fuselage of the Air New Zealand plane that took us to London for the World Cup. The accident with the loo window is the reason I feature in the photo with bandages on my hand and forearm.

Our first All Black training camp was in Nelson immediately after the Super 12 final. My thumb was slightly infected so I was advised not to train. If the media enquired about my injury Hart wanted to say I'd hurt it in a game. Doc Mayhew and I felt we should tell the truth. In the end no one said anything as the media never asked any questions.

The All Black squad was dominated by Canterbury players, and rightly so as they had won two Super 12 tournaments in a row. At practice, during a lineout session, when Mark Hammett was throwing in to the lineout, Ian Jones stopped proceedings halfway through. He told Hammett that he didn't like the trajectory of the ball on his throws. Mark told him to shut up and just catch it. Kamo was like a stunned mullet. The feeling was that Kamo had too much to say. That incident was an example of what I liked about Mark. He is straight, honest and a good team man. What you see is what you get, and he and I always got on well and enjoyed each other's company.

After the Nelson camp we bussed to Blenheim, a lovely drive through forested hills and across the bridge over the jade-coloured Pelorus River. I felt stirrings of familiarity and pride entering Marlborough: it was like a homecoming for me. We went along to my old secondary school and did the beep and other fitness tests there. The forwards first, then the backs. I was sitting with Robin Brooke and it was obvious that Jonah was really struggling. He dropped out early in the piece. Robin said that he often wondered just what Jonah actually felt like on such occasions. No one quite knew what was going on. Was Jonah really tired, or what? Most guys' reactions were a mixture of sympathy and puzzlement. At that time, none of us knew the real nature or extent of Jonah's medical problems. But no one was critical of him: it was apparent he was trying his best and no one accused Jonah of slacking. And John Hart was prepared to cut Jonah some slack in respect of his fitness. John saw Jonah as pivotal to our success. It was hard to argue with that.

Between 18 June and 10 July we played tests at home against Samoa (won 71–13), France (won 54–7) and South Africa (won 28–0). I remember little about them, except that our opposition on each occasion seemed weaker than we expected. Prior to the game against the Boks we trained in the snow in Queenstown. The papers ran pictures of the hardy All Blacks.

Exiting the Athletic Park tunnel for the last time to face the French in the final test ever played at the grand old ground in 1999. It was a fitting finale, the All Blacks winning 54-7.

The locals used a grader to clear snow away so our sprigs could grip. We turned the area around the scrum machine into a sloshy mess. Some of the guys had never been in snow; they frolicked like children.

During this period, pre-World Cup marketing took up a lot of time. I was one of those selected to be in the haka that was produced and run as an advertisement on TV. One night we spent the whole evening at Eden Park practising a new version of the haka. A local Maori group had been called in to tutor us and tell us what the haka meant and how to perform it properly. I knew the essence of it because Daryl Gibson, a friend and roommate, had told me the details a couple of years before. At Eden Park we practised and practised until we were so hoarse that we could barely speak. Up until then I had always felt rather ambivalent about the haka and saw it as an All Black convention so I did it. However, I wanted to perform the haka well and not be disrespectful to Maori culture. The producer wanted intensity, so a Maori haka party was brought in to face us while we were filmed. We were coupled with a member from the Maori haka group and performed the haka directly at that one individual 'one on one'. That drew out the warrior spirit in me. Eyeballing an opponent, sticking my tongue out and opening my eyes wide had the effect of stripping any inhibitions that I may have had. I felt pared back to my essence; all the trappings of so-called civilisation had flown.

By the time the producers were satisfied we were knackered and I had lost my voice. Back in the changing shed we sang Neil Finn's World Cup song *Can You Hear Us*, but I was reduced to lip-synching. The song went down wonderfully well with the team but for some reason it didn't catch on fully with the public.

Before our first Bledisloe test of 1999 against the Australians in Auckland, Robin Brooke, Norm Maxwell, Taine Randell and I did a lot of work on our lineout. It paid off. We had studied their lineout and thought we had it figured out and so it proved. We knew instinctively what was going on and had a superb day. The result was very satisfying considering we had lost to them in three consecutive tests the year before.

My mum had come up from Blenheim to watch the game, and my brother Brent played for New Zealand Universities in the curtain-raiser. All told, a great day and night afterwards.

Next stop South Africa for our second Tri-nations test. We stayed in a lovely lodge a few kilometres away from the crass Sun City. Mobs of blacks were chanting in the streets. They were on strike over working conditions and pay. I asked one of the black workers what they were paid and it was pitiful. When I first experienced Sun City in 1996, it was superficially alluring, but I came to see it as a place where mainly wealthy white people indulged themselves at the expense of others. I won't be going back there ever.

For the first time, I roomed with Christian Cullen and enjoyed it. Backs and forwards don't usually room together — props get to room with props, locks with locks and so on. Rooms often have a double and a single bed. Christian was senior to me, but he's easy-going, didn't pull rank and demand the double bed and we flipped a coin to decide who got to sleep where — he won the double. Christian is quiet and placid, he didn't snore, and I never heard him speak ill of anyone. Backs are just different creatures, generally. They seem to sleep all day. Christian couldn't get to sleep without the TV on, and I am the opposite.

The test against the Boks was to be played in Pretoria and we knew they would be hard to beat on the veldt. Hart had started getting former noted All Blacks along to speak to the team the night before tests. This time it was Andy Dalton, ex-All Black hooker and All Black captain, and as a fellow hooker I was given the task of replying and presenting him with a test jersey signed by all the team. I saw this as a real honour. Why had Hart introduced this practice? I think it was because the management was fearful, since the advent of professionalism, that current players would lose much of the ethos associated with the old All Black traditions. Getting former 'greats' along would, they hoped, keep tradition alive. And the choice of a speaker wasn't random; the former All Black that came along would have had experience of playing our upcoming opposition, and often at the same ground. In Dalton's case it may well have been his captaincy of the 'rebel' Cavaliers side that toured South Africa in 1986. The presentations were initially of good value for the team, but as the year unfolded their novelty wore off and they were generally seen as a rather contrived motivational tool.

I was rooming with Kees Meeuws. He was really sick the day before but somehow he managed to get out of bed and play, which took a lot of courage. We won 34–18 and, as there was a break of two weeks before we were to play Australia in Sydney, we all had a late night out. Some of the team got into strife at local bars where, as is often the case, galoots tried to pick fights with us. There are always a few idiots who decide it would be fun to thump an All Black. I'm not sure whether Reuben Thorne was all that aware, though. He'd just played his first test and, in accordance with tradition, the rest of the boys helped stitch him up. He was sent home early much the worse for wear. The non-drinkers rounded most of the rest of us up and we escaped without serious incident.

We flew back to Auckland to prepare for the second Bledisloe Cup match, then flew across the Tasman a couple of days beforehand. We were thoroughly beaten. After 25 to 30 minutes I knew we weren't going to win. You could feel the palpitating, fierce intensity — the strength and conviction in the Australian team — especially in the scrums. We tried and tried to move them but they were wonderfully resolute. The Australians seem able to drag everything they have out of themselves on big occasions. It's more than sheer grit; it's going to the limit, and then finding just that little bit extra physically and mentally. Around this time, and until recently, it was evident that All Black teams weren't as efficient, as cool under pressure at crucial times. I think Australian teams have tended to be task focused — they play rugby like one would chess, very mechanical and methodical. New Zealand teams get too emotional, we let that get in the way of clear judgement and thought, and in big games at pivotal moments you need to be thinking clearly. The final score was 28–7 to Australia. I've never felt more beaten in an All Black jersey.

A contentious issue surfaced at this time — the presence of players' wives and partners on tour. Partners can be distracting. Some of the players lose their focus, come under additional stress when trying to meet their obligations as members of a team, as well as attending to the needs of their partners. A few — quieter guys especially — get really edgy. Loyalties are divided, and a situation can develop where, in the eyes of some, the team becomes the enemy.

So far, for the All Blacks, women on tours have been a distraction, and have proved to be more of a hindrance than a help. They were a disruption during the 1999 World Cup, especially while we were training in the south of France, and their presence has created problems since that time as well. (In Cardiff some of the women had a few too many and, in the early hours of the morning before the game against South Africa, a group of them were caught in the main lift intent on getting into their partners' rooms.) It's not as if rugby tours these days are lengthy affairs — no pun intended. Three or four weeks maximum is the rule. To me, touring is better than playing at home and on tour it's one bunch of men against a whole nation. Rugby is the principal focus, which is as it should be.

In Australia in 1999 the presence of partners and the pressures that resulted proved insoluble. Collectively we were at a loss as to how to handle the issue and lacked maturity to deal with it. In the last few years massive progress has been made in this area; wives and partners are included far more often, and old-school thought and dogma have finally fallen away. It wasn't that long ago when women weren't allowed to after-matches and test dinners.

I know Josh Kronfeld could see that the presence of women was an issue, in the sense that it was dislocating for some. His view is that players have to be prepared to spell out just what their partners can expect by way of contact — when and where — while a team is on tour. They have to accept, he says, that the team's rules and requirements come first. Some players, says Josh, aren't strong enough in that regard. And while he agrees that dealing with the presence of partners will always be a difficult issue, he points out that 'the Australians had their partners around them at the last two World Cups and they seem to have performed okay'.

We had just over a month before our first game in the World Cup, against Tonga in Bristol on 3 October, so we went straight to the All Black training academy near Palmerston North. The gym's too small, the location's wrong: it's a big lemon stuck in the middle of a cow paddock. John Hart was concerned about the way the Australians had exposed our deficiencies. The coaching staff ran us ragged. This was Hart being hardline. The catch cry was that we all had to be totally committed to either 'shitting' or 'supporting', shitting being vigorously clearing the opposition out of the way, supporting being getting there to provide options for the ball carrier. The view was that there hadn't been enough of either during the test loss to Australia.

One day we had a full-contact practice match. It was surreal: New Zealand's best going toe to toe in a paddock in the middle of nowhere with no one around. Another afternoon we had nearly 100 scrums. Mark Hammett was injured so I did all but two or three of them and after about 70 scrums there were black dots in my vision.

The quantity and intensity of our training was a clear sign that the coaches were in panic mode. At the end of the camp some of us were physically and emotionally spent. A break was needed and yet we were about to play what was, for many of us, the most important tournament of our lives. It felt as if we'd peaked already and were on the way down.

The backs weren't too concerned about the intensity of their training. Wayne Smith was fairly happy that they had the skill and speed needed to best any opposition but Peter Sloane was worried about the forwards. Hart believed we needed to lift our performance and all-round effort if we were to get on top of the likes of England, France and Australia. I think too that because most of the coaching was in the hands of Smith and Sloane, many of the squad had lost some of their faith in Hart's abilities as a coach; they saw him as more of a manager first, coach second. Yet we had a manager, Mike Banks.

At the close of the camp, a couple of former All Blacks, BJ Lochore and Mark Shaw, came along and handed out little black books. Not exactly propaganda similar to the issuing of Chairman Mao's *Little Red Schoolbook*, but certainly meant to inspire us with summaries of memorable moments — tours, teams and series wins taken from All Black history. There was a view that it would help if All Blacks were reminded of the significance of the black jersey and what the culture entailed. At the time there was a concern in rugby circles that the advent of professional rugby was severing us from the traditions and values that had been at the centre of rugby's importance in New Zealand society. That concern persists today. It was asserted that as All Blacks we were members of 'a special club' and that we were required to 'honour this jersey with: Honesty, Humility, Respect, Commitment, Loyalty'. The book had phrases such as 'Once an All Black, always an All Black', 'It's an honour — not a job'. Actually, it's both, I thought. 'All New Zealand men would change places with you tomorrow.' I could certainly nod agreement when I read the one that said, 'Don't believe the hype', and the one that cautioned us to 'leave arrogance on the field'.

I saw the black book as a well-meaning attempt to remind us of our place in New Zealand rugby's history. However, I don't think you can learn a lot from reading about it; you have to live it.

Justin Marshall blotted his copybook, by unintentionally disposing of his little black book within a few hours of receiving it. It got mixed up in his washing and was completely flubbed after going through the laundry. He got heaps for that; his attitude was called into question. A little ironic, really, for few have given more for the All Black cause than Justin.

On our last night in the camp we had a few drinks, relaxed and looked to the future. Tongues loosened and someone said that he could stay in an ice-cold recovery pool for X minutes. Several of us were goaded into trying to beat that time. Quick to take up a challenge, I lasted longer than anyone else. Stupid me — I came out looking and feeling like an icicle.

The All Blacks had nearly won the Cup in 1995 — should have and would have said many, if it hadn't been for the notorious 'Suzy', labelled a food poisoner by Laurie Mains — and the pressure of expectation on the team was considerable. We were well aware of it: the phrase is 'the nation's eyes were upon us'. John Hart clearly felt it intensely. How could he not have?

In the hours before departure I developed a headache and was coughing a lot. I felt quite sick and I became increasingly worried. I saw Doc John Mayhew, who said I had a sinus and ear infection, and he gave me some medication. On the flight I was feeling worse so I started taking double the prescribed dose. Instead of arriving in England without any fanfare, we got off a plane emblazoned with three front-rowers — Carl Hoeft, Kees Meeuws and me — painted along the fuselage. So the three of us were asked to pose for a photo on the tarmac with the image behind us.

Taine Randell poses in front of the 'painted plane' prior to the All Blacks' departure for the 1999 World Cup.

I was feeling awful and continued to take double the dose Mayhew had prescribed, thinking it would make me get better quicker. When, later, we were told we would be drugs tested next day, I didn't even think about it. My roommate was Mark Hammett who kept me awake with his snoring. Staring at the ceiling, coughing away, I took yet another dose. In the morning I had a drugs test, failed to complete the sample, so sealed it and came back and completed it after training. The first part of the sample was very concentrated as the long flight from New Zealand had left me in a very dehydrated state.

Two days later Taine came up to me at a players' meeting. He said something was wrong and the management wanted to see me. 'What is wrong?' I asked. Taine told me it was something to do with the drugs test. I felt like a dead man walking as I wandered down the long corridor to meet in a room with Hart, Mayhew and manager Mike Banks. I was confused and panicky. Once in the room and told that a positive drugs test had been recorded from the urine sample my mind was sent reeling.

The management were very supportive and just wanted to know how such a concentrated sample could have been recorded. Once I had told them of my unilateral decision to take double the required dose and the dehydrated state my body was in a huge sense of relief flooded the room. The next topic of discussion was how to tell the team and what to expect from the media.

We all walked back to the team room where Hart told the team everything and all of the boys without exception were supportive of me and my situation.

The first thing I had to do before the media broke the story was phone my parents and tell them not to be alarmed when they heard that an All Black, a front-rower, had tested positive for drugs. I badly needed to assure them that I was not a drugs cheat. But, and it turned out to be a big but, I was seriously disturbed by the implications for my own reputation and for the team's.

It was hard for me not to feel that I had let the guys down no matter how often they slapped me on the back and gave supportive comments. So now I was ultra-sensitive wherever we went, imagined people were looking at me and nudging each other: 'Look, that's him. That's the bastard. He's on drugs, the cheat.'

Doc Mayhew was annoyed. He knew which drugs were deemed to be performance-enhancing and prohibited, and the pseudoephedrine which had been detected in my sample, a drug found in certain products sold to counter coughs and colds and associated afflictions, was allowable under International Rugby Board (IRB) rules.

We were all aware that in certain quarters in Great Britain, particularly in England, All Blacks were viewed with some distaste. Previous teams had been deemed surly and unapproachable. Is this familiar? My alleged infraction provided our detractors with ammunition. Our campaign, when looked at through my clouded and disturbed vision, had been tarnished before it had properly begun.

I had to front up to the media with Doc Mayhew. I had been told to say nothing. Doc was needled by journalists who kept trying to make him admit that he had erred. In the end I got sick of their persistence and defended him. I said he had told me how many tablets to take and when. 'What was he expected to do, stay with me for 48 hours and give them to me himself?'

Mayhew knew that drug testing would take place during the tournament, but, in addition to the fact that pseudoephedrine wasn't on the IRB's banned list, our management's argument was that the competition had yet to begin — this was, in Mayhew's words, an 'out of competition test' — so we shouldn't have been tested anyway. The Rugby World Cup office accepted Doc's explanation of how I happened to have the drug in my system, said that I was 'technically' in breach of the rules only, and gave me an 'official reprimand'.

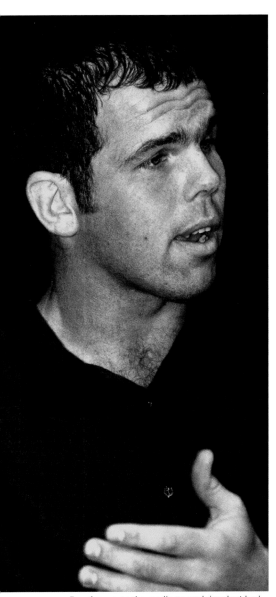

Fronting up to the media to explain why I had returned a positive drugs test at the 1999 World Cup.

In the end it was all much ado about bugger all. But not to me. After the press grilling I was so het up that just before dark I went for a 30-minute run with Justin Marshall. Marshy was fitter and faster than me. But fired by all of the emotional turmoil that I had been holding within, I charged along. He kept up but not easily. At the end he said, 'I'm knackered. You were running on emotion, weren't you?' It wasn't really a question.

On reflection, I realise this so-called 'drug scandal' affected me profoundly. I lost an enormous amount of confidence and my play suffered. I just couldn't put that incident behind me: couldn't separate off-field issues from on-field performance.

John Hart and Peter Sloane kept us working exceptionally hard. Before our first pool match against Tonga we engaged in a lot of heavy contact and smashing into each other in training. There was no tapering off and I thought that, consequently, in our performance against the Tongans we showed signs of fatigue. The Tongans were very emotional and physical. They bashed into us and Tana Umaga was knocked out early on.

I marked a massive guy. Try as I might, initially I could not budge him in the scrums. Later on I began to move the mountain in front of me and had just started to get some ascendancy when, to my dismay, he was replaced by another equally large specimen.

This was the first time Tonga had played a full All Black side. We won 45–9, an unimpressive effort when compared with England's 100-point victory against them less than a week later.

Afterwards, as I was sitting mulling in the changing shed, the door opened and in lumbered a mammoth — that's how big he'd seemed — my first on-field adversary. He wanted to swap jerseys, shorts, socks, the lot. I had never swapped any of my test jerseys and wasn't intending to start then. But he was very insistent so in the end I went along with it. A bit later the reserve hooker arrived, but unfortunately I had nothing left to give him.

Next day, at our team debrief, Tana launched into a speech about how disgraceful it was for us, All Blacks, to have allowed ourselves to be intimidated by the Tongans. All Blacks do the intimidating, he said, not the other way round. I had never seen Tana so upset. He was coherent but only just, and angry. It was clear that he felt that both he and the team had been humiliated. His views were abundantly clear.

Tana's point was valid but I was preoccupied with my own concerns. I was battling to keep myself on some sort of mental and physical even keel. That meant that team matters weren't uppermost in my mind. I still felt stigmatised by the inference that I was a drug-taker.

Looking for a way through the Tongan defence during the All Blacks' opening pool match at the 1999 World Cup. The scoreline of 45–9 looked comfortable enough, but in reality it was an unimpressive performance.

'He doesn't mince words' – Tana Umaga

Tana Umaga first played with Oliver in the New Zealand Colts side in 1994. He has always found Oliver 'easy to talk to, down-to-earth. By the same token, he's very smart, sort of intellectual, and he wouldn't seem out of place socialising in Ponsonby Road in Auckland, either.

'He doesn't mince words and some don't like that.

'He taught me a lot about how to be a leader. I was honoured when he asked me to be one of his back-seat group in 2001.'

Umaga said Oliver was 'all for honesty in the team', and he was one of those players you could rely on 'not to shirk the hard stuff'. He said Oliver was 'a passionate All Black' and 'you wouldn't find a more professional rugby player'.

Umaga was surprised when Oliver was dropped prior to the 2003 World Cup. It was not something he agreed with. Nor did he agree with the criticisms Mitchell made of Oliver's play when giving his reasons for leaving him out. 'Mitchell said he wanted a different style of hooker. A wide-running player. Well, the thing about Anton is that he is capable of playing any style asked of him.'

We moved from Bristol to Pennyhill Park, a lovely country estate near London, to prepare for our crucial pool game against England. A win at Twickenham would give us an easier path to the semi-finals. We had training followed by a very long night at New Zealand House where we were rolled out for a promotion in conjunction with New Zealand Tourism. As captain, Taine had to speak on behalf of the team and gave a lengthy, intelligent speech. Our build-up was tense and on the Tuesday, Norm Maxwell, he of unparalleled heart and determination, got the forwards together and gave us a deeply impassioned address. It was classic Maxey, sincere and heartfelt. He said he really 'wanted this game and it is up to us to front'.

The management team was worried about London's traffic jams, so our bus left for the ground much earlier than usual. On the way we played a video of the boys doing their stuff at the SAS camp months before. The soundtrack was a Fat Boy Slim song 'Praise You' that a few of the team were fond of. There was far less traffic than expected and, with police escorts shepherding us along, we got to the ground about an hour and a half before we needed to. I wandered around the ground then lay down on the floor of our changing room and slept for nearly an hour.

England really believed they would win. We rated them, and their pack had tough nuts like Lawrence Dallaglio and Martin Johnson, who has often been termed a latter-day version of our Colin Meads. Twickenham was bursting at the seams and the noise was deafening. The game was incredibly intense and I felt that I had one of my better games. Nothing spectacular but I did a lot of the little things that often go unnoticed but are essential in the overall reckoning: tackling in close, blocking, cleaning out at rucks and mauls, working with my props in the scrum. Early in the second spell, England drew level at 16–all, and at that stage it was anyone's game. Then Jonah scored a fine try and we kept up the work rate to win 30–16.

It was a bruising, highly physical game and I was physically shattered next day, glad to get into the pool and relax and soothe the muscles and joints. Taine and Craig Dowd, however, were required to train with the other players who were preparing to play the midweek game against Italy at Huddersfield. It was tough on Taine and Dowdy and I admired the way they fronted up and did it. Taine was showing good leadership and, as usual, Dowd never shirked anything. He had a great work ethic. The troops played well against Italy, winning 101–3, and my Otago mate Tony Brown had an excellent game and scored 36 points.

Our quarter-final against Scotland at Murrayfield was 10 days away so we slipped down to Nice in the south of France. Everyone thought it would be a good place to train away from the charged atmosphere and continual media attention in the UK, where it was winter and there was a lot of rain. If we thought we would be out of sight, out of mind, we were mistaken. After a photo of us emerging from the Mediterranean appeared in the papers it elicited scornful and niggardly comment, insinuating that we were on the French Riviera having a holiday. Actually, there were hardly any people around. We trained hard and there was some tension in the party. The whisper was that John Hart and our manager Mike Banks didn't see eye to eye about some things. The consensus was that John was seeking greater control, that he had a secret — or not so secret — hankering to become All Black rugby's equivalent of Alex Ferguson, the all-powerful manager of the Manchester United soccer club. I'm not saying there was a great deal in it, just that in all teams people need clearly defined parameters when it comes to roles and responsibilities. Go outside them and friction often results, and in our case it was beginning to show.

There was some grizzling in the team at Nice because upon arrival Hart called a meeting and said that while we were in France we weren't to drink alcohol at all. Winning the World Cup was our overriding priority. We were there to train and look after ourselves with that object in mind. Given the All Black culture, and the amount of drinking that sometimes entailed, he had every reason to be concerned, so his edict was understandable. But some of the squad felt they had done enough already to warrant a little rope, a bit of time to unwind and relax. Some felt we were being treated like little kids, and you know what kids do when they are told not to do something, they go out and do it anyway. We dined in our mini teams (small groups of eight or so organised for social activities and designed to mix the team up; the management had their own group) then went out for meals together, and, sure enough, three of the four teams ended up meeting at the same restaurant.

There were eight of us at my table and Taine, who just loves his food, and who can be really quirky in a good way, had an idea. We all ordered a main dish. When it arrived we tucked in for 30 seconds, passed it clockwise, ate for another 30 seconds, then passed that dish on. Some of the dishes got smaller and smaller, some were all gone, and the time allowed for eating went down to 10 seconds, then five seconds before you were required to pass it on. We had Taine to thank for that. He could be funny, eccentric and odd at times.

But the inevitable happened. Most of the players got fairly drunk that night in Cannes. I went home early with Taine, Justin Marshall and Daryl Gibson and waited for the rest to arrive. The back-seat guys got sloshed along with everyone else. And friendly cops even brought a few guys back in their car. I got the distinct feeling that Hart felt he was losing a bit of control; his strict command had been ignored.

Soon after we went to Monaco for a meal, and then visited a casino where a certain aura of unreality was intensified for me when I saw one man bet $150,000 on one hand that lasted all of 10 seconds.

In the lead-up to the game against Scotland, Peter Sloane and I put in a lot of work on lineouts. The more I practised the more nervous I became. We beat Scotland 30–18, led 25–3 at the break, but lost the second spell 5–15. I played well but my throwing was not good. The more I practised and thought about lineouts the worse I got. After that I thought I would be dropped for the next game, our lineout wasn't as efficient as it should be and my poor throwing was a large part of that.

We caught the train down to London. The whole carriage was ours and we sang songs and had plenty of fun. I got picked to play the semi-final against the French, but remained nervous and felt lucky to be in the side. My problem was that I thought I'd let the boys down and I was coming down very hard on myself. It was excessive to the point of self-flagellation. I should have said, plainly and simply, 'Okay, I'm playing, just go out there and do your very best and be done with it.' (Something I managed to do on the 2004 end-of-year tour when I was selected to play against France.) But I couldn't quash that nagging feeling that I didn't deserve to be there.

The All Blacks were hotly favoured to beat France in the semi-final. Did anyone pick France to win? I don't think so. Reference was made in the media to our 54–7 thrashing of the French in New Zealand earlier in the year. France hadn't been all that impressive in the Cup so far.

On the day before our clash, I recall going from room to room and finding lots of players watching the semi-final between South Africa and Australia. I got

About to pack down against Scotland in our World Cup quarter-final at Murrayfield.

103

the indelible impression that most were assuming that we would be playing the winner of that match in the final. Few seemed to believe that the French were playing well enough to beat us.

On match day I went out on the ground for a look around before the start of the game an hour and a half before kick-off. The stands were relatively empty, but high up in one stand was a group of All Black supporters. They were looking at me and screaming, 'Go All Blacks.' I just looked at them. I didn't wave, didn't show any emotion at all except for a brief smile, then turned away. I heard them say, 'Oh, yes, well, don't smile. We've come all this way to support you and you can barely acknowledge us.' And I felt guilty that I hadn't acknowledged their support by simply waving back. Because of an All Black habit that went back decades, I couldn't find the good grace to give them the recognition they deserved, and which I, in my heart, knew was the right thing to do. Reflecting on this saddens me, for what it says about All Black rugby as well as about myself. One can be crippled by certain conventions, by the power of the wrong sorts of traditions.

The semi-final; the French. They came out steaming. In one of the first rucks I got head-butted and felt like punching my assailant and in different circumstances I would have had little or no compunction. But we had been told, in no uncertain terms, that retaliation was not on. We did not want to play with 14 men.

Generally, throughout my career, I've gone out of my way to refrain from biffing the opposition in that I haven't gone out there looking for a fight, having something premeditated. However, when I blow my stack, what follows is anything but subtle.

I was outraged, amazed and stunned by the foul tactics of the French. Just why the referee and the touchies let them get away with it I've no idea. Before the match was five minutes old, Josh Kronfeld was eye-gouged and someone had tried to rip his testicles out. Doc Mayhew says that we should have dealt with it — meaning dealt to their forwards in the traditional way. He reckoned the likes of Zinzan Brooke and Sean Fitzpatrick would have found a way to sort them out physically. Possibly; possibly not. Our trainer Martin Toomey didn't think their shady behaviour caused us to lose; he simply says we played badly, and that that came as a surprise to almost everyone. No one sensed, or foresaw, such a lacklustre performance.

The game was a blur for me. And I don't think, either, that their murky behaviour was the principal reason for our loss. We plainly had one of the all-time All Black shockers.

Early in the second half, despite not having played well, we led 24–10. Jonah had scored two tries. Then everything went from bad to worse, and even worse still. Certainly a couple of lucky bounces went the French way, but that was no excuse. Our defence was atrocious and ill-organised and our game lost all sense of an effective structure. We became a team of ineffectual individuals. The term 'headless chooks' springs to mind. It was an utterly surreal experience; there was panic, plenty of people offering advice, exhorting this, suggesting that, but no overall control. Then, once we knew we were beaten there was silence under the posts, no one had anything to say.

The whistle went. France 43, All Blacks 31. That was it, we had lost terribly. Thrashed. The crowd was stunned. The French were ecstatic. They could hardly believe it. I was desolate, mystified and empty. Where was it now, the glory and the dream?

It was a year or more before I could bear to look at a videotape of the game. It hurt to watch it. I knew we'd been bad, but I was shocked to see just how bad.

Who knows whether, in some of our minds, the memory of our 54–7 win against the French in Wellington back in June had left some with a feeling that we just had to turn up and put in an average performance and the game would be ours?

Like most of the team I just wanted to disappear into the shed. One or two players hung

Above: Christophe Lamaison was France's star performer as they ended our World Cup hopes at Twickenham. Here, he leaves me in his wake. Below: I think the French have just scored . . . again!

around and shook lots of hands, but in such a circumstance the losers are utterly superfluous. Were we expected to play with passion, be ruthless in an effort to win, and then, having lost, pretend that it was just a game and be all smiles and bonhomie? To me that is an unreasonable expectation. I was hurting, we were all hurting. It is not ungracious to depart the scene at such a time. It was the French's stage; it was for them to receive the accolades from their fans and let their elation pour out.

In the shed you could have heard a feather hit the floor. There was utter disbelief. I sat next to Robin Brooke. We were both dumbfounded. I said to him, 'Did that really happen?' The last 15 minutes had sped by and he couldn't believe it either.

A busload of dejection left Twickenham and returned to Pennyhill. John Hart's family joined him on the bus — he must have been feeling the weight of despair. Confusion too, one supposes; and possibly the ambivalence that arrives when you are torn between wanting to give it away on the one hand, and, on the other, wanting to find the resolve to carry on and not throw in the towel.

The back-seat crew called Taine to sit with them. He looked spent, dejected. I can't begin to imagine how savaged he must have felt. And after the tournament was over he had to fly all the way home to New Zealand to face the music and the scorn. He fronted up and then took off for the United States, escaping for a couple of months. Who could blame him?

A couple of incidents on the bus were indicative of the atmosphere in the aftermath of our demise. Doc Mayhew, trying to be professional and therefore responsible and realistic, suggested

The fulltime whistle has sounded in the World Cup semi-final and the expressions on the faces of the All Blacks' management team reflect the final score — France 43, New Zealand 31.

we might as well do a roll call to check who was carrying injuries and who wasn't. We still had to play the game for third place against South Africa. This was too much for Hart. He got up and in a very clear, loud voice, told Doc, 'I am still the boss here. Sit down.' Mayhew did as he was told. It must have been hard for Hart to control his emotions at that time. Hart was no fool; already he would have known that criticism bordering on vilification would soon be heading his way like a load of cluster bombs. But I doubt that any of us could have guessed the extent or nastiness of the battering he was actually to suffer.

On the bus Peter Sloane also got it in the neck from Hart whose remarks left Sloaney awfully disconsolate. It had to do with Hart, no doubt in emotional extremis, having accused Sloane of not being respectful enough towards Hart's family. When we got back to Pennyhill many of us went to the house bar, mainly because there was no way we wanted to sit abjectly stewing in our rooms. I'm sure I wasn't alone in thinking that I'd get little sleep anyway. Sloaney was absent. I asked Martin Toomey where he was and he said that Peter was in his room and was staying there because he was so upset by some of the comments Harty had directed at him.

I grabbed half a dozen beers and went and knocked on Sloane's door. No answer. I found a maid, told her it was my room and I'd locked myself out. She let me in. Sloane and I talked for a long time and I thanked him for all the help he'd given me since I'd known him. He's a dear friend of mine: straight-talking, decent, no airs and graces. He believes in hard work and not taking the easy way. I could be frank with Sloane and have faith in the fact that, irrespective of whether he agreed with me or not, he wouldn't bear a grudge. Not all coaches are like that.

The game for third and fourth against South Africa was to be played in Cardiff. When we arrived at our hotel I listened to the rooming list and when I heard that I was with Ian Jones I knew I'd been dropped. Ian had not been in the starting 15 for the last few games and the age-old practice is that reserves room together.

Being dropped from the starting line-up for the first time in my career hurt. I knew I could play a lot better than I had been. My feeling was that I had been doing reasonably well around the track, but the odd lineout mistake and the drug affair had had an ongoing effect on my confidence. Outsiders often say, 'Stop beating up on yourself, get over it.' It's easy to say that when you're not caught up in the middle and unable to obtain perspective. After the semi-final, then, in a sense I was enfeebled. Uppermost in my mind was the thought, 'Four more years before I get another chance to win the World Cup.' Ha, if only we could see into the future . . . or is it just as well we can't?

Before the game I spent time with Josh Kronfeld, who said he was suffering from injuries incurred in the semi-final but that the medical staff and the coaches, despite what he'd told them, thought he'd be okay. He wasn't fit enough to have played in Cardiff and it showed.

The Boks beat the All Blacks 22–18. Afterwards there was devastation in the shed. Some of the boys were crying. This was the culmination of months of effort during which they had emptied the well. Watching a few of my team-mates crying shook me to the point where I realised just how self-preoccupied and defensive I had been for much of the time since the result of the drug test. Those crying had opened up and given everything . . . I had not.

We had a team gathering that night in Cardiff and John Hart announced that he would not seek to continue as coach. I understood his reaction to events but thought his decision hasty. His speech was a bit melodramatic in places — we didn't need reminding of the effort he'd put in.

Most of the All Blacks cut loose after the game against the Boks. But I couldn't get on the booze. Having seen my team-mates' desolation after losing to the South Africans, I felt as if I didn't deserve to be an All Black. It was an over-reaction, I know, but at the time the emotion was only too real.

After the game against South Africa we had to stay in Cardiff for two days to attend a dinner after the final. I decided to go and visit my Dad, who was leading a tour group, and my eldest brother Mark at their hotel about an hour away. I slept on the floor of Dad's room and had a good yarn to him and to the folk who were in the party.

The next day, reunited with the team to watch the final — Australia 35, France 12 — we walked back to our hotel from the ground in our black clothes and ties, all of us surrounded by average Joes and, apart from Jonah, none of us were recognised at all. We were yesterday's news — forgotten.

At the tournament dinner that night it was interesting to mingle with opposition players. One who impressed me as level-headed and intelligent was the Australian prop Andrew Blades. I kept thinking what a nightmare it must be for Taine and saw it as lucky that his partner Jo was there. But I put my foot in it when I told him that if he felt like a spell I'd be willing to captain the Highlanders in 2000. Initially he reacted adversely, thinking that I was challenging him for his position, which was not what I had intended. After he returned from a holiday in the States he freshened up amazingly well and was in a good state of mind to lead us in 2000.

Back home in New Zealand, with the South African loss less than a week behind us, I was in a bit of a daze and feeling oversensitive but no one was caustic towards me personally. Further north especially, John Hart was the one who copped most abuse and some of the remarks were vile. However, those who knew the Otago All Blacks best say they couldn't help noticing changes in us. Peter Gallagher, the Highlanders' physiotherapist, said in 2003 that 'This generation of Otago players was stuffed — severely damaged psychologically — by the 1999 World Cup campaign, the loss, and the subsequent national outcry. They came back angry and despairing, and they felt disenfranchised, savaged by the rugby public.'

A week later in Dunedin I met my middle brother Brent and we went out to celebrate a mate's 30th birthday. Later, we went into a McDonald's restaurant. Although I didn't realise it at the time, awash with alcohol I was loud and swearing too much when talking to Brent. How did I know? Two or three weeks later I received a letter that had been passed on to me by the Otago rugby union. A Christchurch family was returning home from a trip to Invercargill. A young boy in their family was an All Black fan. He wanted to ask me for my autograph but decided not to because of my profane language and generally poor behaviour. The letter spelled all this out, point by lacerating point.

I burned with shame when I read the letter and carried it around with me for three months. Then, when I felt I had had time to reflect, and the courage to write a reply that was heartfelt and truthful, not simply a hasty reaction based on a desire to cover up and make excuses, I sent a letter of apology. I received a reply to my response which was more generous and kindly than I deserved, but I was grateful for it all the same.

I kept that family's original letter in my diary for over a year. It was there to remind me of the need to set and live up to acceptable standards of decency and consideration for others. In the end, though, I had to expunge those persistent feelings of guilt and stop looking back. A year later, I pulled the letter out of my diary, screwed it up and threw it in the rubbish.

So, at the end of 1999, I was at rock bottom. We had failed to win the World Cup, I'd been labelled a drug cheat, I'd been dropped from the test team, had lost confidence in my rugby, been bagged by the media, and had let myself down so badly in public that my character had been called into question. I had a massive repair job ahead of me. I vowed this would never happen again. Over the summer I trained harder than ever before, determined to turn things around in 2000.

Chapter 8
Putting the Wheels Back On

I came home from the 1999 World Cup feeling emptied, devastated. But I certainly wasn't thinking, 'Oh, well, it's just a game'; nor was I thinking of giving up. In fact, quite the opposite; I was aware that there were some problems in the All Black set-up that needed attention, and I resolved to be a part of the solution and not part of the problem.

John Hart was derided, abused, spat on at a race meeting, virtually told that he alone was 'guilty' for our failure to win the World Cup. Not so; it is never one person's fault entirely. He got mauled by both the public and the sporting media, which was unfair. To me there's too much hype, too much hyperbole in our sport. Praise is too often excessive; conversely, criticism is often overly harsh.

Back in England I had gone into Hart's room at Pennyhill Park outside London to find him reading a whole stack of articles on the All Blacks and our activities during the World Cup. I wondered if he might not be too concerned about outsiders' perceptions. For my part, I thought Hart started out well in his term as All Black coach but appeared to spend increasing amounts of time acquiring more and more power, which made his fall, when it came, all the more dramatic. Perhaps that was behind the actions of those who were so savage in their denunciation of him; the same phenomenon would occur when Mitchell's coaching reign was ended.

With respect to All Black management, I believe in collective responsibility and too many in rugby were trying to duck that. I'm all for individuality but it needs to be married to a strong, proud, well-organised and responsible team ethic. For some time it had been clear that while the All Blacks liked to be seen as having a disciplined and unified sense of purpose, an admirable presence and a finely tuned physical and mental focus, all that was really an illusion.

Hart departed with more dignity than most would have mustered. The NZRU appointed Wayne Smith as head coach assisted by Otago's Tony Gilbert. I'd enjoyed playing under Tony

Men of the new millennium. Head coach Wayne Smith (right) and Tony Gilbert were appointed to guide the All Blacks' fortunes in 2000.

with Otago and the Highlanders. Tony wasn't given to histrionics; he was level-headed and reasonable but firm. I liked his dry sense of humour and lack of ego. He didn't see himself as the greatest coach around and he tried to treat everyone fairly, not bare his personal likes and dislikes in respect of players. Wayne Smith came with good reports. He was said to be intense, extremely thorough and well organised. Before the end of the year Peter Thorburn joined them to make up a diverse, informed, agreeable threesome.

Smith's triumvirate decided they wanted to put in place a system that would allow the All Blacks to become a truly professional unit suited to the nature of the game, and both the public's and the players' expectations of it, in the 21st century. They agreed that every interest group would need to be involved: sponsors, players, the rugby public. Most accepted that patience would be required initially — because consultation needed to be wide — and that what was decided would need to be revised and refined from time to time. But the three men, and those of us most heavily involved, expected to lay down a solid base for others who followed to stand on.

Gilbert said the trio agreed that All Black selection would be based on Super 12 form and those involved would be frank and open as to the reasons for their preferences. Also, they decided to sit down and talk with all the divisional coaches on their own patches.

Andrew Martin, formerly a colonel in the New Zealand army, and a better-than-average rugby player in his day, was appointed All Black manager. Dauntingly, and unwisely, Martin was also required to oversee, if not manage, the affairs of under-age New Zealand sides, always at a distance — a workload that was unreasonable. In Gilbert's view, Martin was asked to do a job that 'was too big for one person' and his later loss to New Zealand rugby was 'huge and totally unnecessary'.

Gilbert Enoka, a sports psychologist who had worked with the Crusaders and the New Zealand cricket team, was contracted to plan what work needed to be done with the All Black squad prior to the 2000 international programme. Tony Gilbert notes: 'The major difficulty, I felt, was that we were trying to achieve something important in an environment where players were coming in from a variety of backgrounds, with varying levels of maturity, and we could not keep them together long enough to make some stuff stick. It's different with a Super 12 side or a cricket team or, in fact, the army. You can't direct life shifts in young men, but only set up the environment for them to take place over time.'

While I know that all players are different, I think it's necessary to require that they be willing to act with a common purpose in certain areas. One of the hardest things of all is to strike the right balance, for as Gilbert said: 'The problem is that players need to be selected who can win test matches whatever baggage they bring with them.' I assume what Tony means is that a big part of a coach's job is to take the odd awkward or difficult yet talented player and work out ways of making him fit into the team environment.

'Strong and mature views on many things' – Peter Thorburn

Peter Thorburn was the third All Black selector along with Smith and Gilbert in 2000–01.

He saw Oliver as having 'a great sense of humour, while at the same time being one of the most intense and direct young guys I've met. He had strong and mature views on many things.'

Post-World Cup 1999, then, was yet another transition period. Some senior players had gone, or were leaving; others were undecided as to whether they wanted to play any more: Robin Brooke, Josh Kronfeld and Jeff Wilson, for instance. Smith especially wasn't convinced that Taine Randell was the right man for captain — Taine's career had become a case of being wanted then not wanted then wanted again: no wonder he was seen as somewhat detached — so Smith pushed hard for his Canterbury and Crusaders captain Todd Blackadder. Gilbert liked Toddy, saw him as 'a proven captain and a great bloke', but he doubted whether Blackadder's presence would give the All Blacks enough lineout options. In games against Australia Gilbert thought that Norm Maxwell would very likely be our only reliable lineout option.

Despite his misgivings about Blackadder's abilities, Gilbert said that 'Todd was absolutely committed to the team and couldn't have given more'. Gilbert saw Simon Maling — 'talented, smart and selfless' — as an option to partner Chris Jack, but found that the other selectors didn't agree.

In 2000 the All Black squad tended to stay and work out at the Institute in Palmerston North. We did very useful groundwork there. But the fact that we didn't arrive in host cities until the Thursday before tests didn't please the unions concerned: they prefer it when the All Blacks are there from early in the week so that they can optimise the public relations spin-offs. For many players, the downside of being in Palmerston North was that they found the place unexciting socially, and few had friends or relatives close by. In my case, my father was just around the corner, but I was an exception. (The NZRU recently bought out of its lease of the Institute as it has proved to be ill-equipped and inadequate for a professional rugby team's needs.)

When we weren't out on the pitch training, we had plenty of meetings, facilitated by Gilbert Enoka, to discuss our differing views on what the All Black jersey meant to us as individuals. Some felt no strong connection with the past, and some said that they were principally concerned with the here and now. For me, being a part of a continuum reaching a long way into the past, remembering great deeds and great performances, has always meant a lot. Norm Maxwell told us that he watched people's eyes and that they told him a great deal about the strength of their motivation, the force of their convictions.

We came up with a phrase, 'Enhance the jersey', which soon became, simply, ETJ. This underpinned everything we did both on and off the field. The question each of us had to ask before we drank another round, whether we went and trained harder, whether we needed to be courteous and helpful, and so on, was: Would it enhance the jersey?

So there was a lot of discussion about the need for values: about the need to be honest with ourselves and others; to show respect for and loyalty to each other and to the best of the traditions handed down; to believe in yourself and your mates and be selfless in support of others; to do whatever was necessary to protect the good name of the All Black jersey; to be arrogant on the field and humble off it.

We set our own rules for dress, for the use of sponsors' products, for the provision of medical treatment, for lateness . . . we tried to cover every possible contingency. You were fined $1000 if late, for instance, and while some thought this crazy, the solution was simple: just don't be late. So we came down hard in an effort to rectify some of the discrepancies that had crept in towards the end of Hart's term.

We had an excessive number of rules, but given that we were a rather disparate group, and that we were trying to establish a new All Black team identity, we needed them. The players were involved in drawing up the rules and agreed with them. At the time they were unifying, and there was the intention that they be eased up progressively the next year. I don't think it would have been healthy to continue to have so many rules governing the team. We wanted to create an environment where players had enough maturity and responsibility to make judgements for themselves, and part of that initial process was education. Once what was acceptable and what wasn't was firmly established, then the coaches wanted a team where young men were trusted to do what they thought was right. Rules *per se* though, were seen as part of the 'system', and considering the background of most of the players, I don't think they would have been adhered to; in fact I think the opposite would have occurred.

One of the rewarding things that came out of this period was that for the first time I got the chance to form some close relationships with other players. I recall flying to Auckland to do promotional work with Norm Maxwell. On the way home we told each other about some personal matters that we'd not disclosed before, and we were both in tears. The effect it had on me came as a surprise and I realised that it was the first time I had cried since my grandfather had died in 1997.

Smith, Martin, Enoka, Gilbert and Thorburn all felt that if we were to gel as a team on the field we needed to set down rules in relation to the way we behaved off it. By the middle of 2001, I was starting to see some admirable changes in the conduct of many All Blacks and that was heartening and really encouraging. Players were taking control of their actions and I'm sure that the work we put in during 2000 was behind it. Sadly, the premature removal of Smith, Gilbert and Martin, and the lessening of Enoka's involvement, saw the return of some drunken, immature behaviour. It left me feeling angry and disillusioned.

Andrew Martin was definitely in charge. That was what the NZRU wanted, and so did Smith and Gilbert. They wanted to get on with coaching, and for Martin to run the rest. Unfortunately, before long some in the media were enjoying themselves by calling Martin 'Colonel Cuddles'. If they had known more, and had taken a broader view, they may have been less scornful.

Not a lot of players understood Martin's role. Some thought Andrew was a control freak, that he enjoyed insisting on this and that, and that he thought he was still in the army. We were getting up early in the morning and working really hard. It was a huge jolt when compared with what we had been doing previously, and when that happens reactionary comments are inevitable from certain players. Nevertheless, I was confident it was what we needed at the time. None of us knew, then, that Martin had been given the work of three men managing and coordinating the affairs of all the NZRU rugby teams. He did it all without grandstanding and neither sought, nor got, much thanks or public recognition.

As a manager, Andrew Martin was more visible, appeared more hands-on than his predecessors. Some in the media, and in rugby circles too, thought him too prominent, too controlling, with his fingers in too many pies. Yet all he was trying to do was fully discharge his responsibilities as laid down in the job description from the NZRU, in which the hierarchy was: NZRU CEO, then All Blacks manager, All Blacks coach. Martin took his job extremely seriously, and he made no apologies for setting high standards or for being thorough.

I liked Martin and respected him. He had far, far more going for him than against. To me, his presence was overwhelmingly beneficial. But, unsurprisingly, he wasn't universally appreciated. He irritated a few, including John Mitchell and Robbie Deans. They made that plain. Murray Deaker and Keith Quinn were a couple of senior sports broadcasters who made fun of Martin. Along with some of their younger cohorts, they lampooned him unmercifully. I thought their jibes at Martin were gratuitous and unfair.

What, many were asking, is Martin doing on the sideline? Well, he operated from the bench at the request of Smith and Gilbert, particularly during tests. Other than ensuring all admin matters were flawless on the day, they both felt that he would be of assistance at ground level. Bear in mind that there were up to five support staff and seven player subs on the sideline, not to mention the 'fourth' match official, touch judges, sub recorders and Uncle Tom Cobbly and all! It was Martin's job to coordinate the subs on direction of the coaches, and to ensure that no 'carded player' was in the bin a moment longer than necessary.

Previously all this used to be overseen by John Mayhew in his capacity as doctor. That wasn't really what Mayhew was there for and when Martin took over he noted that Mayhew had his hands full making quick medical decisions. In the modern professional era, there could be no excuse for an error like, say, having only 14 men on the field when a replacement was needed. Smith and Gilbert saw it as Martin's job to react as quickly as possible, whether with a replacement or blood bin sub. All of this has to pass through the bureaucracy of the fourth official and touch judges. In respect to all this, Martin has said, 'I had never wanted to be a blazer in the President's Box and was extremely pleased to be asked to make a contribution somewhat more meaningful than damaging the gin stocks upstairs.'

'Totally self-contained' – Andrew Martin

According to Andrew Martin: 'The first and most obvious aspect to Anton is that he neither craves nor needs the acceptance of others, whether they are peers, subordinates or superiors. In that regard he is totally self-contained. This is both his strength and his weakness.'

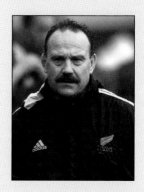

Martin saw Oliver as having 'an unflinching sense, an intuition, of right and wrong and his maintenance of these principles has been consistent through a totally fearless determination. Indeed, with no respect for self-preservation or thought of what others may have felt . . . it is either right and you do it, or it is wrong and you don't. His conviction in articulating his beliefs and moral code was equally as determined and fearless and this is what has from time to time caused those around him to regard him as some form of "turbulent priest".'

In Martin's view Oliver is a 'professional athlete' who 'will question and search until he believes that he has or is able to bring his team-mates up to his standards'. Martin believes that some of those high up in the All Black camp were ill at ease around Oliver, saw him as a threat because he 'had the mana, the respect and credibility to carry senior team members with him' and consequently preferred to be without him.

Andrew 'The Colonel' Martin in customary attire – shorts and a tee shirt.

The shorts and boots incident that some commentators, notably Keith Quinn, made a meal of came about during the second Tri-nations test against South Africa in 2001 at Eden Park. (Keith also made a derisive comment about Martin when the team visited the New Zealand First World War graves in France. Surprising, really, as Quinn is not normally so insensitive.)

Here's Martin's side of the story:

'My usual sideline dress was our Number 1 tracksuit and runners. Very smart and appropriate too, I believe. Anyway, it was a filthy Auckland night with torrential rain. I knew I was going to be subjected to the storm so dressed as usual but with rain jacket, rain pants and boots given how wet and slippery the runners would have become. With about 10 minutes to go to kick-off one of the subs came to me [and said] that he had left his rain gear back at the hotel! I always carried a bit of spare kit and was able to give him a jacket, but no rain trou. What was the priority here, a warm and dry manager and a wet cold sub on the bench? A no brainer, eh? So the sub got my rain pants.

'It was still hosing down and my experience in the

I broke my test try drought with two touchdowns against Scotland at Carisbrook in 2000.

bush always was that if you kept your upper body dry and warm, and didn't allow long pants to sap body heat away, you would always be warm(ish). Just look at any photos of New Zealand bushmen even in their Swanny shirts. The majority will be wearing shorts.

'Anyway there I was, sans tracksuit pants, with boots on and warm as anything as the weather lashed around us and the All Blacks routed the Boks.

'So it was that my rather less than attractive pins were propelled to minor and passing celebrity status! It was all assisted by Andy Haden, who probably teamed up with Murray Deaker to lampoon my apparent attempt to take the playing field.'

The All Blacks' 2000 programme began with easy wins over Tonga (102–0) at Albany in June, followed by more than comfortable wins (69–20) and (48–14) over Scotland at Dunedin and Auckland. In the Dunedin test I managed to score two tries, the first time I had scored a test try and I happened to get a pair. I got concussed early in the game when receiving a kick-off. On video you can see me running the wrong way for about 15 metres until I got my senses again and joined the fray, going the right way this time. Consequently, I only have vague recollections of the tries.

Our first major challenge was the Tri-nations/Bledisloe Cup match against Australia in Sydney. In front of a huge crowd, over 100,000 souls, we won (39–35) thanks to a last-minute try by Jonah Lomu. It was a bizarre match. We had the Aussies on the ropes and one would have thought out of the match, but they crawled their way back into the game and dominated most of the second half. Indeed, they were leading until Jonah scored the match-winner. It had everything a test match could hope to have: skill, pace, see-sawing fortunes and a cliffhanger of a finish. My main recollection was that the game was played at terrific pace. We tore around like huntaways chasing skittery sheep. I got substituted halfway through the second half and enjoyed the final blow from the sidelines.

Afterwards the team was told not to go out and leer up. 'No booze' was the message; there's another test in a week. Todd Blackadder, Justin Marshall, Taine Randell and I went along to our team room, had a couple of beers and played pool. We stayed up later than intended and were privately reprimanded for it. This raised the interesting question: when do players enjoy their wins and how should they do it? Were the All Blacks becoming too fussy about post-match recovery, too preoccupied with worrying about the next game? After-match relaxation and enjoyment is important. I hadn't got drunk, far from it, but I had still gone against management's wishes. Tony Gilbert's view, in retrospect, was that 'we should have stuck together longer as a team that night and enjoyed the feeling. It was too clinical . . . a good time for bonding without getting drunk was missed.'

We flew back to New Zealand and drove up to the Heritage Hotel in Hanmer, about 140 km north of Christchurch. I loved cruising around on a bike in the clear, cold air beneath snowy mountains. In the test against the Springboks at Jade Stadium our scrum got worked over a bit but we won the game 25–12.

Our second test against Australia was a close one and we lost, 23–24, in Wellington. We should have won, but, as Tony Gilbert observed, 'Our lineout deficiencies were to become evident as the game went on even though we coped early on with some sleight of hand.' We

Trying to escape the attentions of Australia's Jeremy Paul during the narrow loss to the Wallabies in Wellington.

made a number of mistakes late in the game and Craig Dowd was involved in three of them. With the Australians on the ropes on their line, Dowdy tried to go for glory from a ruck and knocked on. They kicked the ball out in our half and Dowdy went to the wrong place at the lineout (Hammett was on at the time, not me) and we were short of a lifter. Then Dowdy infringed in front of our posts . . . ah, gutting.

I felt sorry for Dowdy. In the shed he was crying. He knew the gravity of what he had done and I knew how much he respected the All Black jersey, what it meant to him. I was to experience similar wrenching feelings a year later when I contributed to a mistake from which Australia scored and we again lost in the last few moments of a game.

Our next test was against South Africa in Johannesburg two weeks later. We left our reserves behind so they could enhance NPC matches before flying over to join us. We stayed at sea level in Durban and while waiting for our reserves to turn up I think we were in too much of a holiday mode. It was a mistake, too, not to have had a proper debrief after the loss to Australia. The issues that needed fixing were glossed over because, by the time our reserves arrived three or four days before the game, we had to focus on the next test.

We all went out to the airport to meet the reserves. Andrew Martin had arranged for us to get a special dispensation that allowed us to go out on the tarmac and meet the players off the plane. They were last off and we did a haka for them. I recall saying to Andrew as we walked back, 'We are not going to lose this game,' and he concurred, replying, 'You are right, we are not going to.' We were both wrong.

Toddy got up to speak to us at the captain's meeting on the eve of the game. I could feel the intensity of the emotion flowing from him, but he was struggling to express himself adequately and I recall thinking that I should get up and stand next to him in support. I didn't. No one did. In hindsight I wish I had.

We lost the game and it was a bad loss, 40–46. Too much inaccurate football, not enough sustained effort and discipline. The Boks came out passionate and determined and we were simply not at the same level emotionally. They were more committed than us, and consequently won the game.

The loss of two tests in a row was hard to take and many in the team reacted in the traditional way, getting well and truly boozed. A team drink was organised to get our spirits up for they were extremely low. It was the easy way out, to get pissed. We drank the hurt out and replaced unpleasant thoughts with false positive feelings instead of facing the gravity of our performance soberly. Smithy and Andrew Martin said they were disgusted with us. Our management's remarks hit me with tremendous force. From then on I decided no more, that's it. I am not going to be part of an All Black drinking session and get myself into a state like that again. From that moment on I resolved to do what I could to change that part of the All Black ethos.

It was a fairly disconsolate lot that stopped off in Sydney for two days to debrief on the way home. Otago's manager, Des Smith, wasn't happy about that. He phoned more than once, insisting that we be released and get home to play for Otago in the NPC. This was a clear sign that Otago was in trouble, an omen of things to come.

In Sydney, I had dinner with Josh Kronfeld. He and I went back a fair way in both Otago and the All Blacks. I told him straight that I didn't think he should be in the back seat of the Otago bus any more. I said that while I admired his ability, and while no one doubted his courage and commitment on the field, I felt that he wasn't a real team man in other respects. He had reached the end of his career and was starting to take little things for granted and his mind was obviously focused on his future in England. I said that he and Jeff Wilson were somewhat similar: brilliant players but too individualistic to occupy the back seat. The rest of the Otago team didn't feel as if they knew Jeff and Josh very well, didn't have any empathy with them. If you are on the back seat you have to be respected for what you do on and off the field, to have the players' confidence so that they felt that they could approach you for advice.

Josh didn't take it well. He thought that I undervalued his contribution and that I overrated the importance of the back-seat tradition. Perhaps Josh and I had differing ideas about the meaning and function of the back seat.

In my opinion, the back seat is meant to provide guidance to the rest of the players and be a conduit through which individual or collective concerns can be conveyed to management. It's all about traditions handed down by those who insist that it's essential to honour the All Black jersey through honesty, humility, respect, commitment and loyalty. Nowadays the name 'back seat' has lost its allure. But there's still a group of senior players who act as brakes on behaviour, act as go-betweens to the management, and offer wise counsel, especially to the less experienced members in the team. I think Josh, if asked, would have been more than willing to dispense such counsel, as he is one of the most generous people I have ever played with. The point I was trying to make to him was that the other players didn't feel as if they could connect with him for that to happen.

So what about Des Smith and his efforts to get us released to play for Otago? He didn't get his wish and Otago, without its All Blacks, lost on the weekend, 14–18, to North Harbour at Albany.

An air of mystification enveloped Otago rugby. People spoke of Otago's time immemorial tradition of punching above its weight in national competitions. But it couldn't seem to win the Ranfurly Shield any more, and the days of long tours by international teams who, more often than not, got done by Otago at Carisbrook, seemed to be over. Otago and Highlanders teams at NPC and Super 12 level had come to look like horses that made a habit of leading much of the way only to fall at the final fence. There had been success under Mains, years back, and under Gilbert more recently. Under Gordon Hunter we'd beaten the Springboks and the Lions, had done so-so under Peter Sloane and were nowhere near it under Glenn Ross and Kevin Gloag.

The Otago public, generally loyal and sometimes desperate, were perplexed. They felt that Otago's administration, when a review of Otago rugby was undertaken by John Graham and one or two others, failed them by refusing to release even a summary of their findings. This was regarded as a snub, and it exasperated and angered a lot of Otago folk. In recent years there has been much talk about the need for 'open and transparent' dealings in just about every area of New Zealand life. But have we had that?

In the NPC, Otago lost to Waikato, Wellington, North Harbour, Taranaki, Canterbury and Auckland. The 26–29 loss to Canterbury in Christchurch was also a Ranfurly Shield challenge, and another gutting close one that was hard to take.

I had gone to visit Ken Bloxham, very ill with cancer, at his home the week before the shield challenge. Ken had been a long-time Otago hooker. I took along a test jersey and gave it to him as a sign of my respect for him and what he had done for Otago rugby. Ken's helpers told me that he was relatively comfortable and able to talk freely. The visit lasted a couple of hours and we talked about old times and country rugby mostly. When I left his house I promised him on behalf of the team that we would do everything we could to win the Ranfurly Shield for him and all the other ex-Otago rugby players who had tried and fallen short. Unfortunately we couldn't win the shield. Canterbury got up in the last minute.

Another overseas tour was imminent now that the NPC was done with. Tony Gilbert phoned and said he wanted me to speak to the All Blacks about the significance of our tests in France, and especially since the first test was to be played in Paris on Armistice Day, 11 November. Even more significantly, we would be playing for the Dave Gallaher Trophy. I had mixed emotions when considering Tony's request. Elation because I was to be, by implication, still in the All Blacks, but overwhelmed by the amount of work I had on at university: I had three final examination papers to sit. I called on journalist and author Ron Palenski and he proved to be an immeasurable help. It was only a five-minute speech, but I wanted it to be effective and accurate. Without Ron I'd have floundered.

Later I realised that Gilbert and Smithy were probably testing me to see whether I had that extra something that went with the qualities they were looking for in an All Black captain. At the time the touring side was announced, I'd stopped in to see David Latta in Balclutha while driving back from Stewart Island where I'd been diving and fishing for a couple of days. We listened to the team being announced over the radio, just like the good old days. Carl Hoeft, my mate in the Otago front row, had been left out so I called on him in Mosgiel on my way home and gave him some of the seafood I'd snaffled. Hoefty was upset but philosophical. I thought he handled his non-selection amazingly well.

The All Blacks again gathered at the Poenamo on the North Shore. It was the sort of environment that works for me in the initial bonding period: the rooms open out onto a forecourt and the low-key, communal atmosphere and the back-to-basics approach were welcome. We'd drifted away from that in the preceding couple of years. We were given a Rubik's-type cube on which All Black faces from the past — Colin Meads' was one — merged with various shapes, and the cube also had the points to remember with respect to 'Enhance the jersey' (ETJ). We also were given a pendant, with a koru-type design for which Kees Meeuws was primarily responsible. When one of our props got injured, Hoefty was called in as a replacement, then at practice tore a muscle and had to go home. I felt sorry for Carl: that tour just wasn't meant to be for him.

En route to France we stopped in Japan to play a game against a composite side that included a few former All Blacks and good NPC players. My brother Brent was playing in Japan and I took along a big parcel of meat for him. Airport staff took ages to release that package and the whole team waited and waited on the bus until the bloody meat was cleared. At the local Sheraton Hotel we — Jonah Lomu especially — were greeted like superstars. We were mobbed wherever we went. A couple of fans had placards beside our bus with 'Oliver' written on them, however, in Japanese parlance they yelled out 'Oweba, Oweba san.'

The game against the composite team was very physical and we were out-scrummed, a taste of what was to come. In the second half we settled down and won fairly easily in the end. Afterwards we learned that they'd been talking of smashing us, believing they had a chance of winning. That wasn't going to happen even though we had only had a couple of runs. In the airport lounge and on the flight to France management had laptop computers with them showing matches featuring the French. These were passed round and I think that the fact that our boys were doing their own analysis of the opposition so early on was a good sign; players were taking the initiative.

Our hotel in Paris was in the middle of town on the Champs Elysées. I was impressed by the architectural splendour and by an all-pervasive sense of history. I greatly enjoyed being anonymous and strolling around unnoticed and untroubled. Very few, if any, French people seemed interested in, or aware of us. The Arc de Triomphe was nearby. I looked at a photo of Hitler passing underneath it, walked to the top, and visualised Hitler and the German army marching below. The weighty historical significance of the place wasn't lost on a bloke brought up in small-town New Zealand.

Andrew Martin had arranged for us to stay in Lille for a couple of days in the week before the test in Paris. Tony Gilbert says the 'days at the graves and the battlefields drew us closer together than anything else that had happened in 2000'. Of that week he says, 'I will never forget it.' In his view it 'not only gave us a chance to put some honour back into our team but also to honour our nation's contribution to freedom'.

That week was as emotional a time as I have ever known. Todd Blackadder and I laid a wreath at Gallaher's gravesite — he died of wounds received at Passchendaele in 1917. Waves of emotion poured over me and I had to walk away quite a distance to get some privacy. There were cameras everywhere and I wanted to escape them. I was overcome with grief and started sobbing. I recall Tony Gilbert came over to have a chat, then, realising I needed to be alone, walked away.

Suddenly aware of the horrifying sacrifices of my Kiwi ancestors, I felt acutely aware of my nationality. That First World War graveyard, with row after row of small white crosses, affected me terribly. On the way back to the bus I began talking to Andrew Martin about what I had seen and felt; then we both started crying. At that we said, 'Let's get on the bloody bus before it all gets right out of hand.'

Later that day we looked at the site of the battlefield at Passchendaele with historian Chris Pugsley, who was magnificent as he painted a graphic picture of the battle. We stood on the apex of the hill and could visualise New Zealand troops weighed down with all their equipment,

Todd Blackadder lays a wreath at Dave Gallaher's gravesite. It was a hugely emotional time.

struggling through mud, being cut down. The ground, said Pugsley, still gives up the bones of dead soldiers in the wet season every year.

I was interviewed by journalists and said that I was ashamed not to have known about the things Pugsley had described to us. This ought to be part of the New Zealand school curriculum, I said. Some media interest focused on this statement, intrigued that it took a rugby player to say it and help gain some awareness.

Later I learned that a relative of mine, an old digger named Callanan, was buried there. If I'd known I'd have sought out his grave and left some flowers next to his white cross.

We next visited a town called Le Quesnoy where the inhabitants treated us like long-lost brothers. In 1918, New Zealand soldiers, instead of bombarding the town, which was occupied by German military, climbed the walls and went through the place street by street, clearing the Germans out. Todd Blackadder recalls that we were given 'a lavish reception at the civic centre'. There was a sense of mutual respect and gratitude reaching out across the world.

In the pre-match hours before we ran on to Parc des Princes on Armistice Day in 2000 the team had a feeling of intensity about it that I had never felt before. There's no doubt that our visit to the war graves and battlefields had had a profound effect on us all. To me it seemed as if the boys were utterly determined to uphold the honour of all of our predecessors. We were tapping into the power that comes from wishing to honour your lineage. No doubt individuals were affected to varying degrees, but in my case I was galvanised. I wanted this game and I was not willing to be denied. Tony Gilbert recalls Toddy saying on the field after halftime, 'There's enough Kiwi blood lying round in this country. We don't want any more.' And Tony adds, 'We were never going to lose.' Final score: All Blacks 39, France 26. This was the first time the French had lost on Armistice Day.

The morning after the test Jonah was diagnosed with a fractured eye socket and was out of the tour; half of his face was swollen to the size of a Swiss ball. And, unfortunately, Taine completely missed the first meeting of the morning, as he had been staying at another hotel with his partner Jo and had simply thought the meeting was later that morning. Result: $1000 to team funds. Taine decided that because he was on the back seat of the bus he should be setting a better example and stood down for a week and sat at the front. As Jonah was to leave the tour this left only Mehrts back there.

Toddy asked me to go into the back seat, which I accepted without hesitation. It was truly hard to believe that I had made it all the way down to the back of the bus. Memories of my first tour in 1996 to South Africa came flooding back: the utter fear I had of those who occupied the rear seat. It was to be a defining moment for me and my rugby career. I had just received the ultimate sign of respect from my All Black team-mates, and it was this kind of affirmation that I had been subconsciously searching for. Finally, I felt that I deserved to be called an All Black. I had been charged with the responsibility of helping and guiding those junior to me. This was something that meant a tremendous amount to me.

I wasn't aware of it at the time but after the Armistice Day test both Smithy and Gilbert were 'worried' that 'a number of players thought that we had already "won the war"'. That was the reason for the really hard training they put us through on the day we left for Marseilles. The Canterbury boys especially hated it. They felt it was unnecessary, that they wouldn't be fresh for the next test on the weekend. At the time the vibe throughout the team was not good. How fickle teams are. How quickly the mood can change. Smithy was on edge, pushing us hard, and he got into me a couple of times at that training session, for no particular reason. He wasn't picking on me specifically but he was really agitated and I just happened to be on the receiving end of a few of his biting remarks.

Challenging the French defence during the first test of the 2000 series at Stade de France, Paris.

In Marseilles we stayed at a downmarket little pub. The beds were small and, not for the first time, I flopped the mattress on the floor and slept there. For some reason it was decided to train in the afternoons which was a mistake, as disinterest and lethargy set in because of having to hang around in the mornings conserving energy.

The day before the test we tried to get in and walk around the ground. Officials didn't want to open up the gates for us and we were also locked out of our changing shed. There was a particularly arrogant little French guy. Andrew Martin looked as if he was thinking, 'I want to strangle you, you little bastard.' It was unsettling and disruptive. Eventually, we were allowed to look at our changing rooms, but in groups of six at a time, not altogether. Afterwards, the players not in the test squad for the weekend's test went off to a mayoral reception where they kept being told that we'd been lucky in Paris and the French were going to knock us over the next day.

The second test was played at a soccer ground in front of the noisiest crowd I have ever experienced. The French started with immense intensity. All I remember about the first 30 minutes is tackling. Down 0–14 after seven minutes, we managed to claw our way back into the game but kicked away possession at vital times and lost 33–42. Afterwards I was asked by Martin to do some media interviews to help out Toddy, who was shattered by the loss. We had the same scrum difficulties in Marseilles as we had in Paris. Their scrum was simply better than ours, and we were never able to gain even parity on our put-in or their put-in.

The All Blacks have never wanted for support overseas. Here I pose in front of heaps of good luck messages we received prior to the second test against France at Marseilles.

My opposite, Fabrice Landreau, came into our dressing shed and we swapped jerseys. He said some highly complimentary things about my play, the first time an opponent had done that. I thought it was kind of him. Fortunately, I was able to be similarly complimentary to him — because it was true, he was a fine player.

According to Tony Gilbert, the loss 'left Smithy inconsolable'. His gloom grew from a combination of the loss, the pressures on an All Black coach, sniping from the media, and the fact that, Gilbert again, 'we were not showing the consistency of character necessary' to win the tight games.

Disappointment within the squad was plain. The next day's 'honesty session' was meant to put hard questions and get hard answers from within. We only touched on the issues. The management had set up the meeting in the hope that the players would arrive at the conclusions that were obvious to them, but we didn't go deep enough and in the end nothing was resolved. I thought Justin Marshall got closest to the truth, was the most questioning. All of us, including management, needed to look at our accountability.

A group of us bussed to a winery on the Sunday afternoon. At the winery we were given several bottles of wine, some of which were about 20 years old. There weren't enough to go round. It was the same old story: there was a rush to get the prized bottles, and some grabbed two. I got one and, knowing Andrew Martin's fondness for good wine, gave it to him. I thought to myself, viewing the unseemly scrabble, it's only wine, for God's sake. Many in the group were still inclined to think of themselves first rather than consider others' needs. We were still some way from being an unselfish, coherent team.

The bus trip to Genoa in Italy took most of the day and tempers started to fray by the end of it. But our hotel in Genoa was great: it had a lovely spiral staircase, and was right in the middle of town. After real difficulties making myself understood I got a hairdresser to cut my hair, then went out shopping with Tana, Ala and Filo (Umaga, Alatini and Tiatia). I bought some shoes that Filo really fancied. It was a good time and I immediately warmed to Italy, its culture and the people. They seemed to be friendly and accommodating, even more so if you made an effort and tried to speak Italian.

Managers and coaches will never please everyone, and by this time it was clear that as far as Andrew Mehrtens was concerned, Andrew Martin was a pain. I got on fine with both of them, but Mehrts made no secret of the fact that he thought Martin was a control freak. You could equally have said that Mehrts was nit-picking, and near-impossible to please. Many saw Mehrts as having got to the stage where he was questioning everything Martin was doing and finding fault with most things, and he voiced his complaints again and again.

While we were in Genoa I met my father, who was there looking at the prospect of coaching John Kirwan's old team, Benetton. Dad came round to our hotel and we had a couple of beers together. I rang Gordon Hunter in Dunedin on his birthday. Gordon was at home and very ill, battling cancer. Before I'd left Dunedin, Gordon and I had planted tomatoes in his glasshouse. I'd got fertiliser and helped him spread that and string up the plants. Throughout the tour we'd kept in constant touch through emails. He kept me posted on the plants' progress and in one email wrote: 'As I'm typing I can hear the creaking of the growing vines.'

Right up until five minutes before we ran on to the park to play Italy, I was unusually nervous. So I sat down, got out my cube, and stared at it. There was Colin Meads looking at me with a questioning glare. 'Okay, Colin,' I thought, and my nerves went away. I enjoyed the game and our lineouts went like a dream. Once we subdued their forwards, who were strong but negative, and overcame our irritation with the refereeing — the ref just wouldn't police the breakdowns at all — we won comfortably 56–19.

The test dinner was festive indeed. I sat with Taine and his partner Jo Edwards. Doc Mayhew was there and he and Jo debated New Zealand social and political issues the whole time, mostly with opposing views, which made for an interesting and sometimes humorous evening.

Afterwards the guys were frisky to say the least. Everyone was jostling in the aisle when I boarded the bus. I battled my way to the back and saw myself as relatively sober when compared with most. Justin Marshall was fairly full and had a go at me. Three or four other scuffles were going on further down the bus and a few punches got thrown. With the women on the bus too it was bedlam for a bit, maybe chaos. A reshuffle took place: players with partners sat near the front; some of the younger guys further back; and Doug Howlett and someone else sat further back than tradition allowed. I tried to get control and barked at Howlett: 'What the hell are you doing back here?' Howlett said there were no seats. I told them to watch themselves. The next day Doug said he couldn't avoid sitting further back and I quickly apologised for my outburst, explaining that things had been fast getting out of control and I was simply trying to gather the reins in.

When things had settled down and we filed off the bus Toddy came up to me, looked hard at me and said, 'You are ready.' It was then I saw that he had staged the whole kerfuffle, had been needling Justin to provoke him in order to see how I would react. I was dumbfounded by Toddy's manipulation, and rather impressed by his cunning method of achieving his intentions.

Back at the hotel, Mehrts, me, a couple of the other players and Gilbert Enoka had an informal meeting. A few players thought Toddy was a bit too accommodating of Mehrts at times. We wanted to tell Mehrts that he had been pissing people off. He couldn't see it. We tried to make him realise just what a key figure he was in the team, and how influential and crucial he was to our success on and off the field. Eventually, Mehrts listened. He said he'd been unaware of just how influential he was and once he was made aware of this he changed immediately. Andrew has always put the team first and is a very unselfish person.

Everyone went out that night but I came back early. I was tired out from the test and the after-game events so stripped off and slept naked on top of my bed, as it was very hot in our hotel room. My roommate came in later with a woman and I slept on oblivious. He said it was a trifle embarrassing. For whom?

We left Genoa and took the train to Rome. On the journey everyone had a tour debrief with the managers and coaches who conducted interviews in a separate carriage. Unaware of other players' reports I was happy enough at my own assessment, which was a decent pass mark.

We arrived in Rome and, apart from dinner as a team on the first night, the next three days were up to each player to use as they saw fit. The team dinner that first night was a cracker. We had a whale of a time at a restaurant owned by a local rugby enthusiast. Lots of dancing on tables, waving of flags, the Wellington boys singing their favourite song 'Who let the dogs out?' . . . it was a fantastic fun night. Then Andrew Martin and I and a few of the boys went to an Irish bar for a while. Eventually, locals offered to drive us back to the hotel. They were highly emotional and were running red lights and yahooing. The streets in the middle of Rome were empty, and every time they went through a light the Colonel and I were joining in with the good-natured hooraying and whooping and yelling.

Todd Blackadder had a couple of big days where he drank a lot. He'd been feeling the stresses and strains of being All Black captain. Watching first-hand the effect on him had been a shock to me. What with being Crusaders and Canterbury captain as well, he barely survived the tour. Toddy was feeling the absence from his family, especially when he learned the day after the test against Italy that his young son Ethan had broken his arm. One night he refused to go to bed. I was having little influence on him so Mark Hammett, in particular, and Greg Somerville helped me out and we got him into the lift and up into his room. He sat on his bed and started saying he was a Crusader through and through and Hammett, easy with his emotions, started crying too. It all got a bit much: 'Just go to sleep, Blackie!'

Next day involved sightseeing, including a visit to the Colosseum — appropriate if you see rugby as gladiatorial. Then in the evening we met local rugby dignitaries at a rugby club. As the bus was about to move off most of the players crowded over to one side and were wolf whistling and waving at a group of highly attractive women standing on the pavement. Overly eager, somebody leapt off the bus to chat them up. 'Hey hey honey, how you doing?'

'I'm okay, thank you.' The voice was deep and husky. That gorgeous woman was a man!

Before we left for Germany I asked our manager if, now that we were in effect back on tour, and wearing our number ones, I should say something to the team about the need to live by our rules, maintain our discipline and dignity when in public. Our standards had slipped considerably since we had arrived in Rome and with no games to work towards we were quickly losing our structure as a group with a common cause. The tour was over but not over, partners had arrived, and the whole disciplinary fabric was fraying. No one quite knew which rules, if any, still applied. If our partners arrive late, are we late? Do we have to cough up a $1000 fine for that? That was the sort of question requiring an answer. After consultation with Martin I stood up and reminded the players that we were 'back on tour' and that all the previous rules, which had taken a three-day vacation, were now in place.

In Germany we asked to see a concentration camp at Dachau. It was a cool, overcast day filled with foreboding when we visited, and it matched the mood of all of us as we walked around buildings designed to exterminate human life. The clean white rooms where, once, dead bodies had been piled high, engendered macabre and chilling feelings for me.

We also visited the adidas centre, where we were introduced to hundreds of staff, answered questions posed by small manageable groups and did mini skill sessions with them as well. They thought the lineout lifting was great fun, although a number were freaked out once they had been hoisted into the air themselves. The comments we heard later were that the staff liked how friendly and interactive we were, and that no soccer team would have been so obliging. We were asked to do a haka in front of the adidas stadium and the watching workers loved it.

The next day we toured the adidas testing units where we mentioned we'd had trouble with some of their boots and apparel. That night Andrew Martin stayed up late in our hotel, just to keep an eye on things. In the morning there were reports of scuffles resulting from more over-indulgence, and friction between players and partners. Clearly it was time to leave. By the time our visit to adidas was over, all team and management cohesion had gone and it left me wondering whether the public relations effort could have been done with only two or three players rather than the whole team.

In our last meeting before we left for New Zealand Gilbert Enoka gave us all a sheaf of papers on which we were asked to review our team-mates as players and as individuals. We didn't have to comment on everyone, nor were we required to put our names to comments unless we wanted to. This was part of what, as Enoka put it, 'developing a culture where we can convey honestly to our team-mates what we think of what they do and how they play'. He thought this 'paramount' if we were to become 'a consistently successful team'. I received my feedback in the mail just before Christmas and found the honesty from some to be beneficial and I took note of a few comments in particular.

On the plane home to New Zealand a familiar, desolating emptiness returned. Half the team had left to go their separate ways. As usual my first sight of the New Zealand coastline miles ahead and far below brought tears welling to my eyes; it is such a warm, welcoming feeling to see home once again. At Mangere, the Aucklanders meet their families, the rest of us check in our luggage for flights south. I go into the domestic lounge and . . . feel alone again. It's as quick as that.

For a rugby player like me, who has been single for much of his career, home life is a life you don't often lead. You get home and realise you haven't got much to go home to. But a lot of the married lads find it tough when they get home too. Often their partners have finished work, are on annual leave and want to go away somewhere, while the guys just want to stay at home and recover.

I remember standing outside the Auckland terminal building in cauldron-like warmth. The tests on Armistice Day and in Marseilles seemed to belong to an entirely different world, a completely different time. I got to Dunedin just in time for my friend Duncan Blaikie's medical graduation ceremony. In the photos taken then I am a pasty white colour, evidence of that northern hemisphere winter.

It felt good to be home. What a different feeling to 12 months before! How different I was to the disconsolate and unsure person that I found myself reduced to the previous year. I was proud of what I had achieved and it felt so good to know that it all came from some intense soul searching and plenty of hard work. So, to treat myself, I had a whole week off from rugby and then it was straight back into training for the Super 12 competition.

Chapter 9

Captaincy: Challenge or Poisoned Chalice?

Halfway through 2000 an assortment of little things had started to unsettle me. I decided it was time to stop flatting with my close friends Duncan and John Blaikie, and Simon Maling. I'd lived — when actually home in Dunedin and not off playing rugby — with Duncan and Simon for four years, and John for three. We all played footie in the same team and socialised together.

Our accumulated mess, mine and theirs — plates and other stuff lying about — was irking me. Time to leave. I didn't want to argue over trivial matters with my best mates. I felt our lifestyle was stultifying and I was being bullied by a need to grow more. A voice was telling me that my horizons were too narrow; I was cruising along like someone having come back from a Sunday drive not feeling as if he'd seen anything different, anything truly interesting.

Rugby constricts a man too often. I felt I was too often portrayed as being the archetypal Southern Man and was uneasy about that for it means being seen as fitting a one-dimensional stereotype — a stereotype that didn't reflect who I was at all.

My move had a domino effect. Before long Duncan was off to play for the Chiefs; John moved in with his girlfriend and Simon with Tony Brown. I wanted a cosy two-bedroom flat. In the end I had to settle for a three-bedroom place in Shiel Hill from where I could see the Pacific and Tomahawk Beach. It wasn't great but it was clean, and when I cleaned it up it looked like it *had* been cleaned. That had never been the case with any other flat I'd been in.

My lawyer and agent Warren Alcock had been acting on behalf of Carl Hoeft, Kees Meeuws and myself. Previously, we'd all signed fairly similar deals. Now the NZRU had made new offers and Warren said that the union had decided it was time to treat me differently, so when the three of us turned up for our collective negotiations I was sent to another room and came back after Kees and Carl had finished their discussion. Warren said that the union had upped its

Enjoying the festivities at a 'scarfie' party in Dunedin with, from left, Matt Carrington, Duncan and John Blaikie.

offer considerably. 'Why?' I asked. He said that 'they see you as an important part of the future of All Black rugby'. Apparently, Wayne Smith was behind it. He had decided, unbeknown to me, that I was to succeed Todd Blackadder as captain. This came like the proverbial bolt out of the blue. I had spent years trying to become the first-choice hooker and was only just getting used to that, not that I ever felt truly secure.

The NZRU said that they wanted me to sign for four years or not at all. The offer was for a fixed, graduated increase each year for the four years, irrespective of form or anything else. It was either that or a deal which involved a 'performance review' every year. (The usual deal is that you get a retainer, a Super 12 payment, then an All Black payment and so much per test.) I thought about the offer while on Highlander Super 12 duties in South Africa in 2001. I decided it was best to go for fixed payments as opposed to an annual performance review because of the certainty that the fixed payments brought.

Something must have been singing like a bird of warning in my head. Four years is a long time in professional rugby, I thought. Who knows what might happen: coaches might get axed; I could get injured seriously; I might start playing badly; other players might play extraordinarily well. Before long — all too quickly — all of this came to pass. I'm not superstitious, nor am I especially cynical, but given events since 2002 I can see how I could have become so.

Warren met and discussed my contract with the NZRU's negotiator who, at the conclusion of their chat, wrote down some figures on a piece of paper and left it with him. When Warren looked at the note he realised that the union's rep had offered more than Warren had thought I was going to get. Warren phoned me and told me to come in and have a look at the figures. He said that he thought the union's lawyer may not have realised what he had done but that, now that he, Warren, had shown the paper to me, it was legally binding. I accepted as quick as a hooker's strike against the head — how often does that happen nowadays?

Shortly afterwards, Tony Gilbert, the assistant coach under Wayne Smith, rang and said, 'Anton, give Smithy a ring.' I said, 'What about?' Tony chuckled and growled, 'Just give him a ring.'

I rang Smithy and he said that he wanted me to be his captain. I was truly stunned. I had known Wayne for a few years now and built up a strong friendship with him which made the phone conversation all the more special. I told him I would do the job, would be his captain and we promised each other that we would do everything in our power to make the coming All Black season a success. With the phone back on the hook, I sat down for 10 minutes and collected my thoughts and reflected upon my rugby history.

Initially, it was a giant step making the New Zealand Under 17s, and that had made me realise I had the ability to be an All Black. Next step was actually wanting to be an All Black and opening my heart and all of my boyhood dreams to becoming one. After becoming an All Black it was not sufficient just to wear the jersey; I wanted to be a good All Black. More recently I thought my end goal was to be respected by my current and past players as a person who respected the values and traditions of All Black rugby.

Even after being offered the job in 1999 and the incident with Toddy at the back of the bus in Italy on the 2000 tour where he told me 'You're ready', somehow the thought of being the skipper had never seemed a realistic option. I had never aspired to being All Black captain. Having seen what Taine Randell had gone through, and the pressures Toddy had had to bear — and especially the way he had dealt with them in Italy — why would anyone covet the job? That had been my thinking.

I got on the phone and talked to my close family, who were all elated about the news. The announcement wasn't going to be made public for a week or more, so I left instructions of silence with my family and had to hold onto the secret myself until the official press conference in Dunedin.

After the end of the Super 12 and just prior to the announcement of my appointment as captain, I had to go to Auckland on business. On the way back, on a whim, I altered my flights, flew into Christchurch and took a cab out to Toddy's place in Rangiora. The rugby union's CEO, David Rutherford, had just left. Toddy was friendly and, naturally, a bit rueful about the fact that he was no longer going to be the captain. The NZRU, Rutherford and Smithy in particular, had the decency to tell Toddy the bad news before it became public knowledge. He thought he had another year in him. We chatted, drank cups of tea, strolled round his and Priscilla's property. Their two kids, Shinae and Ethan, were with us. Ethan showed me his tree hut, and how he could do jumps on his bike. Then we all went south to jet boat on the Rakaia River — and got stuck on a couple of shingle banks. I joked with Toddy, whose nickname was Mount Rangiora, a reference to his large behind. I said that was the reason we got stuck.

Part of the reason for going to see Toddy — apart from because I thought he was a top man, and I respected him — was to tell him that I hadn't coveted his job.

It's worth pausing here to consider the captaincy question.

When you look at the number of All Black captains there have been in the past five years — Randell, Blackadder, me, Randell again, Thorne, Umaga — it begs the question: why such a turnover? Some believe that it may be because successive NZRU boards have been riven with factions, have not been as strong and as astute, as insightful, as they ought to have been. Are members still pressured by parochialism when it comes to choosing coaches and others? Is there always, to New Zealand rugby's detriment, a war between Canterbury and Auckland on the one hand, and on the other a banding together by everyone else in an effort to deknacker Canterbury, Auckland, or both?

A former senior executive of the NZRU expressed the view that changes of tack and inconsistencies with decision making may well be because of a lack 'of corporate memory'. Newcomers feel an irresistible urge to make changes in order to assert themselves and show that they know more than their predecessors. Maybe it always comes back to the size of the egos.

You could also be pardoned for thinking that our selectors and coaches haven't had a willingness to stick with their choices. The turnover of players has been unusually high. Shining stars in the firmament one month, fizzled rockets in the dustbin the next has been the fate of too many. I remember Fitzy's remark to me about feeling insecure for his first couple of years as All Black captain. I can see now — actually, I could see it at the time but wasn't sure how to deal with it — just how brittle I felt. After one year in the job my mistakes were all too clear to me. That's one reason why Tony Gilbert, for one, *Grrhs*, and says my demotion 'was a waste'. Such support is good to have, naturally, but I try to see what happened to me as indicative of something wider and regrettable, excessive wastage of talent in New Zealand rugby.

Having left Toddy and his family in Rangiora I flew back to Dunedin on Saturday night, with the captaincy announcement planned for the next day. In an effort to relax I went out to a local bar and had a couple of quiet drinks with friends. Several people asked me what Sunday's announcement was all about. I lied and said I didn't know. The public announcement was held at the Leisure Lodge hotel in north Dunedin, and when I got out of my car in the car park I was met with a few flashing cameras from some eager photographers. Smithy, Tony and I sat down in a small room with at least 40 journalists staring straight back at us. To say that was intimidating would be a huge understatement and my nerves gathered in front of the expectant crowd. The coaches told the media that, apart from me, no other All Blacks were confirmed for the coming year and thankfully most of the questions were directed at them and I had to answer, by comparison, relatively few. The worst part of the day by far was posing for all of the photographers. Cameras and photographs have always been an anathema to me.

With great relief that the media commitments were dealt with, I said my goodbyes to Wayne and Tony, headed home, buying a dozen oysters on the way, knocked up a salad, opened a bottle of wine and relaxed. Then I had a damned good and much-needed sleep. At the time it was the sleep of the blessed rather than of the damned.

The next day, Monday, one of my interviews was on TV with Paul Holmes. He wanted to know what I had spoken to Toddy about when I spent the day with him in Rangiora. On the Sunday I had said that we had gone out jet boating, and was annoyed with myself for having disclosed that. I told Holmes that it wasn't my intention to have made that visit public knowledge and that it was a mistake on my behalf to have let it slip. I then went on to say that it was a private matter between Todd and me and that I would prefer if it was kept that way. Many people told me they approved of that remark.

Virtually overnight I realised that a great many people listen very intently to every word you say as All Black captain. It came as a shock. Before this, if asked a question, I had been fairly bullish. It was some weeks before I was willing to accept — call that managed to learn, if you like — that I was expected to be diplomatic, cautious, tactful: being damned careful in other words.

I had been given no advice on what to say, or how to say it. One side of me felt that I ought to be able to say honestly what I thought and felt. Why should an honest response be deemed offensive? Aren't we advised, always, of the virtue in being open and candid? On the one hand,

With my father Frank — New Zealand test captain against Australia in the 1978 series — after I was named All Blacks captain in 2001.

there are people who say, 'Ah, refreshing,' and like it when you are candid; on the other there are those who tut-tut and say 'you shouldn't have said that, that's not the right attitude'.

I'm not saying a captain shouldn't think before speaking. The difficulty I had for a while was in having to give live interviews immediately after games when I was, usually, exhausted. And once or twice extremely disappointed, and now and then shattered. I had yet to appreciate that I was speaking on behalf of a constituency much larger than myself. As All Black captain you are acutely aware that an inordinate amount hinges on the result, in the eyes of very many rugby fans, and that it is far from being 'just another game'.

Once or twice, after interviews, I thought, 'Hell, I shouldn't have said that. That wasn't right. That was a bit ungracious.'

Is there any other country in the rugby-playing world where so much attention is focused on the captain?

The few days after the announcement of my appointment as captain were humbling: cards, letters, faxes flooded in. I've kept most of them. The fact that so many people I didn't know took the trouble to send me congratulations and encouragement was inspiring. That was why in 2004, when curators at Te Papa in Wellington asked me to contribute to an exhibition featuring items valued highly by a number of well-known New Zealanders, and asked that

I provide a few words in a style suitable for children, I sent examples of this correspondence with this note:

'The most treasured items that I own are the letters of encouragement and support sent to me from people I don't know.

'During my career I have had many periods where I've felt alone and sad. Letters like these three (I have lots more at home) made me feel good about myself and gave me strength to meet life's new challenges.

'I think it is truly special for people who don't know you personally to take time out of their lives to support and enhance yours. These are the actions of unselfish and thoughtful people and I try to pass their positive thoughts on to others.'

All Black squad members were asked to assemble at the Palmerston North training centre. The newcomers, those who hadn't been there in 2000, arrived first. The Colonel, Andrew Martin, thought it a good idea that I be there to greet them. This was real captain stuff, and in that sense I was new too. Smithy had a new catch-cry for the year: tika — in Maori I believe it means do whatever it takes in the best interests of the group. Amusingly, most of the boys thought it meant show some ticker, some heart.

Gilbert Enoka gave us an excellent audio-visual display that went through all the protocols we'd put in place the previous year, everything that was intended to help us lift our standards all round. And at Palmerston North Thorbs (Peter Thorburn) asked to have a chat with me. He said he was worried about my perception of him. Peter thought I didn't think much of his role or contribution, and I could see he was nearly in tears. In fact, I had quite the opposite opinion of Thorbs and his work. Peter's job, as well as being the third selector, was twofold. He was to be critical of our own team and provide feedback to Wayne and Tony about anything at all: coaching, training, team atmosphere. He also looked at other teams to see if they were doing things that we could use to gain an edge, and in my opinion he was doing some excellent analysis. I realised then, and it's something I still battle with, that sometimes, when I'm really focused, the blinkers are on and I lose sight of the periphery: I just hadn't paid enough attention to Thorbs.

We practised mauling quite a lot. The three selectors believed that through mauling, keeping the ball off the ground, we would drag opponents in and then, if we timed it right, release the ball and give our backs a bit more time and space outside. Every day for the week or so we were in camp we practised mauling up a hill at the institute. But, curiously, I don't think we actually used the maul much in matches during the year.

Around this time I was approached by one of the women's magazines and offered $30,000 for an exclusive article, on the 'Life and Times and Innermost Feelings of the New All Black Captain' I suppose.

I thought long and hard about the money. That is a lot of loot. I planned to give it all to my mum. It would be almost her entire year's salary in one go. But I was reluctant; it felt to me as if I'd be selling my soul. If I agreed to it then that would mean my privacy, my independence would be gone.

What to do? I asked around. Goldie (Jeff Wilson) said I should take it. 'It's only for one week and then people forget. Besides, it's for your mum.' Another friend, the Otago trainer Matt Blair said, 'Mate, you can't compromise your principles.'

In the end I said no to the offer. This doesn't mean that I disapprove of those who have taken the money for similar stories; it's their decision. For me it didn't feel right.

Every time I think of that $30,000, and what Mum could have done with it, it makes me wince. Was my decision selfish or unselfish? I wonder still.

'A chip off the old block' – Chris Laidlaw

Chris Laidlaw says, 'Anton's a chip off the old block, but more ordered than his father Frank. Actually, "frank" is a good word to describe Anton. His frankness could well have frightened Mitchell and Deans. Many in rugby look for blind loyalty. That's a New Zealand thing.

'In his general play, Anton reminds me of Sean Fitzpatrick.'

Laidlaw sees Oliver as 'an admirable player. I'd have had him in my World Cup squad in 2003. As a person, many in rugby have been deeply impressed by him.'

Our first test of the year was against Samoa at North Harbour Stadium. The lead-up week to any first test of the year is chaos: lots of training, learning new moves, new calls, media interviews and sponsorship appearances. The Black Ferns captain, Farah Palmer, was also in Auckland, as the Ferns were preparing for a game. We were both hookers (no aspersion intended), both studied physical education at Otago, and so the print media and the *Holmes* TV programme featured us. A photographer from the *New Zealand Herald* took dozens of shots and the paper used some that made me look like a spaced-out idiot. I'm not vain; few of us can afford to be. And no one would ever say I'm going to be touted as rugby's equivalent of Mel Gibson or Brad Pitt, or even Russell Crowe, but fair's fair. The photographer turned up at the captain's run a day before the test. He apologised for the pictures and said that someone in the illustrations department had chosen them.

It wasn't the first time this sort of thing had happened. After a while I got madder and madder. Why make fun of prominent people like that? Goodwill gets lost. I was starting to think, if newspapers are going to treat me like this, I won't cooperate with them. When the *Dominion-Post* newspaper made me look like a dolt early in 2003, this time capturing me exhausted in a fitness test with unflattering facial expressions, I was so riled that I was going to write a letter to the editor. Instead, I rang Ron Palenski, who used to be a senior member of staff there, and he advised me against it. His view was it was best to shut up or the buggers will take pleasure in doing it again.

When I became captain it was the practice that the trainer took the team warm-up sessions at the captain's run. I didn't like what I saw as a disorganised warm-up session early on, wanted it done better, so I took over Mike Anthony's role there. He was a bit miffed: captain's runs before tests were still fairly new. Over time they became more balanced, meaning everyone was mentally alert throughout, without the session becoming a 100 per cent full-on physical hit-out. As a new captain, and one who wanted everything done properly, I was possibly a bit too serious. Today these runs are shorter and tighter with a lot of jocularity before and after. But back then I didn't have faith in the boys and others to do the job properly unless they were totally focused. And Wayne Smith was encouraging me to stamp my authority on things.

If I had my time again, I would have relaxed more and trusted the players and Mike to get it right and not tried to act as a quality controller. The result of the test was a victory for us: All Blacks 50, Samoa 6.

Smithy had decided it would be good to have an ex-All Black stay with the team during the week prior to a test — to exchange knowledge from the past and make the ex-All Blacks

Leading the All Blacks out against Samoa at Albany for the first test of 2001. It was my first test as captain.

aware of what being a current All Black entailed. The flanker Graham Williams was the ex-All Black asked to be with us for the week leading into the Samoan test. He sat at the front of the bus where the management sat and where I also chose to sit, so I quickly told him players sat further back and to get down there with the rest of the team, as he was one of them. He liked that and enjoyed himself. Stu Cron, also a former flanker, was another who joined us for a few days before the game against Argentina at Jade Stadium.

On another occasion I recall we had a scrum session with Stu Cron's brother, Mike. He was full of good ideas regarding scrummaging. One plan was that the number eight should start a scrum engagement. The idea was that the number eight held the locks back so that they were only just touching the props and when the number eight gave the signal and propelled the locks forward, the props followed slightly after them so you achieved a sort of ripple or concertina effect. That was the theory but we couldn't quite get it to work for us, so maybe the theory isn't too sound.

Then again, Taine Randell, when he was at number eight for Otago and the Highlanders, was able to make it work. His was a modified version of the Cron theory.

On the morning of the test against Argentina at Christchurch, the fire alarms went off in our inner city Heritage Hotel. We all had to evacuate post-haste. There we were standing around outside wondering what it was all about. Aha, there was a culprit: Norm Maxwell. Our manager, Andrew Martin, had tightened up on spending in several departments, including laundry. Maxey had been rummaging around in his bag and found his number ones all scrunched up in the bottom from the week before. So he put them on a hanger, hung them in the bathroom, turned on the hot shower, and shut the door. It was his way of attempting to get the creases out. Forty minutes later the steam in the room was so thick and hot that the alarms went off.

I may have said it before, but it's worth saying again: I had a lot of time for Maxey, for his courage and total commitment to the cause. He is an interesting mix: at first he appears naive and very relaxed, will respond to many remarks with a 'Sweet as, bro'. But don't be deceived; on the field he plays with reckless, aggressive abandon and little regard for his safety. He could be zany, unwittingly so at times. For instance, once he left his smelly, sweaty shoulder pads on after a match and pulled a white shirt on over the top of them before struggling into his jacket and tie. He said that at the after-match he wanted to look as if he had bigger shoulders. Another time he couldn't find his black dress shoes, so he unscrewed the sprigs from his rugby boots, gave the boots a quick wipe, and turned up at the after-match wearing them. Norm was one of the great characters of my time in All Black rugby.

A new stand was being built at Jade Stadium in Christchurch, leaving a large cavity on one side of the ground. It was eerie and the test lacked the normal atmosphere because of it. We beat Argentina 67–19, but we did have problems. Their forwards were all over the ball on the ground, wouldn't shift, and the referee let them get away with it. I was damned annoyed about it. One of their players eye-gouged me in a ruck so I hit him. It was a good shot too. The ref ordered me to the sin bin. I said to him, 'Mate, I was eye-gouged.' That attempted justification for my indiscretion made no difference; off the field I marched.

After the match in the press conference I was grilled. Punching is not a good example, not what we show the kids, a bad role model. Smithy and Tony Gilbert weren't prepared to censure me and they left it to me to decide what to say. I can't recall what I said, except I remember trying hard not to be too defiant, nor excessively contrite. But think about it: what do you do if someone's got his fingers stuck in your eyes and the ref doesn't spot it?

In 2001 there were no after-match socials. Both coaches were completely dedicated to getting the best out of us. Research showed that social functions after matches, standing

Doing my best to explain to referee Andrew Cole why I belted an Argentine player at Jade Stadium. It was all to no avail and I was banished to the sin bin.

around in crowded rooms for a couple of hours, was crucial time that could be better spent optimising physical recovery. Smith and Gilbert persuaded the NZRU Board to drop after-match gatherings, no small feat given their history. The following year there was a return to after-match events, although they became less prolonged and, in some cases, were attended by fewer people. Cancelling the after-matches in favour of better recovery time may have been an example of how we tried to make a few too many changes. A classic case of rugby becoming too professional for its own good, perhaps.

Next up the French in Wellington. They were said to have an under-strength team even though they had just beaten the Boks in two tests in South Africa. I sat with Tana Umaga on our flight to Wellington on the Sunday after the Argentine test. We discussed the previous week and what we thought about when and where and how we'd trained, what went right during the test and what didn't, how best to divide our time — virtually everything we could think of. I made a note of what Tana and I had discussed and when we got to Wellington I took our views to Smithy and Tony.

Every Monday morning management had a meeting at which they decided our timetable for the week ahead. Management had several meetings each week, but Monday's was the most important. I had the right to turn up whenever I liked. Before this I had stayed away. The normal procedure was that the Colonel, as manager, spoke first and provided a schedule for the week as he saw it. But this time, he'd no sooner got started than Smithy stopped him and told him that I had made a number of suggestions which had arisen from a chat between Tana and I, and that he and Tony had decided that a lot of it sounded good so they were going to run with it. I'll never forget the look on Andrew's face. I guess he realised that he would have to rejig quite a lot and that, understandably, he would have preferred prior notice.

Later, Smith was to say that he was more confident of beating the French than he had been for either of the two previous tests because, notwithstanding they were far and away the strongest of the three teams, our players had taken the initiative and were more motivated.

Ian Kirkpatrick was the former All Black who joined us for the week prior to the French test. Kirky was a likeable guy. He had mana, real presence, and he turned up to the first training with his rugby boots. He sat down among the players, laced up his boots and strode onto the field as if his heyday was yesterday and not 30 years ago. I was amazed; he even ran in some of our grids. My thoughts were that he was still in splendid nick, and that he must have been some athlete in his day. Alas, during a sprint session, he tweaked a hamstring. But no one said anything like 'You silly old bastard, it serves you right.' It was more like 'Ten years in the All Black jersey and a good bastard to boot.' Kirky was well respected.

On the day before a test I like to go to a movie or read a book. Usually it's good to get out of the hotel. On this occasion I went to a movie with Tana and Ala (Pita Alatini). They weren't computer game addicts like some of the players, and away from rugby were very relaxed. The antithesis of me, often, which may be why I found them good company.

The French were tough. They had a good scrum and they put us under a lot of pressure in the lineout. This was partly because Maxey, who had been given the job of calling the lineouts, got sin-binned and there wasn't really a Plan B — a bad oversight. The three French loose forwards were tall, which meant that — given their lineout's eagerness to contest just about every throw, and back themselves to snaffle possession — they were equipped to compete in three (front, middle, back) not the usual two positions (front, middle). Final score, 37–12 to us.

Three games, three wins. I was extremely relieved, for I had put myself under a lot of pressure, having fallen into the trap of not trusting others to do their jobs properly. It was probably the burden of responsibility of being the new captain, and me wanting to make doubly sure I wasn't seen to be complacent.

That night I went out to a nightclub where it was so dark you couldn't see your fist when your arm was outstretched. I met a few people who knew hardly anything about rugby, and whom I'd never met before. I had a few drinks — not many — and danced for a while. It felt good to be anonymous again. Then I thought, time to go home, so I left and looked for a cab. To my amazement it was 5.30 a.m., starting to get light. I had a couple of hours' sleep, showered, sorted out my luggage and rushed off for media interviews. I was a bit late and, subsequently, prompted by the Colonel, the back-seat boys ticked me off about it. They were doing their job, so that was good.

Before we left for South Africa to start the Tri-nations series we had a few days off. I spent some time reading and relaxing with my friend Matt Blair at Rob and Jean Johnstone's holiday home in Wanaka. Time away from footie is always precious to me. I need time and space away from the game to recharge my mental batteries and re-establish my identity as Anton Oliver the person, not the rugby player.

Rob suggested I drive back to Dunedin via the Maniototo. I'd heard about how different it was so I took his advice. Black ice and fog all the way to Cromwell, then, when I turned off up the Manuherikia Valley at Clyde, I entered a strangely beautiful, mystical world. There was a hoar frost; everything seemed brittle and crystalline. Even massive trees looked as if a nudge would send them toppling over. At Omakau I crossed the river and drove up Blacks Hill on the range between the Manuherikia and the Ida valleys. At first I was still in the fog then, near the top of the hill, I burst from mist into a glittering, brand new world of sunshine and a bright blue sky. There was the broad Ida Valley below, Rough Ridge on the far side and in the northeast the pleated Hawkdun Range. There's something liberating about such great expanses of folded empty country. I will never forget the first time I saw this view. Shapely then stolid hills and mountain ranges with subtle tones led off in all directions, and the whole, though stark at times, was curiously seductive. I felt an enormous upwelling of emotion, pulled over, and began to cry. I have no idea why or where it all came from, but out it came. It may have something to do with the fact that when you lead the All Blacks, or any team or organisation that means a lot to New Zealanders, you feel a powerful sense of responsibility that has its roots in a love of country and this transmutes into a strong sense of belonging, and pride.

The small break was invaluable to me, a godsend before we returned to camp prior to flying to Cape Town.

I took my guitar with me to South Africa. It had been made for me entirely out of native wood by a luthier at Purakaunui just north of Dunedin. I was going through a period when I felt extremely nationalistic, and having a guitar made out of local materials and fashioned by a Kiwi was part of that. It's uncommon for New Zealand wood to be used because it's said to lack the normal, or right, resonance. I find my guitar a pleasant, relaxing and, at times, consoling companion. Others have different props. Take Taine Randell and Tony Brown and Justin Marshall: they just loved their white toffee pops with their cups of tea. Loved them so much that they chipped in together and took a small suitcase full of them — over 30 packets — on tour. When the coaches and the nutritionist found out they got a talking-to. A dozen or more players spent a great deal of time playing each other at computer games. The coaches and I were concerned about the amount of time they were spending in their rooms. We thought that they would be mentally drained and would have preferred that they had spent some more time outdoors. However, telling the players what to do and how to prepare was going against the culture the coaches were trying to create: one where young men thought independently and made their own decisions rather than the coaches doing that for them.

Our build-up for the test in Cape Town was fairly low-key but we were worried about our starter moves off scrums and lineouts. It had become apparent that not everyone knew where they were going, or what they were meant to do. With starter moves, a team often tries to put three moves together in order to get in position to attack. We tried to sort these moves out in one-and-a-half sessions. In hindsight we confused ourselves and this put us under extra pressure. Nowadays, Super 12 and NPC sides spend weeks drumming these moves into players pre-season.

The day was wet and the test was tight. Our defence was good, Brownie kicked well — four penalty goals — and we won in a tryless encounter 12–3.

Tony Gilbert was astounded when, as we were doing our pre-match haka, 'about 100 spear-waving Zulus' approached us 'from all sides'. He says there 'was a terrific buzz in the crowd'. He remembers that, afterwards, the South African journalists at the press conference were unusually excited. Their first question for me, he says, was: 'When the Zulu warriors crowded in on the All Blacks while they were doing the haka, did you think there was going to be a fight before the game?'

He says my answer was the 'best and easily the most deflating one-liner I have ever heard'. 'What Zulu warriors?'

I was conscious that Norm Maxwell was keen to be given more responsibility. He thought he could run the lineouts, so I spoke to Tony Gilbert. Tony was lukewarm about the idea, but because he and I believed in encouraging players — the corporate term is 'empowerment'

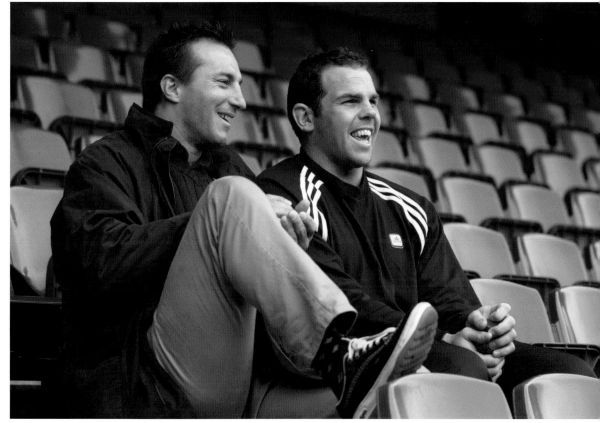

With legendary French centre Philippe Sella at Newlands, Cape Town, prior to the first Tri-nations test against the Springboks in 2001.

— we took a punt on it. As we were to find out, it wasn't a great idea. It is clear that most rugby fans and observers don't realise how hard it is to find someone to organise lineouts and make the best calls. We needed someone with a greater facility and willingness to do his homework, attend to details: someone like Simon Maling, actually, who spent hours examining videos of other teams' lineouts. Maxey is just too laid-back for the job and over the next three tests we were to falter badly.

Before our next test, Smithy brought another idea to me, which I liked. He said he had put together a bogus analysis of our weaknesses and wanted to present it as having been leaked to us from someone in the Wallaby camp. I said 'Okay, but let me see it before you hand it out.' It was just as well because he had used some of our terminology — for instance, the analysis referred to the 'guard dog', the position of one of our defenders close to a ruck. I thought I'd picked up all such giveaways, but, unfortunately, I missed a couple of minor points of style. Guess who spotted them? Mehrts, of course, the clever bugger. He didn't completely blow our cover, just tarnished it. How good an idea it turned out to be is debatable.

Our preparation for the match against Australia at Carisbrook was overly long and we spent a lot of time on rather pointless drills. Usually, with Smith and Gilbert, the practice sessions were coherent, made sense. This week something was awry. Sometimes no matter how much preparation a team and management do, a test week just doesn't unfold how it was planned. It is usually not until a week or 10 days has passed that the reasons become apparent. Picking up subtleties in the team mood is very difficult and issues that need to be acted on get missed. I had

On the charge against Australia at Dunedin in 2001. We played poorly and lost 15-23.

to give Tony and Smithy an honest talk in private and they tended to agree. With them I always felt I could say my piece and they wouldn't become defensive, make me feel as if I'd spoken out of turn.

It came as no surprise to me that we played badly and lost 15–23. This was the test where, with time almost up, instead of telling Mehrts to take a penalty, I tapped and ran. I was frustrated with my performance, the team's performance and the game in general. Kicking for goal, as I saw it, would have seemed like giving up.

I'd been reading Charles Upham's biography *Mark of a Lion* and perhaps this influenced my decision to charge at the opposition; that was what Upham would have done.

Inevitably there were quibbles in the post-match media conference. The media chipped the coaches about my not taking the three points. I interrupted and said the decision was mine alone: if they had a gripe, direct it at me. There were those who agreed with me and those who didn't. The 'didn'ts' believed that a bonus point could be crucial to the result of the Tri-nations. If it had been the final game in the series and a single point would have allowed us to win, I would have taken the penalty kick.

A fortnight later we played South Africa at Eden Park. We hadn't enjoyed training in the cold and wet at Tahuna Park in Dunedin, nor was it pleasant to strike another wet night in Auckland. To me, another loss would have been completely unacceptable. I was tense, determined. Taine was standing beside me during the national anthems. He must have sensed what I was thinking, having been in my position before as a losing captain, and he cracked a joke. That snapped me out of any negativity I had and I was grateful to him for that. When the final whistle blew with us ahead 26–15, relief ran off me like rain, and in a live interview immediately afterwards I made an offhand remark along the lines of, 'That'll keep the wolves at bay for another week.' Again, some people liked that, some didn't. I think, like most All Blacks, I was acutely aware of how scrutinised after-match assessments are. And, yes, it can be said that we too are, at times, oversensitive. It takes a while to become inured to criticism as Fitzpatrick had said, and I was still very much the new kid on the block when it came to after-match interviews.

There was no after-match social function to attend. That was a relief; I don't know of any player who enjoys them. The Boks came into our changing shed and we had a yarn together. I told their captain that we respected their attitude — 'Here we come, you'd better be ready.' Perhaps our relative success over the Boks in recent times is because they play with the same passion that the All Blacks have. Therefore the game has required less thinking and has been more about playing with your heart on your sleeve. Playing the Australians has proved to be far more complex than that and we have consequently been far less successful against them. They don't play solely on emotion.

Later in the evening I mused about how odd test football can be. Here we were elated, whereas two weeks ago we were all right down in the dumps — suffering not just from dejection, but also from self-doubt and a kind of irritated embarrassment. All Blacks, individually and as teams, have seldom enjoyed winning enough. We have always laboured under a colossal weight of being expected to win. The media pressure was unrelenting; there was the rigmarole around recovery sessions, then the training next day. Where, in all of this, had the fun gone?

We are often described as, and required to be, the so-called Black Machine. Inside me I think I resented that: I do not like being seen as a machine. Sometimes I have felt both physically and mentally strong, sometimes I have felt exposed, vulnerable and weak. As individuals and as a group we are conscious of the fact that a significant proportion of the rugby public expect us to suppress our emotions. We are regularly reminded of the great All Black *legacy*. Of course I respected that legacy, and I felt honoured to be part of it and be an All Black. Nevertheless, some of it was repressive, making us fearful of losing, fearful all round — if we were honest.

This is not a whinge. It is stating it as it is. When people say a man has to 'harden up', perhaps we need a wider definition of 'hardness' than that which has bedevilled the game of rugby here, and aspects of other games as well. Need the road be quite so lonely, and the way so fraught, quite as often? The answer, whatever it is, is not simply contained in the saying 'If you can't stand the heat, get out of the kitchen.' There is so much more to this complicated question.

The pressure was on for our last Tri-nations game at Stadium Australia the following week. Even though we couldn't win the Bledisloe Cup — we could still have won the Tri-nations — there was, and is, always a need and an expectation to beat the Wallabies in order to restore or maintain New Zealand rugby's sense of pride. For some reason in New Zealand rugby circles the feeling lingers that the Bledisloe is, or should be, New Zealand's by divine right. Perhaps it goes back to the days when most All Black fans regarded Australia as very much second-rate, rather like how Australian cricket's attitude to our cricket used to be.

"Contain Oliver" was the message' – Brendan Cannon

Brendan Cannon, in recent seasons vying with Jeremy Paul for the number one hooker's position in the Wallabies side, first played against Oliver in 1994 at international under-19 level. 'I rate Anton as having been in the top two or three hookers in world rugby for the past 10 years. There's no more honest forward. His work rate, leg drive, go forward is right up there with the best. Many of us in the Australian team saw his omission from the All Blacks for the 2003 World Cup as a travesty, absolutely ridiculous.'

Cannon said when he asked Oliver why he hadn't left Otago and the Highlanders after the friction involving Laurie Mains, Oliver replied, 'I'd find it hard to play for any other teams except Otago, the Highlanders and the All Blacks.'

'That,' said Cannon, 'astonished me. I doubt you'd find any other guy in rugby today who would say that, who would remain that loyal to one province or team.

'Every Australian team I know held Oliver in the highest regard. In the front row for Otago, he and Hoeft and Meeuws used to intimidate most teams. And whenever the Waratahs were due to play the Highlanders we targeted him. "Contain Oliver" was the message.'

The word was that the crowd was going to sing 'Waltzing Matilda' and drown out our haka. The feeling in the All Blacks was 'Stuff you, if you don't respect our traditions, we won't do it.' So we decided as a group not to perform the haka for that test. I'd been looking into the haka and its history, looking at when and where it was appropriate. My conclusion was that it was being overused, had become more of a commercial marketing tool than anything else, and that we would be better off doing it overseas only in the way All Black teams used to prior to the 1987 World Cup. Many of us thought it had lost its specialness. I remember a whole lot of us sitting around one night discussing the haka with the Colonel, our manager Andrew Martin. Some felt the decision as to whether it be done at all should be left over to each All Black team. But the Colonel disagreed; he said such a decision was the preserve of the NZRU Board in consultation with the sponsors. Sadly, it seemed the haka had become part of the All Black brand.

The Colonel pleaded with me. He said not doing it would be a mistake. I kept saying, 'The boys don't want to.' When we were out on the field warming up before the game, Andrew came over to me again and said we had to do it. The Aussies had given us assurances, he said, that they would respect it. 'If you don't do it, it could cause a trans-Tasman uproar.'

Back in the shed I thought about it as I was putting my kit on. Then I spoke to Taine, told him what Andrew had said. I said, 'I reckon we should do it.' He nodded. 'Okay,' he said.

So I said, 'When we go into the huddle before we run out, I'm going to say, "Let's do the haka after all. Stuff them." And you back me up.'

The boys leapt at that. It worked a treat. Well, yes and no. In fact we were so aroused by it that some of the players indulged in stupid thuggery in the first few moments.

For much of the game we had an edge but Peter Thorburn said that the Australians had cracked our lineout code and were able to contest every throw. With just over a minute remaining we were ahead 26–22. The din was astonishing. Our lineout was a shambles; no one seemed to know where they were going. Tony Gilbert had decided that he wanted Troy Flavell to call the lineouts as they hadn't functioned well with Norm calling them. Troy, though, got a knock on the head and didn't know what his name was, much less which calls to make in the lineouts. So we went to plan B, which we had this time, and Taine started calling them, that was until he left the field injured, then Norm had the baton passed to him. As we lost lineout after lineout the pressure built to the point where the thrower, the lifters, the jumpers and the blockers were in complete disarray, and no one got it right. A schemozzle. We had a defensive lineout about 10 m out from our line with only seconds on the clock remaining and Australia grabbed the ball and from the ensuing ruck their number eight, Toutai Kefu, broke a tackle and scored.

Pandemonium, delirious delight from the Australians on and off the park; shock and despair from our side. Another last-gasp loss to Australia; two years in a row.

Those of us directly involved in such a loss are apt to feel, and are made to feel, useless, unworthy, incompetent. In addition, immediately after the game there was to be a presentation to John Eales who had played his last game for Australia. I had to stand up and say something in front of the best part of 100,000 people and was completely unprepared and lost for words. I felt the management let me down a bit there. They could have let me know in advance that it was Eales' last game and to prepare some appropriate words. I believe I was curt. Frankly, I felt I had single-handedly lost the test — which I hadn't — had let everyone down, and that I was being laughed at. All that was a reflection of how desperate I was to see the All Blacks succeed, and to give my utmost personally at all times. Oh, how one's perspective gets distorted sometimes.

Sometime later a school kid told me that his teacher had used my speech as an example of how not to make one. Harsh, but a fair assessment, and I managed a chuckle when he told me.

I had to say a few words in front of almost 100,000 people at Stadium Australia in Sydney after our second Tri-nations loss to the Wallabies in 2001. It was John Eales' (right) last match for Australia and I was lost for words.

At the after-match, and after I had spoken, Brendan Cannon, the Australian reserve hooker, came over and had a good yarn. He said, 'Hard luck,' and then added that he had always respected and admired me and my ability. He wouldn't have known how much that meant to me at the time.

Back at the hotel our assistant manager, Gilbert Enoka, talked to us about the need for courage. Little did I know that that was directed mainly at Wayne Smith who was already expressing grave doubts about whether he wanted — or would be wanted — to continue as coach.

I received a couple of helpful phone calls from friends who had no involvement in rugby. That balanced the live TV interview with Paul Holmes, who mainly wanted to talk about the lineouts and what went wrong. On the plane home I sat beside Norm Maxwell. Norm said, 'Man, we stuffed up there. If we get another chance, we've got to nail it.' A few months later we were doing just that.

It all seems bemusing and somewhat pathetic in hindsight, but when I got back to Dunedin I was a broken man. I couldn't, and didn't, want to go outside, except to eat. Goldie rang and said he was going to drive up to Christchurch and invited me to go on a roadie with him. So I rang up Smithy and said I was coming up for a day and he kindly offered a bed for the Friday night. I followed Goldie north, driving my sponsored Ford, while Goldie was in his '65 Mustang. We stopped at St Andrews, just south of Timaru, and played 18 holes on a Friday. It was a lovely day by the sea with no one around. We arrived at Smithy's place and he seemed glad — relieved actually — to see us, for he had been in self-imposed exile since his return from Australia.

He'd been digging a ditch in his garden: grieving, demoralised and depressed. He hadn't been game even to go to his local dairy in case he had to talk to anyone. I could understand that. I was feeling like dung myself. He said, 'Right, let's go for a drink. What do you reckon?' I said fine, so off we went to a tavern in Papanui. It was full of mainly rugby league fanatics. I was really apprehensive. But we both put on a brave face and gradually normality began to return. That night was the icebreaker for me.

Later that night I went out with Maxey and we got up early and played golf with Smithy and Gilbert Enoka before I drove home to Dunedin and got home late Saturday night. Next day, on my twenty-sixth birthday, I went to Tunnel Beach with a few friends. You actually descend through a tunnel cut in the rock cliff. It is a secluded and spectacular place, an extraordinary wild spot only two or three kilometres south of the beach at St Clair. More and more I have come to appreciate that time in the natural world away from rugby presents a reality that often makes more sense. Ironically, the events of the following year — being badly injured then dropped from the All Blacks — brought this truth home to me sooner and more profoundly than would otherwise have been the case.

Within a week I was asked to fly to Wellington to meet with an NZRU panel who were to review the performance of Wayne Smith and Tony Gilbert. Indecent haste was one way of looking at it; the fracas surrounding the loss in Sydney had still to fade. I was staying in the same hotel as Wayne and Tony and we went out for a meal and a chat.

There were quite a few heavy hitters on the interview panel. I recall John Graham, Brian Lochore, Andy Dalton and David Rutherford were among them. Prior to the meeting I had pondered what to say and how to say it. I didn't want to tarnish the coaches or anyone else on the management team. I genuinely respected them and their abilities and was grateful for the faith they had showed in me. On the other hand, I wanted to be truthful. There was room for improvement. In particular, I needed to do better myself. We all did. But overall I felt we were on the right track, no doubts there.

I thought I did okay in the interview, okay in the sense that I wasn't too equivocal, didn't fudge it. But what hit me forcefully was the power that players can have when filling in questionnaires. At the end of the campaign 10 or so players were selected to fill out forms and rate aspects of the year's campaign out of 10 and also, although not required to, they could write comments as well. Members on the panel highlighted these comments especially, and had already built an idea of the environment based on the odd two-line response. There is a tendency for players to pen flippant remarks, offer superficial assessments, mostly because they can't be bothered with the paperwork, so jot down the first thing that comes to mind. Players should be more measured and considered, less careless and take more time in articulating their thoughts. If only they knew just how seriously some of their remarks are taken, they would take far more care preparing their answers.

Chapter **10**

The Advent of
Mitchell and Deans

To say that I was despondent after the loss to Australia would be an understatement. I kept seeing Kefu muscle over beside the posts and score the try that won the game. To those who had watched John Eales kick that last-second penalty to beat us the previous year, when Todd Blackadder was captain, this was a shattering case of déjà vu. Now, from North Cape to the Bluff, and out to the Chatham Islands, it seemed as if commentators, pundits, fans — the lot — were agreed that a large part of the loss was attributed to my alleged poor captaincy. As my inclination has always been to look to myself and my own performance first, I tended to agree with my critics. We'd lost some lineouts, failed to maintain possession, and had therefore been unable to sustain pressure. I got so perturbed about the lineouts that I wasn't able to put that aspect of the game aside and the result was I didn't operate effectively as a captain. For instance, when we got a penalty, instead of continuing to kick the ball out, I should have said, 'Kick a high one in the air,' and exerted some pressure that way. Tactically, the ability to think properly was gone. It was like a nightmare. Nothing remotely as bad had happened to me before in my entire career.

I was crestfallen and depressed. Back in Dunedin, I didn't want to start playing in the NPC; in fact, I'd had enough of footie. I just wanted to put my head in the sand. That, of course, would have invited an even bigger kick in the proverbial.

Soon after arriving back in Dunedin, I drove round to Gordon Hunter's house in Andersons Bay to see how he was faring. Gordon's physical state jolted me out of my self-pity. He was in a bad way, his cancer advancing rapidly. Laurie Mains had just taken over again as the Otago NPC coach. Apart from a brief meeting with Laurie when I'd been called over to Australia as a back-up after Norm Hewitt was injured in 1995, I'd had nothing to do with Mains. My feelings about him were neutral. I turned up at practice without my boots. That was intentional and I recall telling Jeff Wilson that I didn't want to play on the weekend and he laughed and said something like, 'You don't know Laurie, do you?' I suppose he meant that if Mains had anything to do with it I'd be playing all right. Soon after, Jeff spotted me again and asked, 'Where are you going?' I said I was off home to get my boots. Jeff laughed again. I'd seen Laurie. His view was that, no matter how hard it felt, I'd be better to get straight back into it. He was right.

Gordon felt the same way. He said that he would dearly love me to get right back in there as soon as possible. My career depended on it, he said. So we made a pact — like blood brothers, almost — that, in return for me helping him fight for his life, I would start playing for Otago as soon as possible. As was so often the case, Gordon's view of what was the correct course was indeed the right one.

The first game I played after the Bledisloe disaster in Sydney was against Canterbury on Carisbrook, where I came on as a reserve. In terms of morale, in terms of confidence and a desire to play, it was largely all about survival to me. We got a hiding. I remember going to a lineout and thinking, 'Shit, where is this going to go?' I felt that, initially, my first few performances back with Otago weren't up to the standard I try to set for myself.

Then as the season progressed I began to play better. Taine Randell got injured, I became captain, and we beat Auckland. It wasn't one of Auckland's best or more experienced teams, but a win over Auckland is always welcomed and thrills diehards in Otago. But it was the game against Bay of Plenty that really lifted me. I made a run down the terrace touchline, beat a couple of players and slipped a pass to our wing behind his marker's back. The wing drew the fullback and we scored. As I was running back Jeff said to me, 'Nice play.' A big smile spread across my face and I thought, 'There could be light at the end of the tunnel.' It was the first time I had smiled like that in a long time. The clouds had lifted.

But not for Wayne Smith they hadn't. He had been hurt badly by the Bledisloe loss. Smithy's contract as All Black coach was due to expire and a review was imminent. He dithered, didn't know whether he wanted to reapply or not, didn't know whether he deserved to be reappointed. The media was speculating: Was Wayne Smith robust enough? Were he and Gilbert, nice guys undoubtedly, tough enough? Was there enough mongrel, as the saying goes? Was there a lack of resolve and composure under pressure at so-called 'crunch time'?

Smithy announced he'd had enough. He wasn't going to reapply. Then, a few days later, he changed his mind. 'The man is too indecisive,' bayed the hounds. 'Think of the message he has conveyed. He's too weak; he's brittle. And it's reflected in the play of the team.' As Tony Gilbert, with no disrespect intended, said later: 'When Smithy dropped the ball, I knew I was gone too.' My view of the rugby union's decision to cut Smith, and Gilbert, was that it was a serious mistake. But at the time I couldn't have known the extent to which that decision would dramatically, and traumatically, affect my future rugby career.

That, briefly, is the bare bones of the matter relating to the sacking of Smith and Gilbert. But because I think it was an extremely bad decision on the part of a jittery NZRU, perhaps characteristic of the nature of New Zealand rugby administrations as a whole, I want to look at what happened in more detail. Every organisation, every sporting code, every sporting team talks of the need for 'wise heads' to prevail. In this case the wise heads did not. Here's my take on what happened during Smith's final days in the job in 2001.

After Toutai Kefu slipped Ron Cribb's tackle and scored, and the conversion was kicked to give Australia the win 29–26, Smith and Gilbert would have heard the crying for blood. After any All Black loss to Australia, you can guarantee that anyone you meet who tells you that 'it's only a game' is not a keen rugby fan. The first thing a sizeable proportion of the rugby public and the media do is, in effect, demand that a sacrifice be made. Successive NZRU administrations have found such calls difficult to resist.

Within a fortnight the NZRU would review Smith's performance. In a debrief with a panel appointed by the NZRU, he said, 'I told them that if they could find someone better for the job, they should.' But he also said that if they advertised the job, he'd apply. He said that, 'I'd doubted myself when I was shattered. There's no shame in that.' If the review had been held a month rather than 10 days after the loss in Australia, Smith would have said he still believed that he had the players and the ability to take the All Blacks through and win the 2003 World Cup.

I believe that he could have done that. But, as the saying goes, Smithy was too honest for his own good. And, of course, he wasn't perfect. By nature he is intense and at times he tended to try to take on too much. Fortunately, both Tony Gilbert and Gilbert Enoka — the latter especially — were alert to that and were able to jolt him back to a less intense reality.

The NZRU review panel talked to me and Andrew Martin, among others presumably, before reporting their findings to the board of the rugby union. As far as I can recall, the panel was: D.J. Graham, Tane Norton (NZRU VP), Lane Penn (NZRU President), Sir Brian Lochore, Andy Dalton (I think) and David Rutherford (then NZRU CEO). Smith often came across in public as a bit reserved, certainly serious and, possibly, a little humourless. Those who knew him well found him determined, yes, and regularly jocular, but with a very dry sense of humour (Norm Maxwell called Smithy 'The Dehumidifier'). Smithy was also seen as intelligent, searching, articulate and selfless. That's how the players saw him and found him as a coach.

But in the aftermath of the loss of the Bledisloe Cup, Smith wasn't like that. The review panel saw only a shadow of the real Wayne Smith. He hadn't had time to reassess matters and run through the various scenarios he needed to view before he could decide what he wanted to do, and how to go about it. The review panel had every intention of reappointing Smith until, as one of them said, he 'expressed so much self-doubt' that they were scared that he might not be able to take the pressure associated with the 2003 World Cup campaign.

Why was Smithy, as one source put it, so 'diffident, equivocal and halting' under questioning from the panel? The view of those closest to Smith is that the All Blacks' indifferent record against Australia during his tenure left him questioning his ability. He didn't help himself by telling the panel that at that moment he wasn't sure if he was the best person for the job, and that they should think of looking to see if there was someone better in waiting. The 'hard men' on the panel saw this as weakness. How could anyone say that they weren't sure if they wanted to coach the All Blacks and be considered suitable? In New Zealand, is candour really welcomed? Whatever, Smithy's performance gave the panel the collywobbles.

Smith clung to a lifeline courtesy of David Rutherford, who gave him a few days to reach a decision on whether or not he would apply. He chose to reapply and by the time he made that decision he had pretty much, with the support of family, friends and some players, recovered from the despair that so dramatically influenced his self-evaluation in front of the panel. However, the panel chosen to appoint the new coach was essentially the same group of men who had seen Smith at his lowest ebb. They were men whose ethos was shaped by post-war New Zealand and the great All Black teams of the 1960s. In their view there was no room for self-doubt or emotional vulnerability. When Smith, after having been advised not to show any reservations in front of the selection panel, vacillated again, the panel lost their enthusiasm for him. It became a two-way contest between Robbie Deans and John Mitchell.

There was another side to it as well. Some people were saying that Tony Gilbert was not up to coaching the forwards. In particular, lineout problems were blamed on him. A scapegoat

Wayne Smith is grilled by the media in 2001. He vacillated once too often in front of the selection panel and was replaced as coach of the All Blacks by John Mitchell.

needed to be found and Tony was it. Look at subsequent showdowns. Were the All Black forwards up to it in general play and at lineouts in the Tri-nations in 2002? During the end-of-year tour against England, and, particularly, against France? In the 2003 World Cup semi-final? Back in 2001 there was some talk of retaining Smith and sacking Gilbert. Smith would not have wanted to coach without Gilbert. There was an honesty and decency about the two of them that set them apart from some others. I never saw them as weak or unable to make hard decisions; they were determined and committed to what they believed in, both morally and professionally. If they had been returned I don't think we'd have had the unravelling that occurred later when the All Blacks staggered through Ireland, Scotland and Argentina.

Let's look at Smith's behaviour from a different perspective. The panel could have seen his responses, and his statements, as testimony of the extent of his concerns for and commitment to the All Black cause. Once they had decided to sack Smith the panel was left with Mitchell and Deans because there were no other credible applicants.

This is not to say that the panel wouldn't have liked a wider choice. Nevertheless, given the panel's experience in rugby, and the fact that Smith's attitude had scared them, Mitchell may well have seemed plausible as an uncompromising, tough-talking forward, the sort who claimed he would run a no-nonsense operation, emphasising that mental toughness was paramount and physical contest was vital. Certainly, that is what the panel would have wanted to hear. But haven't all All Black coaches professed and espoused those things? He is said to have impressed the panel with his 'systems' (none of which came near what had been achieved by mid-2001, but about which the panel knew very little). In the event, most of the 'systems' Mitchell touted weren't new and sounded like stuff that could be spotted in any one of oodles of management texts.

Mitchell is believed to have told the panel that he would institute opposed lineout training. Given the general fixation with lineouts, it was a statement the appointment panel was wanting to hear. The panel had been asking others in the team management if Tony Gilbert had run live, opposed lineout training. No, he hadn't, but neither did Mitchell beyond 2001 in my time under his coaching. We had one before we left for Ireland, with Andy Haden, and that was it.

Many of the programmes Smith and his management team had put in place to challenge the players to think harder about their roles as rugby professionals and privileged young New Zealanders were thrown out by mid-October 2001. Some of the players may have been relieved because it meant they did not have to meet other personal objectives set for them off the field. To me, Smith, Gilbert and Martin were right to insist that off-the-field values required improvement in order to bring more everyday realities into what is essentially a very contrived lifestyle. Clearly, Mitchell and Deans did not think that mattered to anywhere near the same degree that their predecessors did.

To me, Mitchell's work ethic wasn't what it was trumpeted to be, nor was he unusually astute. I think if you are going to be critical of players in public, and make pronouncements about tactics and styles of play couched in esoteric-sounding terms, you have to be absolutely sure that you cut the mustard yourself. Mitchell had been forwards coach to Sir Clive Woodward's England team, appeared to be well regarded in the European club circuit and was said to have done a fairly good job in his first season with the Waikato Chiefs. So while I had some reservations about Mitchell, initially I was not strongly averse to him and his methods. I actually quite liked some things about him. He understood what rugby was like at the sharp end for a player; he knew what was required when the going got tough, and he knew what basics were required to perform well, on the field especially. But he appeared to lack some confidence in himself and took advice from a few who seemed to have programmed him to speak and act in ways that weren't naturally him.

The rugby public seemed happy enough with Mitchell's and Deans' credentials — Mitchell's experience with England, and Deans' relentless success with the Crusaders. For continuity's sake, so the NZRU said, Smith and Gilbert were to be kept on as selectors until the new appointees became sufficiently au fait with the current All Black players and associated personnel. In fact, Smith and Gilbert were nominal selectors only; they had no input at all.

I had trusted Smithy and Gilbert. They were not given to knee-jerk behaviour and they were clearly supportive of me. Later, they told me that some weeks I was in Mitchell and Deans' preferred All Black side, some weeks not. For a time, I was not even in their reserves. Smith and Gilbert have since told me that the team was changing wildly each week, that there were five or more new names some weeks. I thought, 'Far out, what kind of selecting is that?' I was told that at one point Mitchell wanted Scott Robertson as captain. Who knows what changed his mind there?

Peter Thorburn, who'd worked closely with Smith and Gilbert, was bemused when the new coaches appeared to be coming up with a different team every week. Some believed that for a time Mitchell had young hooker Andrew Hore, then Andrew Mehrtens, as possible captains. Mehrts is clever, no doubt about that, but he would have been the first to admit that he would not have wanted the job. Overall, Thorburn found some of the selections Mitchell was considering 'bizarre' and 'ridiculous'. When Mitchell and Andrew Martin came down to Dunedin they invited me round to a meeting at Tony Gilbert's house in Opoho. This was Gilbert's only meeting with Mitchell while a co-selector. I told Mitchell that from my perspective I didn't see that he owed me anything but that, of course, I wanted to continue to be an All Black. He said he appreciated that and also that he would have to make some tough calls. Gilbert was not present when Mitchell and I had our chat, but Martin was.

When Mitch tried to explain a few things it was difficult to understand what he was saying. We were two people, one might say, separated by the same language. It is one thing to emphasise the importance of communication, another to use language that strangles it. I was not alone in experiencing problems with comprehension when Mitchell spoke.

Afterwards I asked Andrew Martin for a translation, and also, 'What was the reason for the meeting?' Neither of us knew. Andrew said he was damned if he understood a lot of what Mitchell had been saying either.

During the lead-in to the NPC game against North Harbour I injured a calf muscle, so I went off to Queenstown, had my first bungy jump, and chilled out with a friend. Out of the blue I got an e-mail message asking me to fly to Christchurch to meet with Mitchell and a few other All Blacks. As I recall, Norm Maxwell, Justin Marshall, Greg Somerville, Scott Robertson, Andrew Mehrtens and Reuben Thorne were among them. After lunch, while we were all walking across to the small room in which we were to hold a meeting, Mitchell took me aside and said, 'I want you to be my captain.' I was stunned. I didn't ask why, I simply said, 'Right.' I thought, 'I've got the job and I'll be happy to do it.'

During this time, in discussions with Mitchell, I said I'd very much like to see Taine Randell in the touring party, not least because I had played a lot with him and, especially, because I trusted his on-field ability to read a game. After all, being buried in the tight as I am, it's easy to miss things. Mitchell said he would think about it. Taine didn't make the team.

For some reason — and I never found out where they got this idea from — the new coaches believed the team 'environment' that they had inherited from Smith and Gilbert left a lot to be desired. Not that I am against change, but I don't like change for the sake of change. To me, and many players, the environment had been magnificent. Some players had been making really significant changes to their behaviour and attitude. But Mitchell and Deans were determined to dismantle much of what Smith had instituted. The word from several sources was that Deans, especially, had no time for Smith. This was just another example of how the so-called 'tight' Canterbury environment was a lot looser than it was cracked up to be. Subsequently, and amusingly, over the period of 2002 and 2003 many of the systems instituted by Smith were reintroduced.

I played the NPC final for Otago against Canterbury in Christchurch. For a long time we had the winning of the game, and then . . . we lost, again. In recent years, many have observed that Otago have had a devastating habit of losing important matches in the last few moments of the game. The question often asked is, 'Why?' I'm not sure. But clearly Otago sides have lacked an ability to control the game at crucial times: control possession, obtain dominant field position, apply the right tactics. Otago has also lacked self-confidence, has been hamstrung by a lack of belief. It is tempting to say that, at times, our tactics have been wrong and that maybe we have lacked sufficient hunger. Every player, every individual has to ask himself, 'How badly do I want this?' On the evidence the answer at times has clearly been, 'Not enough.' Of course, Otago teams have played some terrific rugby, have enjoyed considerable success, so it hasn't been all bad by a long shot. But, nevertheless, the Big Trophies haven't come Otago's way too often. It's been my impression that it is a mistake to become too defence-minded in the last 15–20 minutes of a game. I don't advocate recklessness, but there's no doubt that if you become too conservative you can quickly surrender the initiative. I believe that, more recently, Otago simply hasn't had enough class players. Tactics, desire — well, they are incredibly important, but if the players employed aren't able to perform on the field then there is little chance of success.

In close support of Kees Meeuws during the NPC final against Canterbury at Jade Stadium. We lost to the old foe, 30–19.

Canterbury, the other major South Island union (one with a far greater population and a bigger pot of money than Otago), has a better record. Maybe their players have greater self-belief, and the weight of history and public expectation pushes them to drive themselves and makes them determined to continue to attack rather than to go onto the defence. As with many things, there is a chicken-or-the-egg scenario. Otago and the Highlanders have on several occasions lost narrowly to Canterbury in Super 12 and NPC finals, and in Ranfurly Shield challenges. One could argue that it may have helped the red and blacks having been behind with only a few minutes to play. Attack then became by far the best, if not the only, option.

Our pre-tour All Black camp for the end-of-year tour to Ireland, Scotland and Argentina was based at the Poenamo Hotel on the North Shore in Auckland. Most of the management and support personnel were familiar to me — Andrew Martin and Gilbert Enoka, manager and assistant manager; the physio Paul Annear; masseur Lipi Sinnott; trainer Mike Anthony, and others — but they were not to know that their days were numbered. Before long it became apparent that Mitchell and Deans did not feel at all bound to retain anyone appointed by their predecessors. Martin and Enoka concluded that the new coaches preferred to surround themselves with subordinates, an unhealthy degree of submissiveness. They felt that most of the players quickly realised that, in the interests of self-preservation, it was best not to do or say anything that might rock the boat. Mitchell had his 'life coach', Tony Wynne, with him. He took a session with the team. Few could understand what Wynne was saying. Tana Umaga and Norm Maxwell, for example, asked for clarification. The answers left most of us none the wiser.

The life coach's talk was studded with war analogies. There was a sanctum called 'The War Room'. He had a large store of catchphrases, and it all sounded like palaver to me. It was as if Mitchell truly believed he and Deans were taking over a chronically ill patient and that they saw themselves as our saviours. Were there elements of self-delusion here? Do all incomers have to see themselves as new brooms?

Before long all were familiar with Mitch's frequent New Age speak, with his talk of 'the journey' he, and we, were on. We were going to be taken to 'a new level', which required that 'the inner circle' be 'very tight'. Some pundits got sucked in by the rhetoric in the ensuing year or two. In an article in the *Weekend Herald* (30 August 2003), the novelist Lloyd Jones wrote that Mitchell liked a 200-year-old text by Sun-Tzu called *The Art of War*.

Jones said that Mitch would likely 'enlist Sun-Tzu's "Five Conditions that determine Victory": 1. Correct judgement; 2. Flexibility in troops; 3. Cohesion; 4. Surprise actions; 5. Freedom from political interference.' It's my guess that most coaches and captains would say those aims and objects made sense, but the catch was that Mitchell, when asked if *The Art of War* was a favourite book, replied, 'Never heard of it.'

I was extremely apprehensive about what lay in store for both me and the team. Under Smith and Gilbert I had felt confident that I understood what they wanted and what they stood for. This is not to say everything was perfect; it never is.

Things got worse when Justin Marshall got injured and had to pull out. He was one member of the team I felt I could be candid with — Tana Umaga and Norm Maxwell were others. We shook hands, I went off to training, and when I came back I found Marshall had left me a note. As captain, you need a couple of players with whom you can share your concerns. You don't want to be canvassing too many players for there are some things it's better not to highlight. Justin wrote that I was the captain of the best team in the world and that I was to go away and hold my head high and remain strong, that kind of sentiment. Simple, straight, not profound, but important and I was thankful to him. It also made me feel even more disappointed that he was not going to be with us.

On tour, our first game, a midweek affair, was against Ireland A in Belfast. The All Black team had been named before we left and Tom Willis was to be captain. His first game! I recall saying to Deans something like, 'That is putting a fair bit of pressure on him.' Deans responded to the effect that, 'Captain is a thing of the past. He can cope with it; it's a non-issue.'

Tom is intelligent and he speaks well. But what I felt like saying to Deans was, 'Just let him be an All Black.' I knew from my own experience how important that was in itself without all the additional burdens of captaincy first up. If, as Deans claimed, it 'didn't matter', why not pick a more experienced player?

Deans' remarks were strange. I felt that the significance of the All Black captaincy was being undermined and wondered if this represented an arrogant revisionism, because I knew that in the eyes of most people, the role of All Black captain is an important one and a big responsibility. I thought that downplaying the importance of the All Black captain's role was dangerous. I was beginning to feel isolated and needed to hear things that struck me as more real so I started reading a New Zealand classic, Barry Crump's *A Good Keen Man*. I read it three times on tour, mainly to remind me of the more down-to-earth, unique aspects of New Zealand. And, as the weather was pretty poor, it wasn't hard to imagine oneself back in the New Zealand bush, holed up in a hut while it hosed down outside. I thought that, for the likes of me, given what I saw as the best of the values associated with the All Black jersey, I was feeling as though we were already being rained on by the new coaches. Some other players would have picked up on that, others not. My views were based upon my previous experiences and the hopes and expectations I had privately.

John Mitchell and Robbie Deans . . . silver badges and white gloves never cut it with me.

After our midweek game, Mitch held a new kind of mini court session. Players were given 'awards', titles such as 'Top Dog', 'Tackle Dog', or 'Fierce Dog', or 'Hungry Dog'. Many thought this peculiar, some saw it as stupid. The winners were called up and given a little badge, a silver fern. In private, later, I said to Robbie Deans, 'Mate, they don't mean anything to us. I got given about 300 of them one day when doing promotional work.' He said it meant a lot to go up and get something, even if it was only a little badge. The coaches also produced a pair of white gloves which were given to the player who had missed the most tackles. The recipient was required to wear them at training for the next week, as public humiliation. The white-glove stigma was something Mitch had introduced when coaching the Chiefs. The gloves were intended to remind us all that the recipient was like a traffic officer on point duty waving all the traffic through. Tana was the chosen one. As a senior player, Tana said, okay, he'd cop it, but he didn't believe it was the right thing to do.

One of the 'Dog' awards went to Nathan Mauger who was told that, on the evidence of that performance, he didn't deserve to be an All Black. He was really worked over in front of us all. I kept thinking, 'I can't believe the coach is saying this.' I noticed the body language of many of the players. It spoke of extreme anger and incredulity. At least four players approached me afterwards and said, 'We can't handle that. That's not good enough.' Maxey was very angry, and said to me: 'He can't say that about one of the boys. He's trying his best.' Clearly, though, most players believe submissiveness is the prudent course to follow in most cases.

The normal procedure in such cases would be for the back-seat boys to take their concerns to the coaches and managers, but apart from Tana our back seat was a bit reticent. We went and saw Mitchell and said that we could see what he was trying to do, but it wasn't working. I told him the players were upset about his treatment of Nathan, and that Nathan himself was pretty shattered to be balled out in front of all his mates after his first game for the All Blacks. Mitchell listened and took it on board. He didn't run another Dog Show. I thought that was to his credit. I couldn't persuade Deans to forget the little silver fern pins, though. When we got given our test jerseys, later, in Argentina, I unrolled mine and there, neatly wrapped, was a silver pin.

Many of us felt that both Mitchell and Deans were ill at ease dealing with criticism of any kind. Odd, given that they advertised 'open' relationships as the key to success. It was noticeable that, before much longer, some of those best able to relate strongly and directly with the players — Martin, masseur Lipi Sinnott and Gilbert Enoka, for example — were disposed of. Actually, I believe Deans persuaded Mitchell to keep Enoka on for a time, but with greatly reduced involvement. The bio-mechanist, Mark Sayers, whom the players respected, wasn't so lucky: he was made redundant.

The test squad got down to training for the game against Ireland at Landsdowne Road. I expect training sessions to be well planned beforehand, and that clear instructions be given; also that drills are devised for a purpose and that optimal use is made of the time. This wasn't the case. Players were standing around wondering what they were meant to do. The drills were a shambles. This sort of thing had never happened under Smith, whose planning was meticulous.

I think Mitchell and Deans started out with the view that careful planning, and the issuing of daily schedules, was spoon-feeding. It can be, but planning in advance also cuts down the chances of error, it makes for more convenience and reliability, and gives greater certainty and confidence to those in the touring party. Under Smith and Martin we had a daily sheet scheduling activities and engagements. I believe a daily schedule, or something like it, was later reintroduced, but by that stage I was no longer in the team.

After we'd showered and returned to the hotel, and were having dinner, I was sitting with the coaches, and I asked Deans about what we'd been supposed to be doing with one of the drills. Martin and Enoka were there with us. Deans gave a belligerent response. He said, 'You know, you just have to react.' I replied and said that I felt that we needed better planning if we were to gain the players' confidence, involve them all and train effectively. 'To me,' I said, 'that's what training is all about.' He replied, 'Oh yeah, but it is all about reacting.' I was tempted to say, 'Well, why plan at all? Why don't we just go and throw the ball around and react to whatever happens?' But red alarm bells were flashing so I shut up. I had that sinking feeling that went something along the lines of: I don't think these two coaches are going to welcome anything at all that could be construed as disagreeing with their way of operating. They don't welcome candid response or debate. Robbie would disagree completely with that view. Another case of misperception is how he would put it. He says that any coach who doesn't welcome input and take notice of senior players' opinions is stupid, but he plainly didn't want my views in Dublin.

The test squad had a light training run the day before the game against Ireland. We were on a lower field and, when we'd finished, we went up and looked at the DDs on the top field. They'd been out drinking a fair bit of alcohol the night before and were being put through a lot of what's known as 'shit work'. In other words, menial stuff — tackle bags, press-ups, star jumps — nothing game-specific. It was just hard work to get rid of the previous night's consumption. Mitch was in charge, ranting and raving, showing he was boss. I thought, 'Oh well, we haven't actually come a long way since I first made the All Blacks.'

I was extremely apprehensive before the test began. Ours was a young team and we'd had little time to prepare, 10 days at the most from when we first assembled in Albany to the starting whistle. Before we knew it we were down by 20 points, a big deficit in any match. But cool heads prevailed and the class of the team showed and, in the end, we won convincingly, 40–29. It was, looking back, one of the best victories I've experienced. It was my first test since the ignominy of the loss to Australia and I was acutely conscious of that and the pressure on me personally. Given the degree of preoccupation with lineouts, I knew every rugby fan from Tuatapere to Takapuna would be watching them. They worked really well; I didn't lose one. The Irish crowd was as fanatical and parochial as ever, and the opposition hoed into us.

Before the match a group of us got together and said that we weren't going to have a fiasco in the lineouts ever again. Scott Robertson, Reuben Thorne, Norm Maxwell and I put our heads together and we practised and practised. I remember we were in the car park on the day before the test, and someone mumbled we were supposed to have the day off. The response from Maxey was, 'Well, this is what we're over here for. I don't give a damn if we're here all day.' Maxey didn't want to have another cock-up like we'd had against Australia, and I was heartened to hear that sort of talk.

On leaving the field I would have preferred to sit with the boys, relax and have a beer. But life wasn't like that any more. I walked off into the gloom to do media interviews, then walked all the way back, by which time all the team had showered and dressed. Mitch came over with

The Irish were tough opponents on the All Blacks' 2001 end-of-year tour. After leading us 16-7 at halftime we clawed our way back into the match to eventually win 40-29. Here Irish centre Kevin Maggs lines me up.

an All Black jersey that had been signed by both teams, the Irish and us. He told me he thought the jersey should be given to Richie McCaw as 'he had an outstanding game'. He had, and it was his first test, but a lot of others had played well too. I just bluntly said to Mitch, 'I think Richie has got his jersey, his first-test jersey, and I am sure that is plenty for him. We should hold that for the kitty and wait until the end of the year and maybe give it to someone else.' Mitch went, 'Yeah, yeah, you're right, you're right.' He'd changed his mind just like that. I felt uneasy, again, and wondered what sort of a mind Mitch had.

That night I sat next to the Irish captain and hooker, Keith Wood, and his wife, and they were great fun. My speech seemed to go down well. Up till then I hadn't seriously considered what I said after games. That was before Gilbert Enoka had taken me aside and reminded me that I was representing a whole lot of people, not just myself, and that I ought to put more time into thinking about not only what I said, but how I said it. After the dinner we all jumped in the bus, which took most of the guys to a local pub. Deans and Mitchell went with them. A few of us — Tana Umaga, myself, our masseur Lipi Sinnott and Gilbert Enoka, went back to our hotel. We went to the team room and had a couple of drinks. We sat on tackle bags and chairs, had some toasted sandwiches. Bert and I had a cigar. Lipi and I played the guitar (Lipi far better than me) and we had a sing-along. It was just the best feeling, winding down after a fantastic test victory.

Meanwhile, some of the team came home from the pub on the 1 a.m. bus. The rest, including our two coaches, came back on the bus that got in later. Many of the players who stayed out late said that they were going to come back on the first bus but when they saw that Mitch and Deans were staying they did too. Maxey, with a few beers already on board, hit Mitch up and had him on a bit, told him that some of the boys found it hard to know exactly what it was he was trying to say. 'What's goin' on, mate?' Maxey was one of the few willing to pipe up.

I didn't think it was right for the coaches to be out drinking that late with the boys. I'm one who believes that it's fine for a coach to have a few drinks with the team in the team room, or in the house bar, but otherwise there's a need to keep one's distance.

One of the things Andrew Martin asked me to do was present the jerseys to the midweek team: a number of players were having their first games for the All Blacks. One can't overestimate the emotional importance of these occasions. A number of players were making their All Black debuts on this tour, and one was my close mate Simon Maling in the midweek game in Scotland prior to the test. I saw my task as a real honour and a privilege, and it dawned on me that in this instance I was seen as a type of elder statesman among All Blacks. Each player came along to the manager's room where I was waiting. I chatted to each of them and shook their hands. When I gave Simon his jersey there were tears in my eyes, and when he left the tears really flowed. Simon had been one of my best friends for a long time.

I was a reserve for the midweek game (against Scotland A) and was down behind the posts stretching and warming up when my former Otago team-mate Brendan 'Boof' Laney arrived. He had just taken up a contract to play in Scotland. He was watching Simon Maling doing the haka and he was laughing uproariously. We had a yarn while play was underway.

Prior to the test against Scotland we visited Edinburgh Castle where the words to Laurence Binyon's poem 'For the Fallen' appear on a memorial to Scottish and New Zealand soldiers who fought and died together in war. I recalled Gilbert Enoka's remarks about the importance of giving more thought to the content of my speeches and connecting more with audiences by making appropriate references to the occasion that all had witnessed that day. Alluding to the history of test matches between the two countries, and the players who had gone before, I wove some of Binyon's lines into my after-match speech:

Me and Mitch during a training session prior to the test against Scotland in 2001.

'Age shall not weary them, nor the years condemn.
At the going down of the sun and in the morning
We will remember them.'

I was trying to say that we were all part of something wider than just that day's game, and that the words on the memorial exemplified the closeness of the connections between many of the people in our two countries.

I wanted my speech to be taken as more than merely drawing the analogy that sport and war are similar; in effect I was admitting that thoughts of war and its dire realities have a profound effect on me. Rugby, sport in general, is not war; it is a release and an opportunity to show what one is made of, a chance to display one's strengths and skills and commitment, a chance to confirm one's allegiance to those we live with and among, and to affirm the traditions and values one believes in. Rugby is not life and death. At school, the poetry of the so-called 1914–18 'war poets', Wilfred Owen and Siegfried Sassoon, for instance, resonated with and moved me. Owen wrote, for instance, 'What passing-bells for these who die as cattle?' I am unashamed to admit that, when overseas, being taken to places where New Zealanders lost their lives in war stirs my emotions — awakens gratitude and respect inside of me.

Scotland wasn't a patch on Ireland and we won the test easily 37–6. Afterwards a journalist asked me some questions about the England team's abilities. I said that any questions about England were 'a red herring and completely irrelevant' in the circumstances, and 'Why are you asking me them?' The journalist said that beating Ireland and Scotland was one thing, but how did I think we'd go against England? I wasn't interested in hypothetical questions — since we weren't going to play England on the tour — and suggested he stick to questions about the game we'd just played. Predictably, I received both flak and praise for being so blunt. I wasn't concerned about that in the least.

Back at our hotel after the game we all piled into the team room for a court session. Mehrts and Razor Robertson were the 'judges'. Andrew Martin had been annoying Mehrts who doesn't like anything that, to him, smacks of officiousness or control. Mehrts is something of a free radical. As a result, Mehrts saw an opportunity to put some pressure on the manager. He set out to ensure that Martin was made to look foolish in front of the team. He was asked to consume a lot of beer, rapidly, and soon he was in serious difficulty. I hated what was happening. Unbeknown to me, Martin had been sick, vomiting the night before and had been suffering from diarrhoea as well. Everyone was being asked to drink far too much. Lots of boys were off their faces. But Mitchell and Deans did not move to intervene to prevent Martin's humiliation.

Earlier, Andrew Martin had tried to impress on the team the importance of celebrating a win in a rather more conservative manner than that encouraged by the coaches. The reason was simple. The next day we were to undertake an 18-hour flight to Buenos Aires, re-enter the southern hemisphere summer from winter and six days later play Los Pumas in their very own backyard. Obviously, Martin lost that one.

Halfway through the court session I stopped drinking altogether, I was so disgusted by what was happening. I remember talking to Tana and him saying that he was disgusted too. Tana wasn't drinking at this stage; he had a history of having had one or two drink-related incidents and thought the best way to avoid that was to abstain. We had several young men in the team and I thought, 'We are teaching them that this is what it is to be an All Black — to drink lots of booze.' I can't deny that by this stage I thought that Mitch's social behaviour was inappropriate at times and set the wrong sort of example.

With respect to alcohol, it is true that the All Blacks were perceived as sportsmen who traditionally drank a fair amount of alcohol. But for the previous two seasons we had been trying hard to change that. In my view, and in Smith and Gilbert's view, it didn't fit the image we wanted to convey of the modern-day All Black. We had been trying to lift standards of behaviour all round.

Again, I accept the criticism made of me after my first test. Then, like many on debut, I got plastered afterwards, which I continued to do occasionally thereafter until a test against the Boks at Ellis Park in 2000. After that I felt I had grown and broken free.

Somewhere along the continuum things had to change; there is too much at stake now. To me — and Andrew Martin thought the same — we were going backwards.

Next day, before flying to Argentina, a recovery session was scheduled at the local pool. We were all sitting on the bus waiting. For whom? Mitchell and Deans. Someone had been sent to find them. They came running out through the foyer like two naughty school kids looking a bit the worse for wear.

I was standing talking to David Rutherford, CEO of the NZRU, at the airport while we were waiting to board our plane for Buenos Aires, and when I looked around at the state of our team I was embarrassed. They looked dishevelled, like a rag-tag mob of young louts, not a professional rugby team. Ben Blair was with us. We looked down at his shoes. They were sticky with booze to which muck had stuck. Ben was just a young fellow; it wasn't his fault. We, his seniors, were meant to help the younger players avoid all that. I apologised to Rutherford for the state of the All Black team. He shook his head and said that he was well aware of what was going on. Andrew Martin was frustrated and disappointed with the general state of the team — he knew that we would be in for a long week in Buenos Aires. David Rutherford and Murray McCaw, chairman of the NZRU, were concerned about the team's appearance and general demeanour. Martin got it in the neck from them for they saw it as his territory.

It was extremely hot in Buenos Aires. A lot of the team were still hung over when we got there. I was concerned about the quality of our training and a lack of adequate preparation. Alarm bells were ringing. In the bus on our way back from training a group of us, which included Scott Robertson, Maxey, Reuben Thorne and Dave Hewett, talked of how terrible the tour had been: disorganised. I found Robertson a nice, honest guy with some guts to him. He spoke from the heart and was prepared to go to the wire over things he was passionate about, and I really liked that. I saw him as a good team man who tried hard off and on the field. To most players, self-preservation is paramount; self-preservation in the sense that, whether you agree with things or not, be grateful for being picked and get on with it. But in my case, as captain, it was my job to be an advocate for the others, and I wanted the team to be seen, both within and outside of rugby, as worthy of respect. Some of the more senior players felt that we had become more like tourists than true All Black rugby players, and would be in trouble against Argentina unless we took remedial action and played some real footie. We decided we needed an extra training session by ourselves on the Wednesday without the coaches.

I still look back at the tour — the long haul to Buenos Aires, the hangovers, the heat, the last test of the year, Argentina at home — and think, 'How the hell did we win that game?' It was a miracle. I have to thank Gilbert Enoka for chats and social activity that kept me sane. And I enjoyed playing guitar with the adidas rep Paul Scorringe, and chess with Ross Nesdale, an interesting chap. He and I did some cruising about, taking in the local culture. Nesdale's sole job was to focus on throwing technique — he had nothing to do with lifting or blocking. Richard Loe was with us too. He took a few scrums. Both he and Ross had a rather cushy time of it.

In retrospect I realise that I must have gone into the tour feeling apprehensive and guarded. I knew that, for some time, Mitchell and Deans hadn't been going to select me at all and can only assume that, in the end, they decided — or were persuaded — to retain me in the interests of continuity. So to them I may have seemed a bit standoffish, possibly too serious-minded. Before long they were well aware that in my view their performance and attitudes left a lot to be desired, and they may have noted I wasn't comfortable about the way they had set about dismantling their predecessors' legacy. There was nothing subtle about this, on their part. That things weren't good between Martin and the coaches was plain to most of the players.

Given events to this point, Mitchell now appeared more subdued. A couple of days before the test I went up to Martin's room to have a yarn. He and I were quite candid in our assessments of each other's performance, brutal at times. If you're going to be critical of others you've got to be prepared to take it yourself. He showed me his draft manager's report of the tour, the document all managers have to produce for the NZRU Board. It was quite damning of the coaches. He asked me for my opinion of his report. I asked him if I could take it away and consider it more carefully. I now think that was a mistake. I shouldn't have asked for it; he shouldn't have given it to me. But I didn't look at it again; instead, into my computer case it went and I soon forgot about it.

Martin was of a view that if the All Blacks went down the path Mitchell and Deans were leading them, they would not win the World Cup. Prescience to an unfortunate degree. I tended to agree, but certainly hadn't said that to the coaches directly.

We played the test at a massive soccer stadium. The legendary Maradona was there; the crowd was maniacal. The Argentines are a bit like the Italians in their style of play.

Holding the silverware aloft after our win over Argentina in the final test of 2001.

They dive into rucks, end up off their feet. They're very negative. You need a good referee, otherwise they just kill everything. Their forwards are strong, but if you hoe into them they don't like it and tend to fold. They love to try to best opponents in the scrums and that can sometimes be an end in itself, and it doesn't help them. They played with tremendous passion. Somehow we scored a last-minute try to save the game 24–20.

There was a huge sense of relief — on our side. In a playing sense it enabled certain individuals to claim the tour had been a success, with all the usual, predictable platitudes about inexperience, shaking down, rebuild-ing. Some of us thought we knew better. If we had lost that test it would have made it harder to sell the line that everything was pretty rosy. Soon after the game, Robbie Deans asked Martin if he could use his cell phone, rang Christchurch and had a conversation about injuries and the Crusaders. I still had my kit and boots on, waiting to be interviewed. Steam was still coming off me. In Deans' case, talk about wearing two sets of headgear! While I could easily understand Robbie's interests in the Crusaders, and his concerns for those of them in the All Blacks, I think it's unwise to have a Super 12 coach directly involved with All Black coaching and selection. This allows a coach to influence the development of players from a particular franchise per the medium of the All Blacks.

In the aftermath of the test, the tour over, I and other senior All Blacks told Andrew Martin that, in our view, unless major changes took place we would not win the World Cup. And I have no doubt that to Deans and Mitchell I was one of those prime 'destabilising influences' that they assiduously removed during the remainder of their term. But I had to speak up. After all, under Smith and Gilbert in the preceding two years, the majority of the players had worked hard to create an environment of accountability, self-criticism and honesty that was needed in order to revitalise the All Blacks after the failure at the 1999 World Cup.

The test dinner was a raucous affair; the Argentines got drunk. Many of our team went out drinking. I came back to the hotel and a few of us — Enoka and Scorringe among them — chilled out in Lipi Sinnott's masseur's room and played our guitars. A bit later I went and packed, for I was flying out to Chile next day and would be the first to leave. There is a tradition whereby those who leave ahead of the main touring group have to do a haka, so I strolled out onto the grassy knoll in front of the five-star hotel, took my shirt off, and gave a full-on performance. Members of the public were coming and going and there I was, screaming, going for gold. I lost my voice for two days; it was a real case of let's get it out. Many of the boys, including a few who were seedy indeed, came out to watch. When talking to Greg Feek a year later, he said he would never forget it.

Me (far right) with an assortment of tourists in Chile. I climbed the mountain — or, more precisely, the volcano — Orsono the next day.

It was wonderful not having to wear All Black clothing any more. As most of my stuff was rugby branded, I had to buy a lot of new clothing. When I flew in to Santiago, I checked into my hotel, ordered room service and, apart from a couple of swims, stayed inside for the best part of two days. Three days later I met a friend from Central Otago, a woman with whom I'd spent time years before when we were on an educational trip to South America, and she invited me to stay with some of her friends. I felt like myself again. We toured around Chile for 10 days. It was nice to be anonymous until, of all things, back in Santiago, I met a Kiwi soccer team who recognised me. And guess what? They were from Dunedin.

I flew to Los Angeles and went to the Air New Zealand desk. I felt I'd been isolated for too long from the New Zealand and New Zealanders I knew and loved best, so it was good to hear Kiwi voices again.

By the time I got down to Dunedin I'd been travelling for 56 hours. Before I had time to unpack anything, Tony Brown whisked me away to the St Clair golf course on the cliffs south of the city on a stunning blue day.

When unpacking my gear I found the copy of Andrew Martin's draft report — it was no more than that, and I understand he revised it. Re-reading it, and realising its significance, and the significance of me having it, I went outside, put it on the lawn, lit a match and watched it burn. I never went back to Martin, nor did I write to or discuss it with any staff of the New Zealand union.

It is important to emphasise that under John Hart the coach was king; the manager reported to him and Hart reported to the rugby union. When Hart resigned the union put the manager, Martin, in charge and the coaches reported to him. Mitchell and Deans didn't like that.

Of course, the subsequent loss of New Zealand's 2003 Rugby World Cup (RWC) hosting rights, and David Rutherford's departure as a consequence of his perceived role in that debacle, meant that he was no longer there to advise the board. Steve Tew was acting CEO of the NZRU when the board was told that Martin was the greatest single impediment to the All Blacks' chances of success under Mitchell and Deans at the 2003 World Cup.

At the time that Martin was replaced in October 2002, Rutherford had been removed as CEO and the entire board apart from Paul Quinn had been replaced as well. All this was fallout from the failed RWC hosting bid. Had Rutherford remained in place and several of the board stayed, Martin may have survived.

After all, those board members were the organisation's leaders who had made the decision in November 1999 to appoint a full-time professional manager to lead the All Blacks. This, of course, was based on the perceived failings of allowing John Hart too much control over all aspects of the team.

It must have been frustrating for Martin to observe the board give Mitchell control and then, after the All Blacks' failure to win the 2003 World Cup, return to the model under which he, Martin, had been appointed.

What reasons did Mitchell and Deans give when seeking to have Martin removed? It seems that, primarily, they convinced the powers that be that if Martin stayed, the team's ability to succeed at the World Cup would be under threat. There was a view that Martin talked too much, that he had a 'profile' (a little hard not to!), was too challenging of off-field behaviour, and was unable to relate to elite teams. (Does that imply that running New Zealand's crack SAS unit in the army is not elite enough?) When I heard all that I thought, 'How could he have been seen as worthy of the job in the first place?'

Well, all I would say to that is that I believe Andrew Martin was the sort of man, and manager, the All Blacks needed. I believe Wayne Smith and Tony Gilbert thought the same. One wonders what the NZRU thinks of all this now, and of their role in events prior and subsequent to the axing of Martin. It is worth reflecting on all that when remembering Mitch's post-World Cup 2003 comment that the All Blacks 'lacked maturity', among other things.

Chapter 11

Tragedy, Time Out and Fresh Resolve

I had a sense of foreboding about what 2002 might have in store. This isn't hindsight speaking. I didn't believe Mitchell and Deans had much faith in me and I didn't haven't much faith in them. To me there were unnerving differences between what they professed and how they acted. Aspects of the All Black camp unsettled and exasperated me. I like and welcome open discussion, but I doubted that Mitchell and Deans did.

Which brings me to politics. There's too much of it in sport and it's hard to retain respect for those who engage in it regularly. Unfortunately, captains and senior players sometimes get drawn into it whether they like it or not. Rugby players just don't have the nerve or the power, generally, to play serious politics. So I've been disturbed by the extent to which I have been involved in recent seasons. Actually, at the time I didn't see that I was engaging in politics, I simply thought I was doing the right, necessary things. Laurie Mains has said that I got 'too involved' in the politics. That is rich coming from him. Laurie is widely regarded as having been near the top of the ladder when it comes to ranking the political animals in New Zealand rugby. I would argue that any senior player associated with Laurie couldn't avoid getting drawn into the politics of the game. Captains that Laurie was keen on, the likes of Fitzpatrick and Brewer for instance, were, one way or another, deeply involved in rugby politics. So was Randell, though to a lesser extent. To Laurie, politics is part and parcel of the game.

Humans being what they are, I doubt that you can ever rid sport of politics. In fact, I'm inclined to agree with those who believe that sport and politics are one and the same. Some would say that anyone who believes that sport and politics can be kept separate is naive, and that there's never been a time when the two weren't entwined. After all, look at the size and complexity of the egos of certain prominent people in sport. And, with the amount of money at stake today, is it any wonder there is so much friction, that the environment is harsh, that there are more casualties than there used to be?

In 2002, then, I was greatly troubled by a lot that was going on in and around rugby. Some of it had stolen up on me, partly because I had been given more responsibilities than before. There was also the fact that, clearly, I was troubling to a few others in the game. As a result life for me was more complicated, more fraught and paradoxically more interesting. I could have done without the more interesting bit.

It was a puzzling time too. A year or two before I had been touted as being on the cusp of a — star-spangled phrase — glittering career as All Black captain. Now, the tremors of disquiet were getting stronger. And, although I've always tried to suppress pessimism, I could feel my unease building. I suspected that I was going to get the bullet for reasons not entirely related to my abilities one way or another as a player.

But life for me then wasn't all rugby. While I've been a rugby player for virtually all of my adult life so far — at times it has seemed like for ever — if there's one thing that brings you a massive reality check it is being associated with people cut down by the ravages of cancer. If you want to see just how brave people can be, and just how precious a gift life is, take an interest in the children and families whose lives have been affected by cancer.

There are a number of organisations concerned with children's health. For instance, the Child Health Foundation has an organisation called Cure Kids that is mainly involved in funding research into child illnesses. I am an ambassador for Cure Kids. It was Gordon Hunter who drew my attention to the plight of child cancer sufferers when I heard him talk at a function to mark his leaving the police force in the late 1990s and he asked for donations for children with cancer. I also spoke to Greg Cooper, who had recovered from cancer contracted in his youth. It's bad enough watching adults cruelly debilitated and cut down by cancer, but it's far worse to watch the heart-rending battles of families with children suffering from the disease.

After hearing Gordon speak I thought: I have a profile. I can do some good now, while I still have it. So, prior to the 1999 World Cup, I bowled straight down to the children's ward of Dunedin Hospital and before long was buddied up with Ryan Pigou and Rebecca (Becky) Dixon. Little Ryan Pigou was eight and had leukaemia. At the time his parents Gaylene and Justin were farming near Invercargill and they brought Ryan to Dunedin every few weeks for seven days of intensive treatment each time. This treatment went on for two-and-a-half years. Gaylene says that I taught Ryan all the card games the All Blacks play, and that both he and I know how to cheat. Ryan was very keen on rugby and over time attended many of our games at Carisbrook. Once he even helped our doctor stitch up a head wound of mine after the game in the medical rooms. Ryan was adept at snipping with the scissors. Fortunately, his leukaemia seems to have gone into remission.

Becky, from Central Otago, was in her early teens. I visited her in Wanaka whenever I got a chance. Once she even took me horse-riding and still laughs at my equine ineptitude. Becky has cystic fibrosis and continues to fight it bravely.

When I got back from Chile late in 2001 I learned that another youngster I'd been seeing was very sick. His name was Aaron Otley. Initially he was treated for a brain tumour. Sadly, another had appeared, this time in his spinal cord. This was dire news. The specialists asked Aaron's parents, Mike and Marie, to bring him down to Dunedin from Pleasant Point in South Canterbury. The oncologists said it was a long shot, but they wanted to try some novel radiotherapy treatment.

I was at the hospital between seven and eight in the morning and we spent the whole day with Aaron. He was sedated and kept in intensive care while awaiting his turn at the radiology clinic. I played cards on Aaron's bed with Mike. Aaron's mum, Marie, had to shoot off often to check on their two-year-old son, Mark, who was at a friend's place. In radiology the operators

Me and 'my' kids. Top, with Ryan Pigou. Below left, with Aaron Otley and below right, with Becky Dixon.

put Aaron's head in a weird-looking metal contraption designed to keep him still. By the end of the day I felt bloody exhausted. I went home wondering how Mike and Marie found the strength to carry on.

For the next few weeks I was on the run from rugby, but not from rugby-playing friends. After Christmas in Blenheim with my mother, I met Simon Maling, Tony Brown, Jeff Wilson and John Blaikie in Hawke's Bay. They had rented a house by the beach near Havelock North. I stayed with The Bear, Stu Forster. We all attended a party on a friend's farm. Several friends had returned from London for the summer. It was a great night of fellowship and fun in the Bay.

Further north, at Pauanui on the Coromandel, I visited my father and my aunt and uncle, Jane and Bruce Holdsworth, before driving to Auckland where I had a fun night out with my close friend from university days at Otago, Mark Parker. Parksy crashed on the floor of my hotel room and left for London next day. Although I didn't know it then, it was the last time I would see Mark alive.

I drove back south with my brother Brent, took the ferry across to Blenheim, dropped him at Mum's place, and buzzed down to Christchurch and spent a couple of days with Norm Maxwell. Mum's Christmas present from Brent and me was a few days in Queenstown, so I needed to get there in time to meet her off the plane. On the way I spent an afternoon with little Aaron Otley and his family in Pleasant Point.

Close mate Simon 'Mon' Maling and me at a New Year's party in Hawke's Bay.

I felt a bit like a character — less anarchic of course — out of *Easy Rider*, driven by a desire to be free of the constriction that rugby life can bring. I don't want to sound like an ingrate, for rugby has been good to me, but increasingly I had come to value time off to relax with friends and do different things. Time away from the relentless battering that is so much part of rugby is precious. It's the mental side that has always been the more demanding for me. The body recovers; the real ongoing battle is with the mind. The game is so physically and mentally hard that it gnaws at one's soul; if you're not careful the intellect becomes malnourished. Everyone agrees with those who talk of the importance of developing into a 'rounded' human being but as time has gone by I've come to wonder whether full-time involvement in professional sport works against the possibility of attaining that enviable state.

Laurie Mains had given me an extra two weeks off before I had to report for duty with the Highlanders. Even though I hadn't asked for it, I was very grateful to Laurie for that dispensation — 2001 had been a massively dislocating and challenging year for me, what with the responsibilities of the All Black captaincy, the last-minute loss to Australia that had caused such a ruckus, and the sacking of Smith and Gilbert, two coaches and men whom I respected greatly. Then there was the end-of-season All Black tour with all its unexpected and unwelcome inconsistencies and complexities that had left me feeling isolated. It was no wonder that I was looking urgently about me for solace and new avenues to escape the pressures that went with New Zealand rugby. You can argue that such pressures have always been there, and that as captain of the All Blacks I was bound to confront them, whereas previously I was able to duck away . . . nevertheless, I believe the amount of ruction and intrigue in rugby has intensified in recent years. The irony is that I have been accused of being a catalyst in some areas when, during my career, I have never actively sought out conflict.

The Highlanders bussed to a pre-season camp in Owaka, about 90 km south of Dunedin. I thanked Laurie for giving me the extra time off. I don't know whether he had recognised the pressures I was under, or . . . what? It's hard to tell with Laurie.

The first day of training was a real 'ball-buster'. I had been doing some extra training, but less than my usual pre-season work, so I had a fair bit of ground to make up. It was my first experience of a public training session with Laurie and it followed a pattern that we all became familiar with. We were barked at, whipped along: Laurie showing all and sundry he was boss. To me he was grandstanding. To be obtrusive rather than unobtrusive was Laurie's way. I felt it revealed him as insecure, needy. All of us have our weaknesses, but in Laurie's case I found him disinclined to admit to any.

Taine Randell, Joe McDonnell and Tony Brown organised a hangi to bring us together at the end of the camp. That failed miserably. They didn't get the irons hot enough, so there were too few hot embers and when they pulled the hangi up everything was still partly frozen. The question then was how to feed the 100 or so locals and others we'd invited along to thank for their help. The solution was found when we ended up barbecuing most of the food. Meanwhile, the three bum cooks felt so embarrassed that they purged themselves in order to keep their ancestors at bay. The rest of us were amused to see how drunk they were.

I had come back to Dunedin to find that Gordon Hunter was fading. Clearly he wasn't going to be with us much longer. Every time I called to see Gordon someone else was there and I felt that either I was intruding on their time, or not getting enough time to talk to Gordon one on one. So I decided to go and see him at nights. He was afraid of the dark and didn't want to go to sleep for fear of never waking again. I was deeply saddened and shaken by Gordon's plight.

First I began to turn up around 9 p.m., then later and later. Gordon laughed when I arrived, started jokingly to refer to me as turning up for the 'night shift', as if I was reporting for duty the way he had when he was a policeman. Most nights I stayed till 2 a.m. and every now and then till between 3 and 4 a.m. We reminisced, talked about rugby, life's pleasures, trials, tribulations. I made cups of tea and stoked the fire. Gordon was receiving regular treatment from Jan Watts, a physiotherapist and family friend. If Jan was tired and had been unable to come I'd substitute and give his legs a rub. Gordon's kidneys weren't working properly and his legs were swollen, filled with fluid, so he had to sit with them raised most of the time. The first time I rubbed Gordon's legs I was too vigorous and they were very sore and red next day. I felt really awful about that.

People popped in and out all the time, friends of Gordon's, some I knew and some I didn't, and some whom we hadn't seen for years. Arran Pene was one. He had recently lost an aunty to cancer, so he was familiar with the sensitive psychological undercurrents at work between Gordon, friends and family.

Of all Gordon's friends I was the one best able to do the night shift. I had a little more flexibility in my job. I usually got about four hours' sleep, went off to training, came home for lunch and an hour's sleep if at all possible, trained again in the afternoon, had dinner, then went back to Gordon and Jenni's place. After three or four nights in a row, what with the intensive training at that time of the year, I was shattered and badly in need of more sleep.

My father was another who came down from the north to say his last goodbyes, and although neither of them said as much, both knew that's what it was. One day the three of us got in a car and drove to Lawrence, a bit over an hour's drive west of Dunedin where Frank was born and had grown up as a kid. It had been decades since Dad had been back in Lawrence and Gordon insisted that I sit in the front alongside Frank who was driving. Real father and son stuff. That was Gordon, always one seeking to build rather than burn bridges. We had a day I shall always remember.

The Highlanders' pre-season training was perturbing and perplexing for many of us. A fair bit of physical contact stuff, which some guys like, and lots of Laurie's pet 150s — a series of sprints, or near-sprints, of about 120 m each time with a short recovery break in between. Most of the team managed half a dozen at a fairly fast pace and the rest amounted to little more than an over-long series of slow, boring trudges. Our training sessions were seen as a bit primitive: too long and poorly planned. Not all would have shared my view of them, but I believe most did.

There was a fair bit of disquiet in the ranks. If we decided to go out during the week, Laurie required us to phone and tell him where we were going and what we would be doing. If I was going to go out for a meal with my girlfriend, say, Laurie wanted to know where I was going, when, and what I'd be drinking.

Dunedin's a fairly small place. Rugby players are highly visible. Reports of your conduct, good or bad, get back to a coach and management very quickly. But most of the team were well aware of any dangers lurking in darkest Dunedin. Their conduct in public was pretty good and many of the players thought that Laurie was being unnecessarily controlling. His view was that he'd sooner know in advance, rather than find out after the event.

For most of the pre-season I was either training for rugby or at Gordon's home. One night by the fire, Gordon told me he had always said that he wanted to be buried in his Otago blazer. But where was it? It wasn't in his wardrobe. Jenni thought that, probably, he had draped it around someone's shoulders when somewhere associated with rugby — around someone who was cold and they had never given it back. So I went and ordered him a new blazer. The problem was he had lost so much weight that his old measurements were useless. Jenni got out a suit that had been tailor-made for Gordon for their youngest daughter Andrea's wedding a few months earlier. I sneaked the suit out of the house, took it to the tailor, and asked that he use the jacket measurements when making a new blazer.

Gordon Hunter . . . his last days made an indelible mark on me.

I went round to see him one lunchtime and offered him a muffin. Sometimes he would eat one, sometimes not. He said he really wanted to eat the food that I brought but his appetite was severely affected by his chemotherapy treatment. This day he had taken a turn for the worse and people were milling around the courtyard. The grapevine was clearly working. It was too much for me so I left and returned later in the day. Gordon was still in bed and not well enough to see any visitors.

On Friday, 8 March we were to play the Cats at Carisbrook. I got a phone call at our team hotel to say that the new blazer was ready, so I jumped in my truck, collected it, and took it out to Gordon's home. Earlier in the day, Taine had asked to borrow my vehicle and he had gone out to see Gordon as well.

It was all I could do to control myself and not break down. People were everywhere throughout the house. I got to see Gordon alone for a short while and told him we had managed to find his blazer. His face lit up. He asked me to help him put it on. I did and he seemed happy. But then he became flushed and asked me to take it off: he was too hot. He said to me, 'Anton, they all think I am going to die.' This was a man who never gave up. He was drifting in and out of reality. I sat there desolate and helpless, knowing this would be the last time I would see or speak to Gordon.

I got up, went downstairs and out onto the balcony and had a massive cry. Someone came to comfort me; I can't remember who. I trudged up to my truck and drove away sobbing uncontrollably. A Dave Dobbyn song, 'Beside You', was on the CD player. Every time I hear that heartfelt song, with its intimations of the importance of gratitude, and its insistence on loyalty, I am reminded of what an indelible mark Gordon's last days made on me.

On the bus to Carisbrook I sat by myself at the back. The lights were off and I started to weep again. Kelvin Middleton, who was dating Gordon's daughter Rachel, and has since married her, was just a seat in front of me, and I set him off too.

We both managed to pull ourselves together before we got off the bus, but we had certainly turned a few heads down the back of the bus. Few knew what the hell it was all about. But not a word was spoken then, and to this day not a word has been spoken of that until now.

Gordon sat up and watched the game with his blazer on. Every now and then, his family told me, he commented on the play. In the morning, his daughter Andrea rang me. It was clear she was in tears. She asked me to come round. I declined to go; I had said my goodbyes the day before and had nothing left to give. For a time I felt bad about saying no to Andrea, but soon realised that it had been the right thing to do. I didn't have the strength to say goodbye to my friend again, for another last time. I simply couldn't have done it.

We were flying off to South Africa later that morning. When I got to the airport, Kelvin hugged me, said that Gordon had died. Media were waiting, wanting comment. I felt the setting and the time were inappropriate but knew that someone had to say something on behalf of Otago and Highlanders players before we left, and Kelvin was in no state to do it. Taine asked me to talk to the media, so I did, and it was unbelievably hard. I tried to emphasise what a loss Gordon was to the community as a whole and not allow the focus to turn to me and him. When we got to Sydney and stopped over for the night, a few of us stayed up and had a few beers together in memory of Gordon. We had lost a great, dear friend.

In praise of Gordon

Gordon Hunter was quite simply the most remarkable man I have ever met. I find it hard to capture the words that describe his spirit. All his Otago boys loved him. Collectively, the teams he coached had an overriding desire to win, not only for all the usual reasons – for the province, for team-mates, for family – but also for Gordon himself. It is rare to find such desire in teams. No other coach I have played under has come close to having extracted such desire from his players.

Gordon had a magnetic presence. After his talks the players were charged with a conviction, a zest, a zeal for the game that I have never since experienced.

One of the most unselfish people I have known, that was Gordon. He was always working for the greater good without need of recognition, praise or adulation. And whenever he did receive such recognition he was always quick to deflect it to another, or shift the emphasis away from himself to the collective cause.

His humility was one of his finest qualities; it shone and reflected off him like sun off snow. Gordon never complained or spoke ill of those who had mistreated him or abused his service and loyalty. I personally saw this occur but he steadfastly refused to drop the ball and stuck to the cause. Only at the end did he tell me of his true feelings, and even then sparingly.

He had that amazing ability to make people feel better. After you had spoken to Gordon you left with a feeling of renewed enthusiasm, hope and a sense of just bloody well getting on with it. At least that was often his counsel to me. He never wavered, even towards the end when I witnessed some people at their worst; people calling round to clear their consciences, emptying baggage. That is so damned selfish. Yet he never complained and people always left feeling better about themselves because he gave them a portion of his dwindling reserves of spirit and energy.

I miss you mate, just wanna tell you that. Life is not the same without you.

The Highlanders were to play the Stormers in Cape Town on the Saturday night. During the week we went out one night for a team meal. The menu had been settled in advance: fish and a load of salad to feed 25 to 30 people, and that was it. Laurie didn't like anyone leaving the hotel. The boys jokingly called it the 'lock-in'. In truth having to lie about in our rooms with the air-conditioning on drove most players nuts. Some felt that was no way to acclimatise to the heat. On Friday morning I went to Laurie and suggested we go out to lunch as we were going to be inside for all of Friday and the Saturday leading up to the game.

So why did I go to Laurie? Simple: I was one of the senior players, one of the back-seat boys, which means that when members of the team are unhappy with something they come to the likes of me and ask that their concerns be conveyed to management. A lot of players came to me and said that they hated being locked in. I suggested to Laurie that we stroll along to a little pizza and pasta restaurant 15 minutes away, lunch there, walk back, and take a couple of hours out of the day. I'd been there before on previous tours with the All Blacks and we'd found it okay. Laurie agreed to that.

We ordered our meals but when the food arrived, Laurie flew into a rage. He ranted and blew up our doctor in front of the whole team. Mains told staff to take the pizzas and pasta dishes back, got up and stormed off, saying that he wanted a management meeting when we got back. The players were spellbound by Laurie's performance. Taine, the great foodie, was sitting with me, but he escaped the tirade. Apparently, as the 'organiser' of the lunch, the crime — whatever it was — was all my fault. Laurie said I was irresponsible.

What was his childish tantrum about? Did it have something to do with memories of food poisoning before the final of the World Cup in 1995? Apparently not. Our doctor told me it was all to do with cheese — Laurie thought there was too much cheese on the pizzas and pasta dishes, so they all had to go back.

Greg Cooper defended me at the management meeting but Laurie was in no mind to back down. It was Oliver. The consensus was that Laurie's explosion revealed a total paranoia about food — what else can you say? No one was wanting to scoff KFC every night and, besides, the players have regular meetings with a dietitian, have their fat folds checked regularly and are well educated on what they can or can't eat. An egg or two a week . . . so what? Once, on a trip to a mall, we were allowed McDonald's but only if we took the cheese out of the burgers. Those who preferred a pasta dish to burgers had to say that there should be no cheese on it. Extraordinary, really.

At Newlands we all wore black arm bands in memory of Gordon Hunter and stood and observed a few moments' silence before the game, which we won 21–20. Afterwards we went out to Hussars, one of my favourite restaurants in South Africa, where I had a big feed of warthog ribs. Laurie said we could eat anything we liked: fries, steak, fatty food of any kind. You had to laugh; our coach was so ingenuous. No eggs, butter, cheese, mayonnaise before a game, but straight after, tuck in boys, anything you like. Talk about tossing the dogs a bone after a long day's work. Nutritionists tell us, of course, that what we eat after a match is of major importance in respect to helping our rate of recovery. But I was happy and hoed in: I love a greasy feed with something sweet to follow after a game.

Our second game was against the Bulls in Pretoria where we were 'locked in' again. Taine and Brownie didn't seem to mind. They played computer games all the time. Laurie thought that most of the lads didn't mind being confined to barracks. Not true: most of them hated it.

I was greatly relieved to get back home to Dunedin. I had absolutely hated the trip; for me it was the worst ever. Gordon's death was obviously a contributing factor and it hung over those of us who knew him well.

'Never took a backward step' – Greg Cooper

In 1996 Cooper, an ex-Otago and All Black fullback, saw Anton as 'a rising star. He was powerful, extremely physical, and a very strong runner with the ball.' When Cooper was involved with the Otago NPC side as an assistant coach in 2000 and 2001, Oliver impressed him as having 'amazing self-belief. He never took a backward step on the field. He hated losing. His preparation was impeccable, he did more work than anyone else, and nothing distracted him from his rugby.'

Cooper said he 'was saddened by allegations that Anton is disruptive. I can't say I've ever known him to go behind one's back. But he is direct. After one Otago training session in 2003, he asked to see me and Wayne Graham and John Haggart, and he said, "That training run we've just had was crap. You weren't as well prepared as you normally are." He was right, we weren't.'

'As for Mitchell's criticisms of Oliver's play, I didn't agree with him. Of course, the style of play Laurie insisted our forwards adopt didn't help. They were used as battering rams.'

On the Tuesday night in the week prior to our match against the Waratahs in Sydney, Jeremy Stanley and I went to a fashion parade at the Dunedin Railway Station. We were going to go home straight afterwards but were asked to stay for the party. I had a few drinks, not many, but it was 1.30 a.m. when we got home.

When Laurie learned that some of us had gone out midweek there were fireworks. Four or five of the players, instead of going to their regular cooking classes, had found the cultural lure of Dunedin's premier fashion show too great a temptation. Laurie saw that as evidence of a culture of laziness developing in the team. He tore strips out of the guilty few in front of the team. I wasn't on his list of known offenders, so I went up to him afterwards and told him that I'd been there too. I was fined $500. Others were stung for more than that. I could think of only one previous occasion in my career when I had socialised during the week, and that was on a Wednesday prior to a game against Canterbury. After that I was so scared that I might let the team down that I played a stormer.

In Sydney we stayed next to Coogee Beach. Laurie decided no one was to stay out in the sun too long or to stroll on the sand barefoot. Reason? It was, he said, a well-known haunt of drug users. The boys were annoyed. Half-naked people were running barefoot all over the beach. It was chocker with people, but to us it was out of bounds.

While we were in Sydney a couple of the players stayed out till three in the morning. That really annoyed and flabbergasted me. Mains certainly had grounds to grizzle about that.

The Highlanders had a bye coming up but we trained hard right through to Thursday when I flew to Christchurch to meet Gilbert Enoka and Andrew Martin. We wanted to talk about ways and means of ensuring that the All Blacks management gelled better than they had on the end-of-year tour in 2001. Our wish was to devise ways of working better with John Mitchell and Robbie Deans, not against them. I made the point that I felt strongly that, because Mitchell had shown faith in me by asking me to continue as captain, I needed to work hard in support of him. We all saw Mitchell as persuadable in the sense that he was willing to listen and, at times, alter his approach if he agreed with an argument. Robbie was more difficult to read.

Mitchell had come to see me prior to my discussions with Enoka and Martin. He said I was going to be captain in 2002; he had no criticism of me as a player or a captain. I took that at face value. He talked about his aims for the All Blacks, in effect to win everything up to and including the World Cup in 2003. This was to be our 'journey'. He had an A3-sized sheet of paper — a flow chart of sorts, I suppose — on which he had handwritten the dates and venues for All Black camps and tests and tours following on from the Super 12 final on 25 May. There were to be four camps — each termed a 'Rehearsal' — between 27 May and the end of July 2002. Then '15 players into Transition' for a 26-player 'Development Tour' in November. The December camp would focus on 'skills', 'conditioning' and the need to 'sell vision' and get 'buy-in'. In May 2003 there would be another 'Rehearsal' (one week), and then in September the final 'Rehearsal', seven weeks leading into the World Cup pool games which, at that time, were down to be played in New Zealand. Nothing novel, really, except that some people were starting to find Mitchell's terminology — 'Mitch-speak' as it were — a bit odd. It was as if he had a New Age infection. A few were wondering: is Mitch doing his own thinking or is it coming from sources mysterious? It was clear that Mitch needed to back himself more.

Under Robbie Deans there was a good deal of tension in the Crusaders' camp. In 2003, Mark Robinson, the midfield back and former All Black, had some concerns. Robinson recalls both Justin Marshall and Reuben Thorne phoning him before he went in to see Robbie and reminding him not to forget to say this, and this, and that. He was both amused and disappointed to be largely sailing alone, but saw other players' reluctance to front up to the boss as survival insurance. And, as Robinson conceded, he had decided to accept a contract to play in Japan, so he had little to lose.

Deans has since said that Mitchell 'likes being challenged', and that both he and Mitch welcomed input from players. Deans said that 'nothing is off limits by way of input from players. You'd be a fool,' he said, 'if you didn't welcome input from all those experienced players.' He also said that neither he nor Mitchell had any problems with me. That is not what many others associated with them believe.

Meanwhile young Aaron Otley was ailing. I'd been in regular contact with him and his family. He'd had another operation around Christmas but that had been unsuccessful; the tumours had returned, and we all knew he didn't have long to go. After talking with Enoka and Martin, I hired a rental car and drove to Pleasant Point, spending most of the day with Aaron, before stopping at my favourite fish and chip shop, the Fish Inn at Waikouaiti, half an hour north of Dunedin. A few days later I borrowed a car from Carl Hoeft and returned to Pleasant Point. I slept in the same room as Aaron and we chatted off and on throughout the night. When I left in the morning I knew I would never see him alive again. It was a teary drive home.

When Aaron died less than a fortnight later I attended his funeral as a pallbearer. Some of the players in the Highlanders thought Laurie had objected to my missing a training run by going back to Pleasant Point, that he had asked me not to go. What actually happened was Laurie simply said it was my decision.

At this time I decided to alter my approach to rugby. Personal concerns — Gordon's and Aaron's deaths — were affecting my playing performances. I knew I could play better and one way of doing that was to focus on ways of improving my own game. So I started doing extra training, particularly speed work. The Highlanders under Mains had not done one concentrated speed session. Laurie was fearful of hamstring injuries especially. His view was that we compensated for the lack of specific speed work by doing speed activation drills.

So the competition bye came at the right time for me. The $500 fine for attending the fashion show had been a kick in the bum. Senior players are supposed to set an example to the younger guys. That fine, and the meeting in Christchurch with Enoka and Martin, made me look forward and drilled into me that I needed to play really well.

I thought I had a top game against the Brumbies and another good one in Auckland against the Blues. We hadn't won in Auckland for more than 20 years. Trying a different tack, we went up two days before the game and did nothing but relax in our hotel. It was another 'lock down' — we weren't allowed to go anywhere or see anyone. Well, we won the game, so you can't argue the edict had a detrimental effect on our performance. This was the first Highlanders versus Blues game for the Gordon Hunter Memorial Trophy. At the captain's meeting on the eve of the game, Taine asked me to speak to the team. I gave a passionate talk about Gordon and what rugby in the south meant to him. We played for him the next day. We were always going to win that game; it simply meant more to us than to the Blues.

The next week we were to play the Queensland Reds at home. I was feeling really good and playing some of the best rugby I've ever played. Laurie actually told me that when I was on form, no other hooker in the country came close to me, and that I was one of the best in the world.

The only difference between the way I was playing in 2002 and in 2003–04, after I came back from injury, is that back then — for a time — I ran a bit more with the ball in hand. With tight forwards especially, chances to run with the ball don't come often — luck comes into it a lot. But you can, of course, choose to stand off rucks and mauls and look for opportunities to be slipped passes and shine that way. Of course, if you do that, someone else has got to do the hard yakker. In Otago and Highlanders sides, tight forwards are expected to do the tight stuff. In international rugby if you don't work hard in the tight against strong opposition, you are likely to lose. I have always felt guilty, as a front-rower, if I wasn't doing my full share in the tight.

I raise this here because, under Mitchell and Deans in 2003–04, there was talk about the 'new style of hooker'. Well, the so-called new style is fun to play, and it can make people look good, sometimes spectacularly so, but in my view it only really works against second-rate opposition. Unfortunately, many commentators and journalists — including some of those employed to provide 'expert' comments — are apt to judge players' abilities on the basis of their individual prominence, and to assert that it follows, therefore, that their individual brilliance inevitably contributes commensurately to a team's effectiveness overall.

But back to the game against the Reds. Our physio Peter Gallagher had a premonition. He dreamed that I was going to rupture an Achilles tendon but didn't tell me or think much of it before the game, until 30-odd minutes into the first half . . .

After lunch on game day, Peter, Donny Cameron (our masseur), Kelvin Middleton and I were talking about life after rugby, and what we would do if, all of a sudden, we couldn't play. I think it was Kelvin who asked what would have happened if any one of us had suffered a massive injury at the beginning of our careers, and what would we have done for the last few years instead of being involved in rugby. Most players try to push such thoughts into the back of their minds, but they are there all right. Once rugby was a part of your life only; now, for most professionals it often seems to be just about all there is.

A few hours later, three-quarters of the way through the first half, something happened that was to change my perspective on life completely. I could not have foreseen the extent of those changes. In this game against the Reds, in front of a typically ardent and parochial home crowd, the ball seemed to be following me around. (No, it wasn't a foreshadowing of the 'new style of hooker' stuff, it just happens that way sometimes.) I had been making several decent runs. On this occasion I got up off the ground near the opposition 20 m line at the Hillside Workshops end of the ground. Someone gave me the ball again, and I took it to the defensive line, stepped the first guy off my left foot, then met another defender, so I started to step again. I felt the stretch at the bottom of my right ankle, then went to make the step again and the full weight of two people came bearing down on my right leg. As I tried to drive myself forward my ankle felt numb, the way your arm feels when you get hit on the 'funny bone'. I went to ground and fed the ball back, everyone got off me, and I got up and tried to run. I couldn't. My foot was flopping about uselessly. I stopped, tried to move my ankle but nothing; absolutely nothing responded.

One or two friends, watching on TV, said they knew something awfully serious had happened. The medical staff were there before I had time to consider anything. I was sitting down. Peter Gallagher took one look and said, 'Off the field.' He and others went to support me, but I waved them away and limped off unaided. For some reason, I felt I needed to muster some dignity. I'd hardly had time to sit down in the shed when John Matheson, a former Otago halfback and leading orthopaedic surgeon, was with me. He'd been sitting in the stand. He pressed where my Achilles was meant to be. Instead of meeting resistance his finger went into a big, scallopy gap in the back of my ankle. Quickly and matter-of-factly he said I'd ruptured my Achilles.

Having done anatomy as part of my physical education degree, I knew immediately the seriousness of the implications. As a video-watching kid I remembered having listened to John Kirwan's sobering remarks regarding injuries on the rugby video *The Good, the Bad, and the Ugly*. Straight away I asked Matheson how long it would take to heal after surgery, and if I

Pondering a long lay-off from the game after rupturing the Achilles tendon in my right leg in the Super 12 match against the Reds at Carisbrook.

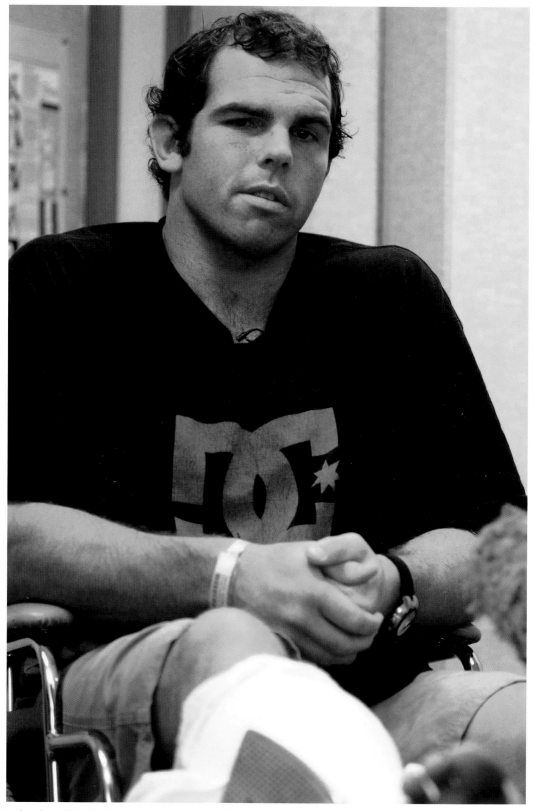

Facing the media after the operation on my Achilles. I told them what they wanted to hear . . .

would be able to come back in time to make the All Blacks' end-of-year tour. He said there was a 'chance', so I perked up immediately.

The team came in at halftime and I listened to the talk. But there's always the thought that, once you can't actually contribute any more by playing, you might as well be somewhere else. Some of the boys came over and asked me whether the injury was serious. I mumbled a response and yelled encouragement as they left the shed to play the second half.

Silence, emptiness . . . except for me and John Matheson. A nauseous spell threatened to overwhelm me. To stop being sick I lay on my back until it passed, took off my wet jersey, pulled on a dry polyprop top and took hold of the crutches that Matheson had managed to find. It was cold and I hopped out to the sideline bench and sat there with a rug draped around my shoulders. The team played well. I sat there feeling and looking, no doubt, disconsolate. It's a short journey from potent to pitiful in sport.

Among those who phoned that night were Andrew Martin and David Rutherford. It was nice to receive consoling calls from the big cheeses.

John Matheson came round in the morning, took me down to the hospital, and operated on me in the afternoon. Next day meant media interviews galore. Annemarie Mains, our media liaison person, had told the media I would be available between certain hours. Unfortunately, according to nursing staff in charge of the ward, she hadn't consulted them. I just did what I was told, unaware of the ding-dong between Annemarie and staff in the front office.

I told the media what they wanted to hear, that I was keen to get back as soon as possible. In reality I just wanted to disappear for a while. The patient next to me was a farmer whose legs and hips were shot. The man opposite was unconscious. My own condition seemed somewhat insignificant in comparison.

Back at the house I shared with Simon Maling, I had visitors galore. Would I rather there had been fewer? Not really. It was humbling, so many people expressing concern, wishing me well. I was instructed to keep my leg up for much of the first 10 days. The Otago rugby union paid someone to cook for me, which I appreciated. I slept on a fold-out couch in the lounge, watched some TV and videos, strummed my guitar and received visitors, feeling rather like a crippled royal.

I also thought I should sit an exam in finance that, prior to the Night of the Rupture, I'd put into the 'some other time' basket. I'd thought I'd be off somewhere in a black jersey, playing for the All Blacks. Although I have never been complacent, from that time on my life in and out of rugby has been, emphatically, a case of never such innocence again.

I rang some lecturers, worked out that I had a couple of weeks to acquaint myself with the course material and arranged to sit the exam.

At the hospital my plaster was changed to a fibreglass cast — in Otago colours. Now my showering procedure involved pulling a large, black, plastic rubbish bag over my leg, taping it at the knee, hopping into the shower on crutches, and sitting on a stool with my leg stuck out awkwardly. The crutches slipped easily on the wooden floor, so showering was hazardous. The whole business could so easily have turned into a scene from a slapstick movie featuring rugby accident victims.

Having been told I could move around a bit more, I started going to the gym and tried to lift weights as if nothing had happened. On my third visit, halfway through a set of weights, I put them down and thought, 'This is bloody ridiculous. You're stuffed. You're miles away from playing again. Face it, go home.'

I knew why I'd started back at the gym; I didn't want to front up to the injury, so I obdurately continued my normal training, or at least what I was now restricted to, as if nothing had happened. But hopping round a gym on crutches, acting like a real tough guy, was farcical.

A couple of weeks later the cast was removed and I was fitted with an articulated boot angled down at about 20 degrees. This is called the 'Aquinas' position. Around this time I had a run-in with a traffic warden. I set out for the university to sit my exam but couldn't find anywhere to park. It was raining hard; if I didn't find a park soon I'd be late. So I went to park in a spot reserved for disabled drivers. The traffic warden wouldn't have it. Park there and you'll be fined, he said. He was insistent, would not be swayed. As far as he was concerned it was black or white: unless there was a sticker on my vehicle to say that I was disabled, I couldn't park there. I felt crippled enough to leave it there, said, 'Stuff it, the guy's a wanker,' and left the vehicle where it was. The exam was passed with a credible B.

After the exam I planned a holiday in the Pacific Islands. I'd never been to any of them. One of my team-mates, Ryan Nicholas, hailed from the Cook Islands. His father lives in Rarotonga, where he is a dentist. Ryan's aunt, who lives in Sydney, has a home in Rarotonga and Ryan arranged for me to stay there. My girlfriend and I flew business class from Auckland. I had a bunch of unused airpoints.

We arrived in Rarotonga in the early hours of the morning. Ryan's stepmother was there to meet us and took us to the house. All the essentials were there: fresh fruit, bread, milk, and an idyllic setting in the trees not far from the ocean. This was the first of many examples of the openness and kindness of both Ryan's family and Cook Islanders in general during our stay.

The Cooks still have that fabled, sun-drenched island paradise quality. We had a fantastic time. Alas, I was so hobbled that diving and swimming and snorkelling were an impossibility. Also, the people are rugby mad, so I was instantly recognised wherever my limping frame went. I took the local team for training and spoke to members of the national sevens side who were there as well. People everywhere wanted me to meet their friends. It was humbling and surprising, but at times it would have been good to have been anonymous.

One afternoon I worked alongside Ryan's father in the family's taro patch, up to my knees in the marshy, muddy ground harvesting taro. My protective boot was falling apart by now. The doctors would not have been impressed.

We flew to a beautiful small island, like a big atoll, about 40 minutes away. The locals treated me like some great god arrived from on high. I was presented with a fishing spear, gave a talk at the school, autographed this and that. It could have been overwhelming; it was certainly completely unexpected. We went out fishing, marvelled at the flying fish, and caught many other fish from lines cast off the boat. Back at the Nicholas' house in Rarotonga, on the eve of our departure, we were treated to an umu, a feast similar to a Maori hangi. Never before had I experienced such open, warm, unaffected hospitality. Leaving the island was like leaving family behind.

I was knackered when I got back to Dunedin and rested for a week. It had taken me a few weeks after the injury to adjust to a completely different style of living. Once I accepted that recovery would be a long haul, I resolved to treat the enforced lay-off as a great opportunity for new experiences. For the first time in seven years I was able to see life outside the parameters set by study and rugby football, the latter especially. I stopped training and thought that as long as my weight was kept in check my general fitness levels wouldn't decline too far. I saw a natural foods person in Auckland and started trying different types of foods, not just my standard meat and vegetables.

There was time, too, to do more work for the Cure Kids organisation. At the same time I also spent hours looking more carefully at my personal investments. In the past, mostly I had taken other people's advice with respect to business ventures. That's not how I prefer to work; I'm happiest when I've got time to thoroughly investigate proposals myself. Two years before my injury an investment, buying shares on the advice of others, went badly wrong. A lesson harshly learnt. So from July to November I was like a high-flying business consultant, travelling everywhere, like a tycoon who couldn't sit still. With the benefit of hindsight, my first break in so many years would have been far more enjoyable if I had simply slowed down and not tried to experience everything all at once. No wonder I was absolutely exhausted by the time December arrived.

The dark clouds of 2002 had yet to disperse. One of my closest friends, Mark Parker, was on his way home from London. I had arranged to meet him in Auckland on 19 October as I would be there doing a promotional job. We were going to have a night out. On 12 October a massive bomb exploded in Bali. Nearly 200 people died, mainly Australian tourists, but also three New Zealanders.

Mark had told me he was stopping in Bali for a few days. News of the Bali bombings was plastered all over the Sunday papers. Later that day I rang Mark's parents, Murray and Verna Parker. They told me they had spoken to a doctor at the hospital in Bali and within 30 seconds he had said Mark was dead; then, within a few moments he took it back and said that he had been mistaken. Shockingly, time was to reveal that he had been right the first time.

But, as it was so hard to find out exactly what had happened, and who and how many had been killed, I spent all of Monday ringing hospitals in Australia and Bali, and emailing friends around the world. With no job and plenty of spare time I spent the next two days on the phone and became the hub for people all over the place. Somehow media organisations got hold of my email address and badgered me, wanting to interview me. I knew that they were trying to do their jobs, but for me it was neither the time nor the place and I never responded to any of the enquiries.

Although I didn't think of it this way at the time, with hindsight I can see that from the time Wayne Smith and Tony Gilbert were replaced, life for me had been a sequence of tumultuous emotional and physical . . . well, in many ways 'catastrophes' is not putting it too strongly.

The next day I did the time-honoured and typical New Zealand thing, that which is deemed a virtue: I tried to get on with it — it, in this case, being pulling down a shed at Tony Brown's house. Tony was recovering from a back operation and was right out of commission. But while I worked I had one ear on the radio and my thoughts were with Mark all day. Was Mark really dead, or was he, could he, be alive still? Then I heard a track on the radio by the group U2. Mark loved U2. I sat down, head in my hands, desolate.

Later that night, Simon Maling and I watched the TV news where it was announced officially that it was true, my dear friend Mark Parker had been one of the victims of the Bali bombing. We couldn't believe it and soon the phone began to run red hot.

We're often told to keep ourselves busy as a means of not stagnating. Okay, but shouldn't time be set aside for reflection or contemplation? I was required to be in Auckland for a fund-raising dinner for Team New Zealand's America's Cup campaign. Then I went to the Cambrian Valley near St Bathans in Central Otago. I had become friendly with the artist Grahame Sydney and had stayed with him a few times when buzzing about in that grand and airy part of the country. I put in a tender for a block of land in the valley — which I didn't get — but shortly after I bought a historic little mud-brick cottage and a few tree-lined acres just up the road from Syd's place. Also, Grahame and I went and had a look at Sam Neill's Red Bank vineyard near Clyde. Neill and Sydney are mates from way back, and both are very keen followers of sport. Many rugby players would be surprised to learn just how many artists and writers are astute and enthusiastic fans of rugby and other games.

Above: With Grahame Sydney, enjoying another stunning Central Otago summer day. Below: Picture postcard scene in Central Otago. That's my cottage in the background.

Meanwhile, Mark's body had been eventually released by the Balinese authorities and Murray and Verna's eldest son was, at last, home in Timaru. Friends from all over the world were gathering for Mark's funeral. I had been asked to be a pallbearer and give a eulogy at the funeral service. So I spent a day at home in Dunedin preparing for it and in the end the words flowed fairly easily, for Mark was such an intelligent, friendly, good-hearted person. But I was apprehensive. Having never spoken at a funeral before I didn't know if I was going to be able to hold it all together and get the words out.

In Timaru I joined other pallbearers for a practice run and then went round to the Parkers' home. Mark's father Murray took me to the room in which Mark lay in an open casket. I was glad of the opportunity to have one last, private moment with Mark, for it was clear to me that everything that mattered most about him, everything that characterised him in life — his vitality, wit, sense of fun and his abundant decency; in other words the essence of his spirit — was not there. The Mark in front of me was not the Mark I would remember. And it hit me, seeing him there, that we place too much importance on the physical and that, relative to so many other things, the physical is far more superficial. Eventually, I laid my hand on the forehead of my old mate, said goodbye, and left.

Outside the other pallbearers were waiting and expected me to be a mess. They told me that going in to see Mark had been shattering for them, and all of them feared that they would be left with a vision of Mark as they saw him in his coffin. I was the opposite and realised immediately that there would be no more springtimes for Mark. The man I knew had long gone. And yet I felt strangely comforted by the thought that he was somewhere safe.

Eulogy for a Friend

It is rare to find a man as fond of sleep as Mark Parker was. If he wasn't actually asleep then he was probably waking up from being asleep, preparing to go to sleep or thinking about how good it would be if he could have an afternoon sleep.

Mark's philosophy was that if you're hungry you eat, if you're tired you sleep.

I first met Mark in 1994 at Unicol hostel in Dunedin some nine years ago. At six foot three and 75 kilograms he had to be anchored down in a strong southerly, and so would have been pretty inconspicuous if it wasn't for him wearing the tightest pair of vacuum-fitted trousers, which he wore religiously, earning him the name Terry Tight Trousers.

I can still remember the first time I met him, a firm handshake, then a look straight in the eye. I remember it because I thought to myself, there's something in this guy, he had something a little different to most that I had met in those first few days at Unicol. Something that only time spent with him would help me define.

Mark had an uncanny ability to label people with nicknames: Stag, 100, Bow Back, Fog Horn, Mincer, Gorse, Guts, Boomerang and Bucket were all his handiwork and invariably they all stuck.

Mark was a listener, and very perceptive, and so his nicknames were very accurate descriptions in a comical way of his mates.

Honesty, loyalty, compassion and caring formed a melded backbone of values that ran through Mark from head to toe. Self-deprecating and the master of euphemism, Mark always downplayed his achievements.

If you asked him how many runs he had scored he would say 'a few'. If you asked him about a casual acquaintance from the evening before and were enquiring about an honest appraisal, he would say 'above average'.

Mark was a handsome man who all the girls liked, much to the amazement of most of us given that his nickname was taken from his body's remarkable similarity to a certain garden implement (Rake Parker), but adore him they did.

One of the oldest clichés often used in eulogies is the description 'no one had a bad thing to say about him'. Well, in Mark's case that cliché is utterly true.

He took his time to form opinions of others and was never quick to judge, or if he did he never said it publicly, preferring instead to keep his own counsel.

I think one of Mark's truly great qualities was his constant unwavering ability to think of others before himself. He did this time and again and it is something that I have always admired about him and have tried to learn from.

A wise man once said to me if you really want to understand someone then go and meet his or her parents. Mark Parker wouldn't have been the beautiful person that we all knew if Murray and Verna Parker didn't pour all of their love and energy into him, establishing a system of values and beliefs that would make any parents proud.

Stories about Mark's antics are endless, and we all can picture him with that funny quizzical look upon his face retelling his own yarns, which were always hilarious.

Mark Parker

My private gag with him was that I thought he had a wonky eye and that it didn't look straight. I thought it got wonkier the more hung-over he got; he disagreed but being the worrier he was I think he got it checked out at his next GP visit. When Mark felt the flu coming on he would, two days prior to it possibly arriving, retreat to his beloved scratcher, turn the heater up full bore, open the window and sleep. Needless to say his room always had a varied choice of odours.

Here is my small wish list:

I wish that I could hear him tell me about Wild Honey, his beloved school band, one more time. And how he would point the neck of the guitar he was playing at pretty girls in the audience, so that they knew he had seen them; I wish I could hear another retelling of *Top Gun* quotes and others from *A Few Good Men*; I wish I could sit down with him and laugh at his silly antics and idiosyncratic ways; I wish he and I could talk over a beer of our halcyon days at university and of the stuff we got away with and the stuff we didn't; I wish he were here with me and us.

Those thoughts make me incredibly sad, but then after a while I smile because he has left us with many wonderful memories.

Such was his gift to us.

Talking with those who had spent a lot of time with him recently, they say Mark's life was getting better and better.

He was spending a few days in Bali by himself when, a few years earlier, he hated being alone in Thailand. He was scoring runs, more than ever before. He was enjoying life in London as a young, confident man who was blossoming from the Timaru bud that he once was.

He would have been a loving husband, a proud father, and supportive and wise granddad.

Mark Parker will be my friend for ever.

After the funeral I was interviewed by the media again (as had been the case when Gordon Hunter died), and again I was acutely aware of the need to put the emphasis on Mark and his family, not on me.

That night we had a wake — lots to eat and drink. Next morning I drove to Dunedin, flew to Auckland, then to Napier in time to attend the wedding of Taine Randell and Jo Edwards. It was a tough day for me: 48 hours ago I had been speaking at the funeral of a friend who had died in a terrorist bombing on foreign soil, and here I was in a chapel near Napier watching two people making a life commitment to each other. My head was full of thoughts of how Mark would never experience this, would never have the chance to express his love in the way that Taine and Jo did. Such thoughts kept resonating in me throughout the day, but I tried to hide them, and, when the speeches were all done, I swallowed a few drinks in the hope that they would keep me going. It didn't work, so I got a ride back to the hotel with a mother who was leaving early to pick up her infant from a babysitter.

A few days later I spoke at the Sportsman of the Year dinner at my old school, Marlborough Boys' College. I had been asked just about every year since I'd left but rugby commitments had always intervened. I'm told my speech was far from romantic — that I emphasised the need to take your opportunities, live life to the full, take nothing for granted. I was in no mood to be nice and cuddly; my experiences in the previous year or two had left me edgy, occasionally bemused, and more inclined to temper optimism and idealism with what people sometimes term cold, hard realities.

This was the tenth Marlborough Sportsman of the Year dinner and, to my surprise, I was honoured with their Sportsman of the Decade award. The presentation left me both humbled and proud that my old school had recognised the last decade of my sporting life with this accolade.

When I got home to Dunedin I jumped straight in my truck and drove inland to Cambrian. Increasingly, that part of Central Otago — big brown and dry shapely hills, gloriously wide skies and clear air — had become a retreat, a bolt-hole. No phone, no rugby practice, no gym training, no speeches, no palaver. Once into the Maniototo I always felt cares and pressures lift and take flight. I stayed with Grahame Sydney, again, as my cottage was being renovated and added to, and at three in the morning went along to Rick Beattie's homestead to watch the All Blacks play England. Rick's a local farmer between St Bathans and Becks, one of the many farming families in the area that go back generations. He has Sky TV, of course; farmers tend to have all the luxuries!

I found watching the game a weird experience. It was the first time since 1995 that I had not been on tour with the All Blacks. But the scary thing was that I had no strong desire to be out there. People were saying, I suppose you'd love to be playing. I felt the reactionary need to say, 'Well, yes, of course, I want to be playing,' but that was not what my heart was telling me. I felt remote from rugby, and realised that I had shut myself off from the game.

It was as if blinkers had been taken off and I had been exposed to a whole new world. I hadn't realised the breadth of the possibilities open to me. I'd met new people, made new friends, had had stimulating conversations and my eyes had been opened to a greater range of activities and ideas.

But I had to start training again, the Achilles had mended well and now it was time to put in plenty of hard work and get my fitness back to where it should be. Initially, it was hard to establish a good routine. Previously rugby had always come first, so it had met little resistance from other activities. There hadn't been as many other interests vying for my attention. Quickly, though, training assumed its old significance. I was nowhere near the level I'd been at before the injury, watching my weight had not stopped my fitness decline as much as I had hoped and my long training base had been eroded more quickly than first envisaged. I've always tended to measure myself against my previous best-ever performance levels and that's sometimes unhelpful. It was not until the end of 2003 that I was able to strike a balance between rugby and slowing down and enjoying other, less dominating things in life.

For the first time ever I had stood back from rugby and critiqued it from the outside. The process was both intriguing and enlightening. I was flatting with Simon Maling and was able to compare his reports of what was really going on in the All Black camp with what was being reported through the media and elsewhere. Up till then I had been rather dismissive of the rugby public and their eagerness to read and believe, as I saw it, reports and comment that struck me as superficial and, sometimes, ill-informed. Now I found myself to be more understanding of the pundits, the critics. There was a greater understanding looking from the outside in.

As for the vexed matter of Life after Rugby, for the first time I had begun to think seriously about that. I had two university degrees and had shelved them, mainly because there are so many variables that affect a future in professional rugby that it is well-nigh impossible to plan ahead with any certainty. What characterises rugby today is its uncertainty: injuries; one's own form and that of one's rivals; whether a coach is on your side or not; how your team is performing; your family relationships.

Somewhat foolishly I had avoided thinking about life after rugby. The pay was and is very good and I simply hadn't thought about anything else other than being an All Black. But the extended lay-off after rupturing my Achilles taught me plenty. I realised many of the best things in life would pass me by unless I took the initiative, extended myself more and grabbed opportunities. It had, at last, dawned on me that life was far more interesting than I had realised.

Throughout a large part of 2002 I had been focused on ways of making more money, and then, in 2003, I woke up to the fact that there are limitations: sooner or later you have to say, 'Stop, enough is enough.' The costs of improving my cottage in Cambrian taught me that. How far do you go? There's always something better, something more expensive. Doing up the cottage in Central Otago taught me a great deal about how surroundings shape thoughts and attitudes. Central Otago, the down-to-earth, practical but also thoughtful and unpretentious people, and the spare loveliness of the landscape had changed me. Trying to cope with the deaths of three dear friends and a career-threatening injury had exposed me in a cruelly concentrated way to life's vulnerabilities. I started to question what was truly important to me and what wasn't, for so much in my life had been turned on its head in the space of 12 months.

I would never be the same again.

Chapter 12
Highlanders Hullabaloo

No matter how you look at it, since the uproar and venom surrounding the All Blacks' failure to win the 1999 World Cup, rugby in this country has been in turmoil. Teams that have played brilliantly one week have been a jittery mess the next. Selectors, coaches and administrators have come and gone. Infighting, back-biting, conniving, politicking . . . you name it, it's been all on. Reluctantly, I got caught up in some of it. Often I felt bewildered by it all, and also indignant at times. Overall, there have been many losers and very few winners. In the end, you can't really overstate the drama and the tumult in the aftermath of the World Cup.

By the end of the 2003 Super 12 competition the Highlanders franchise was an acrimonious mess. To some on the periphery of rugby in the south, the whole situation seemed farcical. Within the franchise region the rugby public were angry. It seemed as if some were more interested in suppressing than in seeking the truth. Whenever I hear people talk of the importance of a 'process' being 'open and transparent' I think, 'Good idea, but how often does it happen?'

Yes, the Highlanders' 2003 season did end in a shambles. As far as most rugby people were concerned, they were left with the impression that it boiled down to Oliver, the ringleader, versus Mains. So-called disaffected, precious player versus hard-nosed, old-style coach: that was the broad picture being painted.

Disquiet had been brewing for some time. After the 2002 season, many of the players were extremely unhappy; some were disillusioned. They felt Laurie was too often petty, needlessly picky about some matters, and was manipulative in ways that frequently left them feeling uneasy and insecure. So near the end of 2002 the forwards and some of the other senior players sat down and talked with Laurie. We aired our concerns about the style of play we were following and the overall level of fitness in the team. The Highlanders were seen as less sharp than the other New Zealand teams in the competition — 'one-paced' was a phrase often used. Our style of kicking for territory, keeping the ball in the forwards and exerting pressure only really worked when it was wet, or when the tempo of a game was slow. Most of the senior players believed that this style doesn't win the big games in Super 12. To beat the top sides you have to have more attacking options. Some of my Crusaders friends said that our style of play was entirely predictable, that they knew exactly what we would do and, also, that as a game wore on we fell off the pace required.

I am assured that, in the mid-1990s, relative to other international sides, Laurie's All Black side was very fit, possibly the fittest of all the major international teams. But that was prior to the start of the professional era, before players had extra muscular bulk and prior to the rule changes that have greatly altered the way rugby is played. Other teams have become fitter and stronger than they were, and the leading players have to turn out more often. Mains, understandably, was inclined to want to stick with what he knew, what he saw as tried and true. To most of us, a lot of it just wasn't true any more.

Laurie appeared to hear what was being said to him late in 2002 and undertook to make changes in 2003; in particular he would abandon the more mindless aspects of practices, especially the running up and down and the physical stuff that had little specific purpose. Kelvin Middleton and Simon Maling said their piece and were buoyed by Laurie's response and assurances. We all left the meeting feeling optimistic.

Our December training camp involved a great deal of anaerobic work and no emphasis on game plans. Some self-confessed lazy trainers thought it was good for them because it made them train. But for the players who were more disciplined, it was just training that we could have done wherever we liked. Most thought that our trainer, André Richardson, whom Laurie had brought back from South Africa with him, and who the boys grew to like personally, wasn't up to it. Laurie turned up sporadically, said little. The whole camp was largely a waste of time.

After surgery to repair my Achilles in 2002 I had been forced to take a long break from training. I had watched my weight, so that was fine, but in November/December, because my trainer Rob Nicholson and I had decided to increase the intensity of my aerobic work only gradually so as to minimise the risk of re-injuring my calf and Achilles, my 3 km run time was a lot slower than usual. Nevertheless, when all the New Zealand Super 12 hookers (Blues, Chiefs, Crusaders, Hurricanes) were fitness tested in December/January 2003, and I compared my test results with theirs (Speed over 10 m and 40 m; Phosphate Decrement Test; 3 km run; Power Clean Lift; Bench Press Lift; Squat), my results overall were better than anyone else's. By the time the Super 12 competition began I had improved further in some of those areas.

When the Highlanders started practising and training in earnest in the weeks prior to the start of the Super 12 in 2003, Mains stuck with his insistence on his beloved repetition 150s, and we did little rugby-specific work until a fortnight or less out from our first game. Meanwhile, friends in the Crusaders and Blues teams had been telling us that for some time they had been working on their sequence plays, so we knew that relative to others we were well off the pace. For us, then, it was business as usual with Laurie, and the senior players thought that he had broken promises made in November the previous year. This is where the rot started to set in.

At one point Laurie called for an extra training session. He was late arriving, his excuse being that he thought *his* time was accurate.

We set off on our pre-season flag-flying trip through Central Otago. A team meeting had been scheduled for when we got to Alexandra. After arrival we were told the meeting had been postponed. I talked to our manager, Des Smith, and asked him if anything else was planned prior to our next training session. He said no, so I drove up to check on work in progress at my mud-brick cottage near St Bathans, about 55 km away. When I got back I learned that a snap meeting had been held and I was ticked off for being absent. If it hadn't been for a general fear of missing snap meetings most of the team would have missed it too. Many of them just happened to be nearby playing cricket when they were informed.

'Has time to listen to anyone in a team' — Kelvin Middleton

Like many players of his generation, Middleton's first memory of Oliver was of 'this big buy, far bigger than most of us in school rugby. I played against him in an under-18 tournament in Westport. I was just a little guy, and fearful of him.'

When Oliver started playing for Otago, Middleton found him 'free and easy. Over time he's become more philosophical, more thoughtful. He's certainly one of the more intelligent guys. Anton looks at things in depth, more than most players do.' As a player, Middleton saw Oliver as 'hard-nosed, highly physical, with a work rate second to none in our rugby. Other teams talk about him, see him as a major threat.'

Middleton, one of the hardest and most consistent workers in the Otago and Highlanders forward packs, found it difficult to play under Laurie Mains. He saw most players as being pretty upset about the atmosphere in the squad. Middleton says that 'Anton has always been one of the most approachable of all players. To say that he would browbeat others into agreeing with him is bull. One of the things that characterises him is that he has time to listen to anyone in a team.'

Middleton thinks Mains would have seen Oliver as 'difficult and uncooperative', therefore 'disloyal', whereas Randell would have appeared more compliant, something that Mains could have seen as indicative of loyalty. But Middleton was convinced that Oliver's views on the Highlanders' set-up were shared by the majority of players, and that he was singled out as the messenger, ultimately, because many players felt Randell was unwilling to put their case to the coach forcefully.

'That article in *NZRW*, depicting him as the "ringleader" in a "revolt", killed his chances of going to the World Cup. That's if they weren't dead already. You'd find very few players who believed those criticisms Mitchell made of his play had much validity. Yes, Anton's had times when his throwing in to lineouts has been a bit off, but that's been overstated. I just don't believe he's worse than others. And with regards to his work in broken play, his tackling, and with the ball in hand, he's awesome.'

Such management issues were a bane for the entire season. Laurie's rationale for frequent changes was that we had to be a flexible organisation. The result was serious disruption. It was well-nigh impossible to plan your week. A few player/students found it difficult to know whether they would be able to attend lectures. The support staff — doctor, physio, masseur — just about everyone had to operate in accordance with what seemed like the unpredictable whims of the coach.

For instance, when at home in Dunedin, training was set down for 3.30 p.m. Laurie's decree was be at the park by 3.00 p.m. in case he wanted to have a meeting beforehand. But days,

Chatting with one of the locals during a Highlanders' pre-season camp at Owaka.

sometimes a fortnight, went by before Laurie decided actually to have a pre-training meeting. One day Byron Kelleher turned up after 3.00 p.m. and it just so happened to be one of those occasions when there was a meeting and he got hauled over the coals, told he was unprofessional. But most of the time Laurie turned up in his civilian gear 15 to 20 minutes after everyone else, sent us out to warm up while he went off to his office to write a few things down. Many of the guys thought that indicated he hadn't prepared properly and they grumbled about it. They wanted more certainty, more settled organisation.

At one point I took this stuff up with Des Smith, told him a lot of the players were exasperated. Laurie happened to be close at hand and picked up on what I was saying. He told me to, in effect, butt out, and reiterated his line that we needed to be 'flexible'.

We held a public training session in Alexandra. Laurie put on a loud, animated exhibition with lots of talk about technical matters. This was an established trend that we had first become aware of in the Highlanders' pre-season camp at Owaka the year before and was to continue whenever there was an audience. In the absence of a crowd of onlookers he was, usually, the opposite.

In Alexandra, repetitions of Laurie's hallowed 150s were given pride of place. After about 20 of them, because a number of players were pulling up with sore calves and hamstrings, Laurie called a halt. Our trainer seemed unsure as to why so many were having trouble. Basically, we weren't conditioned to tolerate that sort of training. The results made life more difficult than it needed to be for our physio Peter Gallagher, who was very good at his job, the best physiotherapist I have ever had. He is an innovative thinker and he spent a lot of time trying to work out different ways of injury rehabilitation.

We played pre-Super 12 games against the Chiefs, Brumbies and Hurricanes. At the time Laurie was telling me that in his view I should be back as All Black captain. Mains said that the Crusaders and Robbie Deans had too much influence and he would like to see that reduced. He asked me to play golf with him and Des and a couple of others. I had a game with them then decided that it was best to keep my distance. There were a couple of reasons for that. One was that the disquiet within the Highlanders' squad, both on and off the field, was worrying me. Another was that I didn't want it to appear that I had joined Laurie's team. There was a view that those in Laurie's camp, so to speak, were likely to surrender too much autonomy. Later I realised that my choosing to keep my distance was in itself a source of friction. The way I saw it was that unless you showed Laurie clear allegiance he was apt to see you as an opponent.

At one point during the season I remember meeting with Alex McKenzie, the NZRU's local professional development officer, and asking him for some strategies to help me cope with and set aside what was going on in the Highlanders' camp. I was having trouble sleeping and the inconsistencies in Mains' doctrines left me feeling exasperated. Alex was a good help and a listening ear and his advice was sound. I introduced a few thought-stopping techniques he had taught me. Even in 2002 it had become pretty obvious that, from a management perspective, there was a division in the ranks and the management team had become a divided unit.

When travelling it was mandatory to wear our sponsor's adidas gear. At Auckland Airport en route to play our pre-season match against the Chiefs, Laurie was spotted wearing the wrong clothing. Our fines' committee — chaired then by Pete Bowden, one of the cleverest men ever to have played in Otago, if MENSA testing is a reliable gauge — put him on the fines list. Fines may seem trivial but if a rule has been agreed upon by the team it has to be adhered to. Coaches don't have dispensations in this area. Sponsors have expectations, end of story. Laurie took umbrage and let Bowden know it in no uncertain terms.

According to Bowden, known to the team as either 'Bow Wow' or 'Booky', Laurie 'felt that the fish-heads were exempt from being fined. Not on Bow Wow's watch! And his next excuse was that he did not get the list of fines, and I should have told him personally.' Laurie, who said that no one was allowed to use the term 'fish-head' when referring to administrators, paid up, but only, says Bowden, 'after much arguing and disapproval. However, he only paid the initial fine, not the doubled amount for late payment.'

If it's a fine for one, it's a fine for all. That was Pete Bowden's philosophy when it came to team discipline.

Bowden remembers that there was another fine, 'for being late for the bus. You know how regimented (some people would say anal) I was with fines. He was late by maybe one minute, so of course a fine was slapped in "Bow Wow's Book of Fines". He straight-up refused to pay that one.'

For pre-season away matches we travelled to the venue two days in advance. The team had to remain in the hotel and have our breakfast and other meals in the team room. Laughing and fooling about was frowned upon. If we wanted to have a bit of fun we had to confine it to our rooms, not the team room. Laurie's line seemed to be that larking about in the team room might affect other individuals' preparation for games. But prior to Laurie's return to Otago, especially under Hunter and Gilbert, the teams I played in had had fun together. Often quirky things happened that kept spirits up. Now, with everyone shut away in their rooms, any enjoyment we had from being together as a group dissipated.

Laurie also had a major thing about food: the rule was no fat, no cheese, no eggs, no mayonnaise, no butter, but margarine was okay, for some reason. If not quite all of that, damned near it. I found Laurie's food-restriction fixation excessive and plainly ridiculous. He picked up on the fact that I was disgruntled — when I'm unhappy my body language, facially and otherwise, tells it all — and wanted to know what was wrong. It was a fair question. I told him it was true that I didn't like or agree with some of his dictates, but that I would do my best to mask my feelings.

One reason for that was because, at the time, apart from my flatmate Simon Maling, I didn't know what the rest of the team was thinking.

Maybe, I thought, it's just me and Simon; maybe the rest of the players aren't anywhere near as perturbed as we are. (I wasn't sharing my concerns with anyone else but Simon.)

Our Super 12 opener was against the Chiefs in Hamilton. We'd beaten them by a wide margin in our pre-season encounter. This time it was close, 29–16, and we were average. The Chiefs had had some heavy pre-season losses and, human psychology being what it is, it's not surprising that they appeared to put more effort in than we did. In the shed afterwards, the boys were jovial, happy to have won. Laurie wasn't at all happy. He said we had been out-muscled; it wasn't good, we'd been lucky. The mood among the players was: 'Well, that's true but it was a win, and an away win at that. Can't we work on our deficiencies when we've had time to debrief and think about what needs to be done to improve?'

When Laurie got out of his car prior to Monday's debrief we could tell that a theatrical performance was imminent. The frowning, the striding said it all. A hush descended in the room. Laurie was very good at the Big Man on Campus stuff. Everyone copped it. He took us through the video and pointed out a lot of mistakes by a lot of players. He hardly had a positive thing to say about anyone.

Training was worse. We were barked at; players were constantly being singled out and abused. I felt like a dog that had just been kicked. Nothing we did was good enough.

The next day was entirely different. Sir Brian Lochore and John Graham, sent by the NZRU to do an appraisal of Highlanders' rugby, came along to training. Laurie smiled and joked, delivered compliments to individuals, stopping proceedings often to give technical advice. It was Alexandra all over again. Balie Swart, who usually took the scrums, was relieved of his role for the time being. Kelvin Middleton was one of a bunch of guys looking at each other as if to say, 'Far out, this is so different from yesterday.' At this stage I thought a lot of things were becoming farcical.

Middleton, who got his nickname 'Bone' after he was described in an article as being 'raw-boned', was brought up near Queenstown in the Wakatipu Basin. Bone had a great way of making players feel part of the team by being brusque without being unkind to them. Kelvin — Filipo Levi was another — was one of the boys occasionally guilty of inadvertently injuring others at training. Our term for this was 'friendly fire'. Middleton and Filipo were the worst offenders. I admired Middleton; he was honest, put the team first. A good bastard.

After training, when Lochore and Graham were in the physio's room, Kelvin chuckled and, smiling, said, 'Shit, you two should be around more often.' They wanted to know why. Kelvin said, 'Well, today everything is just so nice and friendly. You should have been here yesterday.'

Or the next day as it turned out. After the forwards had done their lineout session, which Maling ran, Laurie called the whole squad together. It was Monday's bollocking all over again. 'Last week was terrible, if we play like that again the Stormers will smash us,' he said . . . then he introduced comment he was getting off a South African website. We heard about what was being said over there, what they were going to do to us, and how none of us were in the website's best Super 12 side. I remember leaving the meeting and thinking the whole situation had become absurd, and I wondered if I could last a whole season of such infantilism. Again, apart from the odd remark between me and Maling, I should emphasise that I hadn't talked to any of the others about what was going on. I didn't want to get involved with Mains and his politics and didn't want to be seen to be influencing the opinions of my team-mates. Doing nothing was extremely hard for me, as I saw my role as a senior player being to take these sorts of grievances to the coach.

The captain's run prior to matches at Carisbrook was something I really looked forward to. In 2003 the surface was excellent and it was good to get out there early, kick the ball around, have a few passes, run about and then do your own stretching before starting organised training. Mains stopped that; he said he didn't want to see or hear any jocularity; he didn't want to see props kicking the ball before training, or any of that sort of stuff. Only the backs were allowed out on the ground to run and pass the ball. The goalkickers could practise their kicking. The rest of us? Tough. I used to go to the stand and sit there like a homesick boy, watching the kickers practise, all the while wanting to be out there throwing a ball around. And previously, at the end of training, we'd do our final stretches, have a jog until someone would start a sprint to the halfway line. 'There'll be no more of that,' said Mains. He said someone might pull a hamstring. At that stage I had played nine years for Otago and eight years with the Highlanders and no one had injured themselves when winding up the captain's run that way.

'Demanded the highest standards of himself and others' – Alex McKenzie

Alex is a former lecturer in the Department of Physical Education at the University of Otago. As an employee of the NZRU charged with player professional development, he guided players towards areas of study that might help them gain employment outside of rugby.

McKenzie taught Oliver sports psychology and was coach of the Otago University under-21 side in 1994 that included him, Duncan Blaikie and Simon Maling. He says, 'Anton would sometimes disagree with what I said, or proposed. We'd speak about it afterwards. I always found his comments constructive. Sometimes he'd say something and regret it. But he'd admit that.'

McKenzie thinks that where Oliver has had trouble relating to some in more recent times, 'it's because he has a lot of the more selfless amateur rugby player in him. Society is different now, and many players and some administrators are more selfish.'

I met with Alex McKenzie again and told him that I felt Mains was feeling threatened by me and that I wanted to know how, legally, Laurie could eject me from the squad. He had looked to do the same thing the year before to a player who was seen by him as problematic. So I obtained a copy of the rugby players' collective employment agreement in order to check what I was, or wasn't, entitled to say or do as a contracted player. It seemed very real to me that, under the circumstances, if I chose to act and in so doing broke the terms of my contract, Mains was likely to see to it that I was axed.

In Invercargill we beat the Bulls, although they got closer than they ought to have. We played reasonably well for three-quarters of the match and poorly in the last 20 minutes. Laurie was clearly unhappy afterwards, sullen and brooding. We jumped in cars, drove back to Dunedin and flew to Sydney the next day where we stayed overnight before taking the long flight to South Africa. We always travel business class and, as happened occasionally, we were allocated a few first-class seats. The convention was to give these to the two or three players troubled by injuries. The night before we flew out of Sydney we had a team meeting and, among other issues, sorted out the injured guys and told them who would be in first class. It's 15 hours in the air from Sydney. Laurie and his wife, Annemarie, sat in first class the whole way. So a couple of players missed out. That did not go down well with the boys.

Annemarie was our media liaison person. Why did we need such a person in South Africa? Does a Super 12 team need one at all? Annemarie travelled about with us the whole time.

Laurie Mains.

In Durban, at our first team meeting since the game in Invercargill, Laurie gave us a roasting on what I came to refer to jokingly as 'Black Monday'. The team was a mess, and our performance against the Bulls had been lamentable; that was the verdict. He ripped into Willie Walker, Sam Harding and Paul Steinmetz especially. Then he said something completely unexpected; he threatened to chuck in his job as coach, declaring that he felt we didn't show enough passion and he didn't want to coach a team that didn't want him. He accused us of having no soul, no desire, and that he was embarrassed to be our coach. To me it was melodrama. He gave us an ultimatum: we had to decide whether we wanted him to be coach or not, then he stormed out of the room taking the rest of the management team with him.

This was early in the evening, around 6 p.m., when we were all about to go out for dinner. I remember thinking, I don't know what the others are thinking but wouldn't it be fantastic if the consensus was to tell Laurie we didn't want him. Taine Randell saw that he had to do something and to general astonishment all round acted as if he was completely oblivious to it all. He said something like, 'Well, what do we do for next Saturday?'

Joe McDonnell was first to speak. He said, 'Hold on, we have to deal with what just happened. That was bullshit. He can't treat us like that.' Taine replied that we all knew what Laurie was like, that was the way he was and as we were never going to change that, what could we do?

I said that Laurie's behaviour was absurd and unacceptable, that he went way beyond the limits. A couple of other guys said much the same thing. Basically, Taine wanted the meeting to end and for there to be no further discussion or conflict.

It was a classic knife-edge situation. Lots of the boys were incensed but no one was willing to insist that we sit there and have a really open and frank discussion about what had been going on and, as individuals, how we felt about it. I didn't know what the rest of the team were thinking and didn't want to influence them and override Taine's position as captain. If someone had asked me for my honest opinion I would have suggested we stay where we were, take our time, sort out what we collectively thought, ask Mains back into the room and tell him straight. Imagine if the team decided to take him up on his ridiculous offer of resignation. What could he have done then? I am sure that would have made the team an incredibly tight unit and we would have played accordingly.

For a time there was a sickening silence, as people were a bit shell-shocked. Then Byron Kelleher said that the best thing we could do in the meantime was to look at ways of playing well against the Cats on the weekend. After a while there was general agreement about that and we got on the bus and went off to dinner.

Laurie slowly moved down the bus, sheepishly chatting and smiling. Hard man one minute, mate the next. I think Laurie knew he had really crossed the line. When he got to Kelvin Middleton and me in the back seat we said nothing about his outburst in the meeting, nor did he. We simply talked about tactics to employ in the game on the weekend. Hypocrisy on both sides was the order of the day.

Just before we got off the bus, Laurie announced that we could eat anything we liked at the restaurant except shellfish. We all complied with that. Laurie himself ordered a great big crayfish. Then he moved around the tables telling everyone that we could have a beer if we liked. Life in the Highlanders was becoming more ludicrous by the day. I was going to have a beer anyway, so I did. Middleton reacted differently; he said, 'Bugger it. I'm not buying into that crap.'

Pettiness prevailed: on the Tuesday we were told that there would be no more swimming in the sea before our game later in the week. The ocean was 300 m away. And no one was to leave the hotel after 6 p.m. except as part of a group. There was even a log book in which we were supposed to fill in details of where we were going before we left the hotel.

We flew up to the veldt and were beaten 33–21 at Johannesburg. Laurie said little after that. Having lost his rag after the previous game, which we'd won, he had nowhere to go. Later, Laurie attributed his erratic behaviour to the sleeping pills he'd been taking. He said they had been making him grumpy.

I went out with Paul Steinmetz. During the evening he told me that he hadn't been sleeping. He said he'd been worrying about getting a rocket at debriefs if he missed tackles or dropped the ball. I'd also been having trouble sleeping, and like Paul, was constantly worrying about making mistakes for fear of being singled out in the de-brief sessions. I remember missing a tackle and thinking instantly, 'Oh, shit, I'm for it.'

Steiny said he was agonising over whether to sign up with the Highlanders for another year. He said that unless Laurie changed his ways there was no way he would sign up again. I was flabbergasted to hear this from Steiny. The general feeling in the side was that Laurie had more time for Steiny than for most.

In the lead-up to our next match, against the Sharks in Durban, I roomed with Middleton. Several members of the team knocked on our door and wanted to talk over their concerns about the way the team was being run. That was when the depth of the dismay at what was going on in the Highlanders really hit home to me.

But the boys were determined to give of their best, and in a close match we got home 23–19 over the Sharks. After the game Taine Randell and I were having a swim in the hotel pool. I hadn't said anything to him about Laurie's performance on 'Black Monday'. In the pool I said that I thought Laurie's carrying on had been unacceptable and very destructive. I assumed that Taine must have been perturbed, to say the least, and that he would have been wondering what the hell was going on. But no, Taine said he believed Laurie had the goods, that he was right and that he believed in the approach Laurie had taken. He was unfazed. So, he wasn't on Laurie's side because as captain he felt he was obliged to support the coach, but because he actually approved of Laurie's methods. There is only one word for my feelings at that point: I was dumbfounded.

I puzzled over Taine's position. What, I thought, about the need for mutual respect and the right to open debate; the right, as employees, to be treated civilly?

Utter relief flooded over me when we flew out of South Africa. Thank God, we were on our way home. It was wet at Carisbrook when we played the Crusaders. This slowed the game down a bit and we beat them in the forwards but still lost the game, 16–17. Oddly, perhaps, it seemed that the ructions had instilled a greater degree of unity among the players. After the Crusaders match I recall one of the players laughing and saying, 'Here we go again, another bollocking's on the cards.'

Playing halfback against the Crusaders at Carisbrook during Super 12, 2003. We suffered yet another narrow loss to our South Island nemesis, 16–17.

Our next match meant a great deal to many of us, a game against the Auckland Blues for the Gordon Hunter Memorial Trophy. When the phone went one morning during the week it was Carl Hoeft. A relative in Auckland had rung Hoefty and told him that the *New Zealand Herald* carried an article by Wynne Gray which put its finger on the dissension within the Highlanders. It also included reference to the fact that Gray's source — or sources — disclosed that in some respects Mains and his assistant coach, Greg Cooper, who was in charge of the backs, didn't see eye to eye. I went online and read the article. It was pretty accurate. Both Simon Maling and I were astonished by the accuracy of the report and relieved to think that the truth might emerge and that we might get some help.

Laurie had publicly said that our problems were mainly in the backs, not the forwards. This was seen as a criticism of Greg Cooper. It was common knowledge that their relationship was strained. Concerns were so great there that at one point in 2002 Sir Brian Lochore had been brought down from the North Island to act as a mediator in a meeting between Mains and Cooper, which led to Cooper's reappointment for the 2003 season.

Taine wasn't happy with the backs' performance either, and he pointed to statistical information to support his and Laurie's contentions. By this stage most of the players saw Taine and Laurie as 'tight', and as a consequence few were willing to take their concerns to either of them. Laurie was quick to tell the world what a good captain he had. And any interest Laurie had in promoting me as captain of the All Blacks had long gone.

When I arrived at Logan Park in North Dunedin for training, Laurie called me into his room. He wanted to know if I had talked to the media, or had been involved in the *Herald* story in any way. I said I hadn't, which was true. He said that the team wasn't working well and asked me why I thought that was. I replied that things had been rocky for weeks but that it had all come to a head when, as well as criticising individuals' play, he queried their personal integrity in front of the rest of the team, and then threatened to walk away in South Africa. I said he may not have been aware of the extent to which players took exception to his behaviour but that he had crossed the line big time there. I said all that confrontational stuff just doesn't work. Laurie thanked me for my honesty and that was it, really. We hardly spoke from that time on. Before the season ended, Laurie was to say to some Highlanders' board members words to the effect that I was 'unstable and suffered from violent mood swings'. When I was told that, I recalled how, during his coaching stint in South Africa, Mains had had a falling out with Rassie Erasmus. According to Frikkie Erasmus, who acted for Rassie, 'I can tell you that what Mains has told the board members about Oliver is a copybook of his incident with Rassie.'

It was around this time that our back-up hooker, Tom Willis, an All Black, was injured. If it hadn't been for that I think I would have been dropped. I turned in a couple of really good games and the public and media commentary was that my play was back to my best and I was a certainty for the All Blacks.

In the aftermath of Gray's article in the *Herald*, Des Smith suggested Laurie should apologise to the team and he asked my advice on the matter. I told Des that it was a bit late: more than three weeks had passed since the outburst. But Des didn't agree. Mains did apologise. It was cursory and came at the end of a lengthy team meeting. Afterwards some of the players remarked that it had seemed pretty token, and joked about it.

After Gray's article appeared, Laurie is believed to have wanted the Highlanders' board to investigate who had leaked information to Gray. One upshot of all of this, though, embarrassed Middleton and Maling. They were required to issue statements to the effect that the Gray story wasn't accurate and that things were quite okay in the camp. They felt pretty stupid doing it, but what else could they do? Mains told them to. There were several games to go and they were unsure of what would happen to them if they refused.

On 4 April we beat the Blues 22–11 on Carisbrook. The wet conditions helped us, restricted the Blues. And, when our fine young fullback Paul Williams' leg was shattered as he attempted to muscle across and score in the corner, the ensuing huge delay helped us some more. To this day, Hoefty believes that the delay helped us more than Auckland. He said that the game mirrored the way we trained: stop, start, sit and talk. We were conditioned that way, said Hoefty.

Mains was cock-a-hoop with the win. He strode onto the bus holding the Gordon Hunter Memorial Trophy. A few players who knew Gordon well found that hard to take. The rest were thinking 'Where was the humility?' It was around this time that Kelvin Middleton said he had heard that Laurie was considering seeking reappointment. Kelvin said that when he was at Logan Park receiving treatment, Mains entered the room and, when standing to one side, was overheard to say that 'they' had offered him another year. Kelvin and two others of the Highlanders' support staff heard this.

Subsequently, three board members, including two who spoke to Laurie, said that the board was concerned about the reports coming out about disaffection in the squad. Board members said that prior to Wynne Gray's *Herald* piece they were unaware of the extent of the friction in the camp, but now realised they needed to make some enquiries. Mains had not been offered another term, they maintained, they were simply sounding him out, wanting to know what he thought and what his intentions were.

But all Simon Maling and I — and also Carl Hoeft and Tony Brown — knew was what Kelvin and those nearby had heard. We discussed it. The cold, hard, blunt truth was that, if it were true that Laurie was going to be reappointed, a significant number of the players contracted to the franchise would not have signed to continue to play for the Highlanders. Those who wanted to get out needed time to make it known to their agents and others that they were interested in offers from other franchises.

We agreed that we needed to talk to Rob Nichol of the Players' Association to check on what procedures we had to follow, warn him that he might be called upon to look after our interests. We also wanted to document our concerns for presentation to the Highlanders' board — but only after most of the players, especially the Otago-based ones, had seen and discussed the issues.

In our next game we lost to the Hurricanes by 22 points in New Plymouth, where we were outplayed in the second half. This was worrying because our next game was to be against the Brumbies at Carisbrook. At this stage Mains' game plan mainly revolved round working the ball towards the middle of the field and then continuing to attack down the blindside. But Cooper, Tony Brown and one or two of the others, after looking at videotapes of the Brumbies, said, 'Hell, if we do that, they'll smoke us.' On the day of the game, Cooper, Brown, Danny Lee and Willie Walker got together and said it would be wrong to go the blindside all the time, so they . . . well, we won 45–19. The videotape of the game showed that the Brumbies forwards sat there waiting for us to go on the blindside and we seldom did. Afterwards, when Laurie claimed credit for the tactics employed, Brown and his associates could only laugh.

By now, perhaps surprisingly, there was a lot of unity and unanimity among the players on how best to prepare for games, which often meant ignoring the coach's plans. There was also growing anxiety about when we should meet to discuss taking our concerns to the Highlanders' board. We had to do that before the Super 12 ended because players disperse within a day or two once the competition ends. But we didn't want to do anything that would upset the apple cart while we still had a chance of making the semi-finals.

Away from rugby I was extremely upset about the whole climate in the franchise. It was harrowing. Here I was, after a decade of devotion to Otago and the Highlanders, determined to leave the province to which I had given heart and soul. For years I had been proud to play for Otago and had rejected several higher paid offers from elsewhere. Now I was loathing the prospect of continuing in Otago. I still wanted to play well for the Highlanders but it irked the hell out of me, and many other team members, to see the coach getting accolades that we felt were undeserved. Baldly, I had decided that if Mains was asked to continue, I was going to play elsewhere, and I wasn't alone in making that decision. There is no doubt that Middleton was right when he said that if Laurie was reappointed there would have been an 'exodus'.

'He has the fear factor' — David Latta

'There's a lot of the traditional, pre-professional old-style rugby player in Anton,' says Dave Latta. 'I don't believe that stuff about him being disloyal to anyone.'

Latta, Oliver's predecessor as Otago hooker, sees rugby today as 'cut-throat' and having 'too much of a focus on so-called personalities'.

'As a hooker, I'd have rather played against anyone but Oliver. He would have scared me. No one else scared me. He's very competitive and powerful. He has the fear factor.' Latta recalls attending a training camp in Oamaru in the early 1990s where in just about all tests related to power, strength and speed, 'Anton was the best of all.'

Mused Latta, 'Gordon Hunter talked of the need to commit oneself utterly for the team cause on the field. Today, how many players are willing to push past the pain barrier? Josh Kronfeld did; Jerry Collins does; Oliver does.' Latta ought to know. His level of commitment was legendary.

In the week before our home game against the Waratahs, Laurie told me that he was going to play Tom Willis instead of me. He said I had been playing well but that he wanted to give Tom a chance to press his claims for All Black selection. I asked him to make sure he told the media that I wasn't being dropped due to poor form, or injury. Why? Because, earlier, there had been an instance when Paul Steinmetz went to his local dairy and the woman behind the counter said she hoped his ribs were okay. He asked her to elaborate and she said she'd read in the paper that he wasn't playing on the weekend because of a rib injury. That was news to Steiny. He was angered to have learned of his omission this way. As far as he was concerned he was fit to play and had been dropped. By announcing that Steinmetz was unfit Mains had avoided any critique of his decision not to play a fit and eager player.

We had the Waratahs beaten until silly mistakes and a lack of concentration gifted them the game when they scored in the final moments to win 27–23.

Even then we still had a chance of making the semis if in our final game we beat the Reds in Brisbane. We had just about run out of time to sort out what we were going to put to the Highlanders' board. So Maling, Brown, Middleton and Hoeft rang around something like 23 players — those contracted to Otago because they were the ones most directly affected by what went

A win over the Waratahs would almost certainly have guaranteed us a spot in the semis in the 2003 Super 12. We lost our concentration in the final moments and blew it.

on in the province — and we arranged to meet at the flat Maling and I shared in Ross Street. The meeting was scheduled for the Monday before our game against the Reds. We agreed that someone needed to put together a document detailing and discussing our concerns and that it should be given to all those who attended the meeting so that they could read it and respond. The hitch was no one wanted to write it. I didn't offer to do it. In the end we decided what we wanted to say and I was asked to write it up.

Some noise arose, later, over our decision not to invite Taine Randell to the meeting. Why didn't we? We saw him as having divided loyalties and that would have put him in a difficult position. Some senior players thought, too, that many at the meeting would have been inhibited by his presence. After all, he was soon to leave to go and play in the UK.

Brownie rang Rob Nichol of the Players' Association and he came down from Wellington to attend the meeting. We wanted him to hear what was said and to gauge the mood. I got in touch with Alex McKenzie and invited him to come along as an observer, not to contribute, but as one who would be able to report on whether anyone was being unduly pressured. McKenzie was independent in the sense that he was employed by the NZRU, not by the Highlanders. Player welfare was what he was employed to oversee, and Mains had no influence over him.

Nichol's view is that the players were happy with the document handed out. Alex McKenzie felt only three players showed some hesitancy: Brad Fleming, Danny Lee and Tom Willis. Alex said that while Fleming and Lee agreed that much had gone awry, because this was their first year down south under Laurie they felt as if they needed more time to make a better judgement. As for Tom, McKenzie concluded that he shared many of the concerns but was unsure of the process. He didn't want to see a witch hunt.

Rob Nichol allayed their fears and said no one would be required to sign the document as had been mistakenly reported in some circles.

Everyone else appeared in full agreement with what was being said in an open forum where some of the tension was eased by Carl Hayman turning up with two dozen Speight's and saying gruffly that 'he didn't want anyone to get thirsty'. Both McKenzie and Nichol said that I was one of those who had least to say at the meeting, and that they were surprised at the intensity of the overall concern most players had for the coach's approach before and during the Super 12 campaign.

Pete Bowden, one of our locks who came to us from Canterbury, says he found Mains frosty and the atmosphere he engendered uncongenial. Early on he decided, he said, it was best to 'switch off' and keep his 'head down'. That, he felt, was a strategy adopted by many of the loan and draft players. He said that he 'had nothing but respect for the so called "instigators". I respected them for their play, as well as their camaraderie.' Never 'once' did he think that 'they had put the best interests of the team in harm's way. During the few weeks of the "media interest" Anton, as well as the other senior players, gave the facts and nothing but the facts from my point of view. None of them forced a decision from us and at no time did I feel compelled to do what they said. Because the facts were put in front of me, I was able to make my own decision. I thought this was the case for many. Those that had objecting ideas were welcome to put them across and were also left to make their own decision.'

I'm pretty sure that Laurie Mains didn't see it that way. He has said that Brad Fleming, in his view the 'best' of the wingers we had, and Paul Steinmetz 'totally disagreed' with the players' views and actions. Mains contends that's why the Highlanders failed to renew Fleming's contract. Greg Cooper, the Highlanders coach for the next campaign and the man responsible for Brad's non-selection, point-blank denies this. Laurie also believed that a number of players in the Otago and Highlanders' sides disagreed with me but 'dare not say what they think'. That's tantamount to accusing me of behaving like a playground bully terrorising a bunch of meek, puny little kids. What does that say about Laurie's knowledge and opinion of his own players?

Mains, who subsequently made no secret of the fact that he agreed with the decision to drop me from the All Black squad chosen for the 2003 World Cup, said that both he and Mitchell thought I should stay out of the politics and focus solely on rugby. Mains said that I had done some 'unsavoury' things in the Highlanders. Laurie believed that I had told one of the Highlanders' board members that he had been 'greasing up' to them in order to enhance his chances of reappointment. I can't remember if I said that or not, but if I did it hardly ranks high on the rugby world's scale of what is deemed unsavoury behaviour.

According to Laurie, there was a time when he was willing to recommend me to play for the All Blacks. He contends that he had to talk Mitchell into keeping me on when Mitch wanted to drop me in 2001.

One night during the week before our final Super 12 game, which we lost to the Queensland Reds 23–28 in Brisbane — it was the game when the match referee declined to consult the video ref when Tuilevu appeared to have forced the ball in the corner in the last movement of the game — I received a phone call saying that Laurie had announced his retirement and that confirmation would be in a story in the *Otago Daily Times* next morning. When we turned up for training everyone had read the paper and knew that Laurie had decided not to seek reappointment. To our general astonishment he never mentioned it. The players thought, well, Laurie's grabbed the headlines all right. Grandstanding till the end.

But, of course, it wasn't the end as far as Laurie and the rugby union were concerned.

In the week after the game against the Reds, Nichol, Middleton, Hoeft, myself, Steve Tew of the NZRU, the chairman of the Highlanders' board Colin Weatherall, and the CEO John Hornbrook, met to discuss our concerns and, in particular, what became known as the infamous 'players' letter'. Nichol says he considered proposing I not go along because he knew the knives were out for me. Nichol also asked Taine Randell along to that meeting. Randell's view of the contents of the letter — seven typewritten pages — was that he didn't share most of our concerns, which we all knew anyway, but that there were some areas that could be improved upon. Most of the team had been disappointed in Taine for some months. They felt he wasn't willing to speak up at all on their behalf. This may have been because he believed that a captain should never openly take issue with a coach's methods or behaviour towards his players. But what I knew for certain was that what most players found intolerable was tolerable to Taine.

Tew, Weatherall, Hornbrook and Nichol had another meeting and it wasn't long before it seemed that, in discussion with Mains, an agreement had been brokered that would have allowed Laurie to retire with dignity. The players sincerely wanted that to occur. They did not want to see the public humiliation or denunciation of anyone.

But then, just when it looked as if the agreement would be signed, John Hornbrook publicly came out with his comments that the players had been living in 'a climate of fear', and that the players' letter was like a 'letter from Dachau'. Unsurprisingly, Mains hit the roof and contacted a lawyer. The agreement was off.

Rob Nichol immediately issued a statement saying that Hornbrook's remarks did not come from the players, but nevertheless there were some 'significant concerns' that needed addressing. For reasons that weren't clear, Laurie told Nichol he took exception to his use of the word 'significant'.

In respect of the phrase 'climate of fear', if that means that I and others felt that freedom of thought, action and ideas was restricted, then for many of us life in the Highlanders was perceived to be like that. I was just one of many who thought that to show signs of opposition or disagreement was to risk damaging your career. That was a climate of fear all right.

In 2005 I was best man at Tony Brown's wedding: we are obviously very good friends. However, in 2003, until Middleton had heard that Mains was going to be reappointed I didn't know what Tony was thinking. No one talked to each other. To me, we were 26 isolated individuals, each one fearful of being the only one who felt dismayed.

Mains' lawyers went to the NZRU, as Hornbrook's employer, and alleged that their client had been defamed by Hornbrook. Rob Nichol, hearing that an agreement was being drafted whereby the parties to it would agree not to publicly discuss any of the events or issues in the Highlanders leading up to Hornbrook's now infamous remark about a climate of fear and the comparison with Dachau, expressly asked that the players be excluded from the terms of the agreement. An agreement was drawn up and a settlement reached. None of the players ever saw the agreement or agreed to anything in it. There is a contention that, as we were employed by the rugby union, we were bound to adhere to the terms of an agreement we hadn't, and still haven't, seen.

That struck many of us as outright gagging, unfair and tantamount to bullying.

At the time, the players in the Highlanders felt the NZRU had hung them out to dry. Publicly, our concerns went unheard, unreported. We were depicted as whingers and felt disenfranchised.

Hornbrook was only trying to publicly support the players as up until then no one had. We were not speaking to the media as mediations were taking place so Mains and his allies were taking pot-shots at us. We were like sitting ducks. The boys appreciated Hornbrook's intentions but to compare our problems to a Nazi concentration camp was ridiculous and offensive to many people on every level. I'm sure Hornbrook didn't find defending the players' integrity a chore. The rivalry between Hornbrook and Mains goes back decades and is said to have had its genesis in bitter encounters between Hornbrook's Zingari-Richmond and Mains' Southern club sides.

If the Highlanders' 2003 season had been one of earthquakes culminating in an eruption, for me the aftershocks were just as serious. In some quarters a concerted effort to discredit me continued.

In June, John Matheson, the journalist, not the surgeon and member of the Highlanders' board, published an article in *NZ Rugby World* in which he said that 'A form of insanity was spreading through Otago rugby like a virus.' He claimed that the 'lunacy was contagious' and that 'madness reigned'. The tale's characters, said Matheson, included a 'disgruntled former captain who held court over some of the team'. No prizes for guessing who the so-called 'disgruntled' guy was.

All Black coach John Mitchell got wind of the article before it went to print. He is said to have wanted 'to slam it down in front' of me at an All Black camp and warn me that if I so much as tried anything like that on there I'd be out on my ear.

The first thing to be said about Matheson's piece, which muddied me and my name all over the place, was that he never contacted me about it. And I can't find anyone within the Highlanders playing or management staff who will admit to having spoken to Matheson. The likes of Tony Brown, Simon Maling, Carl Hoeft, Kelvin Middleton, Sam Harding, Peter Bowden, Tom Willis, Josh Blackie and James Arlidge and Filipo Levi all say they didn't speak

How *NZ Rugby World* headlined their damning article on Otago rugby in 2003.

to Matheson; nor can they recall hearing of anyone who did. One tale doing the rounds — widely believed — was that Matheson got a substantial amount of his material courtesy of a long tape sent to him by someone closely associated with the coach. Mains himself says he was not Matheson's source.

Matheson's story was excoriating of me. It contained a mixture of fact and speculation — which is often the case with articles of that length — and was very much slanted Mains' way. Oliver the Bad Guy; Mains and Taine Randell, his 'loyal' captain, the Good Guys. The fact that Mitchell had seen the article just prior to its publication, and that the *Otago Daily Times* was invited, but declined, to run a section of it before it appeared in *NZ Rugby World*, tells quite a lot about the climate of rugby at the time.

Some people see him differently, but I never saw Laurie as one who appreciated being challenged. He bristled when confronted. More than one person in rugby has said to me that Laurie will not rest until he has prevailed over anyone who stands in the way of his aspirations. I think it more than likely that Laurie saw me as such a person. I think he also viewed me as someone who sowed the sort of disharmony that disturbs and works against the prospect of unity in a team. My response to that would be that in the Highlanders in 2002–03 Mains' coaching style, his attitude towards players, his training methods and his general demeanour created a general aura of disquiet and the steady erosion of morale. Of course, not all players felt exactly the same way, but I know that the majority were deeply dismayed, especially the senior players, including most of the Otago-based players. As for the draft/loan players, because they tended to be unfamiliar with the local scene and knew less of the history, they were inclined simply to take what was on offer and leave it at that.

The truth is that in 2003 players were coming to me; I wasn't going to them. For some time, if anything, I was trying to back away. Having people come to me was draining and really I needed all the energy I had to try to get back into the All Blacks. My heart was set on being a member of the winning team at the 2003 World Cup. Pissing coaches off is not the way to enhance your chances of selection, although you hope that playing ability will always be the principal criterion behind selections in any team.

There's no doubt that Laurie has given a lot to, and gained a lot from, rugby over many years. Simon Maling says he is sure that, in his way, Laurie sincerely believed that he was right and that he was doing what was best for Otago rugby. No doubt, too, that Mains has always been someone who polarises; some respect him and his methods, others don't.

It's interesting to read the blurb on the jacket of Bob Howitt and Robin McConnell's *Laurie Mains* (Rugby Press, 1996). There it says no coach has 'endured a greater love-hate relationship with the media' and none, 'probably, has been misunderstood more by the public'.

Mains, say the authors, was 'one of the game's great innovators'. That seems true of his heyday of coaching the All Blacks in the mid-1990s.

Clearly, some rugby people of consequence had, and still have, a lot of time for Laurie's abilities. All I can do is record what I felt about what I saw and experienced under Mains. In the end, my difficulties with Laurie cost me a great deal.

Most players and coaches have, or feel, a 'love-hate relationship with the media'. That usually comes from wanting to keep the media at arm's length a lot of the time. Most players are wary of the media because they see journalists and broadcasters as having the power to make or break them, and because, when they think criticism unfair or wrong, there's not much they can do to correct it.

Mains seems to have found the media insufficiently compliant at times. Unfortunately, others won't always sing our song. As for being 'misunderstood' by the public, I wonder. Some in Otago liked to see him as the quintessential Southern Man, a Messiah come back to save us. That *was* a misunderstanding, in my opinion.

As for Laurie being innovative, that was not my experience, nor was it how most of us found him in the Highlanders. To me, what he preached was often very much at odds with what he practised.

Chapter 13

Back to Beer and Fish 'n' Chips

After the Super 12, I thought my chances of returning to the All Blacks were minimal. And this was before the publication of John Matheson's infamously destructive article in *NZ Rugby World*, the Matheson who in an issue of the *Sunday News* in October 2004 called me rugby's 'bad boy'.

In 2003 I believed I was playing well enough to get back in, but it was clear that my playing ability wasn't the only — and possibly not the main — consideration. I felt a bit like a man with a criminal record, including a history of alleged coach molestation, turning up to apply for a job interview in front of a panel that nurtured grievances related to me. I had heard that Mitchell had his reservations about me on several counts, and it was clear that Mains was now strongly opposed. What I didn't know was how much notice, if any, Mitchell took of Mains' views of me; nor did I know what the other selectors thought.

What I did know was that none of the All Black selectors or coaches had contacted me during the Super 12. It was also disturbingly clear that some in rugby had put it about, or decided, that I was divisive and a troublemaker. I was sure that the majority of people in rugby didn't subscribe to that view but, as is often the case, it's not how many people are on your side, it's who.

As the Highlanders were not in the semi-finals of the Super 12 I had a couple of weeks in which to catch up on some business and visit a few friends. In Wellington I did some training with Andrew Beardmore, an old friend and trainer from Otago, and did a 3 km run to see where I was at; I had made some good improvements on my last effort.

I then went back to Wellington to spend time with my girlfriend. In the aftermath of Mains' resignation and John Hornbrook's unhelpful faux pas, there was a bit of a media frenzy. My cell phone was ringing on and off all day but I chose not to answer most calls, kept my head down and got on with my training. But Radio Sport reported that I had been seen at Wellington

Airport, therefore the likelihood was, it was said, that I was going to be reinstated as captain of the All Blacks. Another rumour I heard was the rugby union had had three or four different suits made just to be sure they'd have one that fitted whoever was appointed.

On the Sunday night after the Super 12 final I rang Simon Maling to ask if he'd heard from the selectors. He hadn't, nor had I. Previously, Mitchell had got flak after failing to call Taine Randell and tell him he'd been dropped. When it was suggested he'd been a bit insensitive and discourteous, he'd made the infamous remark that went something like 'Taine has my number.'

Maling and I were nervous; neither of us ever felt secure of our places in the All Blacks. The team was due to be announced at noon on Monday. I got up and went for a run, bought the *Dominion Post*, then went and had a few cups of tea with my girlfriend. When my phone rang I saw it was Simon. He was upset, more emotional than I'd heard him in the 10 years I'd known him. Mitch had rung and told him he was out. I was a bit shattered for him too. I thought he'd be a definite selection. We guessed that Brad Thorn had been preferred.

This was late in the morning. When my phone rang about half an hour later, and showed a private number, I knew it had to be Mitchell. He said, 'Congratulations, you are in the team.' I was both happy and amazed; I wasn't expecting to be picked. I was later told that up until the night before I had not been in the mix.

The All Black squad assembled at the Millennium Institute, the high-performance centre on the North Shore in Auckland. I was nervous, wondering how I would be received by many of the players, and, more especially, about what Mitchell might say. Understandably, given the friction in the Highlanders, I assumed I would be watched carefully by both management and senior players and was expecting to be told to shut up and shape up, or something like that, by Mitchell.

After photo shoots a group of us, Reuben Thorne, Richie McCaw, Dave Hewitt and Greg Somerville among them, went for coffee at an adjacent golf driving range. I was asked what had been going on in the Highlanders, so I gave them a run-down. Thorne slapped me on the back and said that I should take heart from the fact that the environment in the All Blacks was different. That was good reassurance from the skipper.

Soon after our media liaison man, Matt McIlraith, took me aside and said he'd seen a copy of an article about to appear in the monthly *NZ Rugby World*, and that it portrayed the Highlanders players, and me in particular, in a very bad light. This was the piece I referred to earlier, written by Matheson. I thought, 'Wonderful, at this time and in this situation, I need this like a hole in the head.'

I was in an unenviable position. Here I was back in the All Black squad but not as the captain that I had been before I'd ruptured my Achilles. I was unsure of what was expected of me. Though I tried to suppress it, I had this 'you're on borrowed time' feeling. And now, in a national rugby magazine, I was about to be depicted as the chief troublemaker among the players in the Highlanders.

When I took part in a photo shoot for Air New Zealand, somehow I ended up in the cockpit with Reuben Thorne and Richie McCaw. I saw that picture again in a paper after the World Cup team had been named and laughed at someone's suggestion that, unbeknown to me, I had been in the ejector seat. Before we went off to a training camp at Mount Maunganui, Reuben told myself, Tana Umaga and Justin Marshall that we would be his back-seat trio. I agreed to that and, initially, said little. But I did make a point of trying to get to know the younger players. I also sensed the team dynamic had changed. The Blues had beaten the Crusaders in the Super 12 final and the team featured quite a few very self-assured and confident Aucklanders. The Canterbury dominance had been broken and the balance of power seemed to have moved back to Auckland, though Reuben was still the captain.

At training I was not my usual self mentally, was unsure of what to say, how much or where and when to say it. Don't step on any toes was what I was thinking, and I became withdrawn. At lineout practice I soon found that both Chris Jack and Ali Williams got up much higher than our Highlander boys, so I adjusted to that. At training, both Mitchell and Deans offered confusing advice regarding my tackling and ball-carrying techniques. Later, I asked them to clarify what they were saying. That didn't go down well: my question was met with blank stares and few words, so I decided not to do that again. Then on our day off I went for an extra run up the Mount with Carl Hoeft and trainer Mike Anthony, my fitness improving all the time.

Tana, Justin, Reuben and I had a meeting with the manager, Tony Thorpe. There were a few issues that needed sorting out, including Doc Mayhew's contentious recommendation that players be breath-tested on Sunday mornings. We all disagreed with the proposed breath-testing. Just how much booze would be deemed too much? Given the culture, it was a really grey area.

Justin was dead against telling the players what they could or couldn't do. He said let the boys go out and enjoy their wins and have a good time. I didn't disagree with the sentiment behind that, but said that seeing we were only together for about three weeks, giving up excessive alcohol intake for that period of time wasn't much to ask. The discussion centred round the fact that we had a few players who would be playing their first tests and that the tradition was that they got properly pissed afterwards. I said that it would be a good idea if we dropped that practice. But Tana reminded me that I'd got pretty drunk after my first test. I told him and the others that Tana's memory was correct but, surely, times change and, as professionals, shouldn't we be acting accordingly? Not all traditions are worth maintaining, I said; we should be looking to progress. I was very much in favour of a bit more moderation, while leaving the decisions over to players until they stuffed up. For some, working out just how to celebrate and enjoy their wins remained a problem. I said I had no objection to the guys getting drunk, if they really wanted to, but couldn't it wait until after the third of our three tests, the game against the French?

Justin wouldn't go along with that at all. Reuben had said very little.

I left the meeting feeling that I was a bit out of step, certainly with Justin, and possibly with Reuben. They were obviously comfortable with the way things were. Afterwards I tried to mollify Justin a bit as he clearly felt strongly about it, and I hadn't meant to offend him. I wished we'd had an informal chat about it before we met the manager. It looked as if senior players had divergent views and I feared that I could be seen as stirring up a happy camp, and that this would be taken straight back to the coaches. But I wasn't trying to rock the boat, simply setting out to be constructive. That's what meetings are for.

At the captain's run before the test against England in Wellington I was tense, very nervous. After I had finished my work I sat and watched some of the others do their drills. Most were relaxed, were enjoying themselves. Some were laughing. What a contrast to the Highlanders. I recalled our physio Pete Gallagher saying, in reference to the Highlanders, that 'we were a sour lot in 2002 and 2003'. A coach's mood is often reflected by the team.

Ah, the lull before the storm. The weather on match day was terrible, some of the worst in which I had played a test. The wind was all over the place, which made lineouts exceedingly difficult, but all things considered they weren't too bad on the day and we got our share of ball.

I played adequately but it was a case of 'could have done better'. Too much thinking and not enough instinctive reaction perhaps. The England forwards piled into breakdowns in numbers and killed a lot of our ball. I'd been told to make myself available, to stand off as a possible runner. In the conditions, and against the England side, I'd have been better to get stuck into rucks and mauls and move a few of them out of the way.

I tried not to rock the boat with Mitch and Robbie in 2003. On this occasion I failed.

When their scrum was a man down — they had a forward sent to the sin bin — we had scrum after scrum on their line. We all huddled around Reuben and he told us to scrum them, push them back over the line. I was dying to say, 'No, that's silly, let's manipulate the scrum defence as they don't have a full back row.' We were eating up valuable time trying to out-scrum them. And it was a very tight game, England leading 15–13, so it was there for the taking. But I didn't want to usurp Reuben's position so I said nothing. Yet another example of me being uncertain of my role. I should have spoken up.

In Hamilton, Wales offered little opposition: 55–3 to the All Blacks. I roomed with Richie McCaw and, as is always the case, if you room with one Canterbury forward you room with them all. They all visit each other. As a team they appear close, seem to care about each other. Stories abound of them calling in to see each other when at home in Christchurch. All this is at the root of their success; that and the fact they have very good players. Richie has his pilot licence and took some team-mates flying on his day off. In Hamilton, he hired a plane, flew to Raglan for lunch and was back by 1 p.m.

When we got to Christchurch I learned that I would be in the starting 15 again for the test against the French. We were wary of their lineout because they have tall loose forwards, which makes a big difference, and as a group have a habit of terrorising opposition lineouts. They pose a lot of problems for the player — in our case Thorne — who makes the calls, and this often means that the lifters, jumpers and the thrower have to rush. Hookers get quite anxious about all this because the blame for imprecision at lineouts is invariably dumped at the door of the throwers.

Helping Justin Marshall from the field after he tore a hamstring in the test against England at Wellington in 2003.

Less attention is paid to errors elsewhere, possibly because most other plays aren't starting from a static situation. But lineouts are far from static; there's a lot of haring about and varying degrees of confusion.

After the pre-match media session on the Wednesday I had a chat to several of the journalists. The *New Zealand Herald*'s Wynne Gray was among them. I told him that his piece on the tension and disquiet within the Highlanders during the Super 12 had given the team a huge lift, opened the door to the possibility that some relief might be on its way. I heard quite a lot of chuckling around us. The years of infighting within Otago rugby had been a constant source of amusement and bemusement for the media outside the region.

At the kick-off in the test I got a helluva boot in the thigh and it was extremely sore. Players call such a blow a 'charlie'. I was limping from then on; I definitely couldn't sprint. If it were not for the unwritten law that in tests players don't go off for such things, I'd have considered more seriously how effective I was and perhaps have come off. Despite the injury I thought I was playing better and had greater energy, was in the game more than I had been in the test against the English. But our scrum was poor that day, exerted no pressure on the French scrum and our lineout was scrappy. My first throw to Chris Jack wasn't high enough, their jumper got in front of him, and from then on they were very disruptive at lineouts. Calls were being changed and we were rushing them. But overall my throwing was poor.

It came as no surprise when I was subbed 10 minutes into the second half, but when Thorne

Above and opposite page: Making progress against the French at Jade Stadium in late June 2003. This would be my last test start under John Mitchell and Robbie Deans. I was surplus to requirements for the Tri-nations tournament and the World Cup in Australia.

immediately started calling for flat throws to number two in the line, I was pissed off and thought, 'Why didn't you start calling them earlier?'

Usually, players are not pleased to be subbed off. I'm no different. But on this occasion I felt calm as I walked off the ground. A sense of serenity swept over me. In a way it was a welcoming feeling, and it came, I think, from a pre-match premonition that tonight might be it. Leaving Jade Stadium I felt certain that this was to be my last test for the All Blacks. I didn't feel defeated, didn't feel despairing or embittered or angry, I just felt . . . well, that's it.

My leg was seriously sore. Once it cooled down I was hobbling around and couldn't jog for a week. An eerie throbbing kept me awake at night as well as for the next two weeks. That first night after the game I sought relief in the hotel pool. Ali Williams and I wallowed around and waffled. Ali said, 'Mate, I'm a goner.' I said, 'Mate, you're okay. But I am definitely a goner.'

Next day, at a team meeting before we dispersed, the coaches gave us framed photos of ourselves. As Mitch handed me mine I knew by the look on his face that it was all over for me.

Once home, and as soon as I was able to train, I kept doing the extra work, for I knew that my fitness was almost back to where it should be.

On the Sunday morning I was lounging around the flat with Simon Maling and Goldie (Jeff Wilson) when Simon answered the phone and handed it to me. He said, 'I think it's Mitch.' The memory is vivid. I took the phone and went to my room. Mitchell said, 'Just ringing to confirm your non-selection for the Tri-nations.' I thought that a strange way of phrasing it. He said that

my lineout throwing was poor, my defence was poor, I wasn't running with the ball enough and lacked dynamism, and my work rate needed improving. Now, I accept that at times my lineout throwing has been iffy, but when he came out with all that other stuff I felt like it was a set-up. Then I asked him who had been picked instead; he said Mark Hammett.

Mark is a mate of mine. We've spent a lot of time together in All Black teams. In fact, most of my career was spent fighting for the hooker's start berth with 'Hammer'. But I reckon I would shade Mark as a runner and defender. He was a good front-on defender but not as good laterally. Our work rates were about the same and over the course of the year my throwing was better. I just thought that Mitchell's reasons didn't make sense.

It hit me that there would probably be no World Cup campaign for me. That was pretty devastating and it hurt. I must have been clinging to a faint hope after all but I also knew that Simon and others had been through this, and that I just had to accept it and move on. The phone went all day. Greg Cooper called and suggested I should talk to all the media next day. It was the last thing I wanted to do but I obliged. At training the place was crawling with media people. One of the interviews was for the *Holmes* show, aired at seven o'clock later that night, where my words and attitude got a big tick from the public.

As always seems to be the way, I took refuge in Central Otago. Chippies and a plasterer were working on renovating my cottage near St Bathans. The plasterer in particular needed a labourer so I worked with him for most of the week. The simple labouring-type work without extra worries was just what I needed at the time. On the builder's radio some fans were for me, some against. Rugby's great when it's going well, cruel when it isn't. Sure, I was getting criticism, but I took the view that I got paid plenty, so tough bickies.

One day, when working away by myself, I took a shovel and had a toilet break on the hillside among the trees and, on a very quiet, crisp and still winter's day, thought, 'It's not the end of the world.'

'One of the toughest' – Andrew Mehrtens

Talking about some coaches' propensities, Mehrtens reckons that one or two he's known have 'obsessive preoccupation with video analysis. If you look at video replays for long enough you will always find evidence to support your preconceived views of any player . . . As for Anton, of course you could find video clips to show he got stopped with the ball in hand. But everyone does. Anton's still one of the toughest all-round forwards we've got. The opposition target him because he's so feared, respected.'

'Wayne Smith is straight up. You knew what he expected.'

Mehrtens said that he's been in teams where 'most players' were 'scared to speak up' because they knew that if they did they would be 'vulnerable'.

Oliver was 'renowned as a thinking person, one who spoke his mind. He led by example.'

Mitchell went public with my perceived weakness — the four areas of inadequacy — and while it hurt a lot I realised that he was in a no-win situation. Some of the public would have criticised Mitchell justifying his decision through the media, just as they had when he talked about Christian Cullen's perceived weakness. On the other hand, he was going to get hauled over the coals for not saying anything, leaving the non-selection open to heated debate and conjecture. Mitchell and Deans were in a bind and I didn't and still don't hold any grudge over the incident. It is part of being a professional rugby player: you are in the spotlight and unfortunately have to take it on the chin in front of four million people. We get paid a bloody good wage compared to the average income and it simply goes with the territory. It's all 'character building', as they say.

In my media interviews I said that I would be working on improving in those four areas of deficiency that Mitchell had mentioned, but knew these words to be futile: I mean to say, of the 26 players chosen for the recent three tests only one had been dropped for the upcoming Tri-nations — me. Despite this I kept training really hard and by the time the World Cup squad was chosen my fitness levels were back to their best. In some cases they were my personal bests. This was what had always been in my mind from the time I returned to rugby after injury, that I would be in peak condition for the World Cup. Not much point, though, if you're not in the team.

On the Saturday, a fortnight after playing a test for the All Blacks, I turned out in a second-division country rugby match as the blindside flanker for my old club Toko in Milton in South Otago. Up until then I had played for the University club in town but thought I could do more to help rugby in the south if I went back to where I used to live, and play for my first ever club. It was a hard decision to leave the University club but I told the administrators that they had enough 'profile players' and as I hadn't played for several years they were not going to miss my services on the pitch. They were fine with my decision as they could see that I was trying to do what I could for rugby in the country, raise its profile, and pass on whatever rugby knowledge I had. The word had got around and 500 people turned up to watch, the biggest crowd in years. This voyage back to grass-roots rugby was opportune. It refocused me at a time when I was battling to cope with rejection. The fact that the All Blacks started to play some very good rugby heightened my sense of loss. I asked Tana Umaga what he attributed their good form to and he said that the public squabbling over bonus payments for the World Cup had had a strong bonding effect. When they won the Tri-nations and the Bledisloe I was pleased for them but also envious; I'd been wanting to do that double for so long. And when I saw some comments from Laurie Mains saying that Mark Hammett's presence had had a major positive effect on the All Black team culture, I took that as another low blow from him, and typical.

But back to playing for Toko. I turned up to training and realised I'd forgotten to bring a towel. I was used to being supplied with everything. Same with the club socks; I borrowed a pair for the game then bought them. The local boys were mostly unknown to me and, even though the fact that I'd dropped by for a couple of sessions with them the year before had helped break the ice, I was still a bit nervous as to how I would be received. And where to play? I told the coach that I'd play anywhere. That was just as well as our captain, one of the best players, was also the hooker. The last thing I wanted to do was oust him.

The Toko boys really enjoyed their work at training. They had each other on and seemed sincerely to like each other's company. At a time when I was struggling to retain my connection with the game it was just what I needed. The first training session astonished me. Full contact, no holds barred. I thought, 'What are these idiots up to? Shouldn't you be saving this for the weekend?' Brothers were smashing into brothers, workmates were barrelling into workmates. But it was all gusto; they were immersed in the game and enjoying themselves fully.

The coach's team talk included more than 30 'fucks' in almost as many seconds. We all made do with whatever gear was available; strapping tape was pretty scarce. There were still seven or eight big empty beer bottles on the table in the shed from the previous week. The Toko boys struck me as passionate for their team. I loved that. They weren't there because of money, or fame, or to score a good-looking chick, things that I had grown to dislike intensely about some in the scene I'd been part of for years. All the old so-called clichés about the essence and spirit of the game residing in grass-roots rugby rang true: here, in the Toko club's shed under the old wooden grandstand on the outskirts of Milton, South Otago, population about 2000, at a ground where my first vivid memories of rugby belong. There were no journalists and broadcasters, no microphones, and no sponsors looking for attention or exposure. It felt as if I had tapped into long-forgotten memories of rugby as it was for me in an age long ago. In representative and All Black teams players are often scornful of grass-roots rugby. I had occasionally let slip a disdainful comment of my own. Now I felt a touch of shame remembering that, and a need to make amends.

After Thursday training the Toko boys usually had a few beers in their changing shed. As the new boy it was up to me to shout. They may have been having me on, I'm not sure, but I went and bought a couple of trays of Speight's. When I plonked them down a few guys moaned about there being no DB. I pondered for a few seconds then said, 'Get stuffed. I'm paying, I'll decide.' This was met with raucous laughter. Before I left I asked the boys which was the best fish and chip shop in town and grabbed a parcel to eat on the 40-minute drive back to the big smoke, Dunedin. Ripping a hole in the wrapping paper so the chips didn't get cold reminded me that I did the same thing after practice in Blenheim, only in those days I was riding a bike home. Nonetheless, it felt like I had come full circle. There's something to be said for nostalgia; it can alter your perspective for the better, and in this case it reminded me of my own roots, and the roots of the game.

My last game for Toko in 2003 was against Clinton. We all chipped in for the cost of taking a bus to Clinton about an hour's drive south-west between Balclutha and Gore. Several wives and partners came along. For the first 40 I played open-side flanker; in the second half I was at tighthead prop. Saturday was a real family rugby day for the Toko team. Some of them went and watched their kids play in the morning, or coached them, then turned out for Toko in the afternoon. There was quite a lot of travelling required but they seemed to thrive on it. In the country the changing sheds were rudimentary, the rugby balls were different, and the grounds idiosyncratic. When a goal was kicked in Clinton the ball had to be retrieved from among stock in the nearby paddock. After matches both captains stood up and said pretty much the same things — the infamous thanks to the ladies out the back was a given — and there was always a decent meal available to fill you up for five dollars. No affectation or pretension here.

Some South Otago teams had their own song which they sang after the speeches. I had to learn ours quickly. I kept realising how long I had been away from this. Swept up in professionalism since the age of 19, I hadn't even played a game of club footie for six years. And as a student in Dunedin I'd hung out mostly with young people who weren't faced with the pressures and responsibilities of paying the mortgage and bringing up children on usually modest incomes. It was a foreign world.

So playing for Toko was an antidote and a welcome interlude before I began playing for Otago again in the NPC. It was a tense time, initially, for many if not most had been gutted by the events throughout and at the end of the Super 12 series. To me, and others, Laurie Mains' legacy was a kind of collective depression which we were having to struggle through.

The players still felt hung out to dry by the NZRU, the Highlanders' board and the Otago union. No one was prepared to air our specific complaints and concerns generally. The Otago administration had sheltered behind the fact that it wasn't responsible for the affairs of the Highlanders franchise, and we were left to appear a bunch of thin-skinned, disaffected, pampered and petulant smart alecks with our personal interests only at heart. A lot of the guys felt drained by that and thought, 'What's the point?'

The new coaching staff, Greg Cooper, Wayne Graham and John Haggart, worked hard both to settle things down and stimulate the squad. Cooper and Graham, initially, decided not to drive us too hard. Basically, the Mains way was not the way it was going to be from then on.

Personally, the experience of playing for Toko re-energised me and I played some good football in the early rounds, especially in our wins against Auckland and Canterbury in Dunedin. I was determined to play well in that period before the World Cup team was announced. We won our first four games in the competition.

We had training on the Monday the All Black squad for the World Cup was to be announced. Maling, McDonnell and Tom Willis turned up in the morning and said they had all had the wrong phone call. I was surprised to hear that Tom hadn't made it; I had expected he would.

After practice my cell phone showed that I'd missed a call. I assumed it was Mitchell. When I got home I called him. His line was engaged — some other hopeful was probably getting the message — and left a message to say that I think you've been trying to get me, to say I'm not in the team, and thanks for ringing. He rang me back and we had a frank talk. I wished him all the best for the World Cup campaign, said I was pleased we had the Bledisloe and the Tri-nations back. I said at the time I was quite jealous, then happy for the boys. I think we were both pleased by the tenor of the conversation, even though I still didn't believe that my omission was solely based on playing ability.

At training that day I said to the boys who had missed out, 'It's not every day you miss the cut on making an All Black team for a World Cup. We'd better give it a nudge today.' A memory from eight years before flooded back. Then, I didn't see myself as in the hunt for a place at the 1995 World Cup, but my team-mates Stu Forster, Arran Pene and Stephen Bachop had had high hopes. We were in the North Island when they got the bad news so we had a few consolatory drinks and then a few more at Stu's place when we got home to Dunedin. So after training in 2003 a crowd of us headed off to the Gardies Tavern to sup and watch for the announcement of the team on TV. We wanted to know who *had* made it. As neither Tom nor I had been picked, we assumed Andrew Hore would have been. But, no, Corey Flynn's name was read out. That was certainly a surprise. In an interview, Paul Holmes asked Flynn when he first knew he'd made the team. Whereupon Tony Brown, always quick with a quip when he'd had a few beers, yelled out, 'When I signed up for Canterbury.' A lot of the Scarfies in the tavern cracked up when they heard that. What Brown was alluding to, of course, was the widely held view that the Crusaders boys always had a better-than-even chance of making All Black sides.

From then on the season was a struggle for me and, even though — with a couple of bad losses — we ended up top qualifiers in the NPC, my spirit was broken. When I was dropped from the All Black squad for the Tri-nations, even though I knew I was a goner, I couldn't let myself give up trying both physically and mentally. For four years I had been looking forward to playing in the 2003 World Cup but now all really was lost. I had started out the number-one choice in the first test of the year against England; now I wasn't even in the back-up squad for the World Cup — my ranking was about sixth best in the country. That was a clear indication that my axing wasn't all about on-field issues; Mitchell and Deans simply didn't want me. Instead of putting a line through my name with a biro they did it with a paint brush.

We lost to Waikato in Hamilton, an-all-too common occurrence, then were humiliated 49–18 by North Harbour at Carisbrook. Cooper told me he had begun to doubt whether our captain Kelvin Middleton was playing well enough to retain his place. I had only just enough energy to keep myself going, and barely that at times, but saw the need to do something there. Armed with a dozen Speight's I went round to Kelvin's place, had a chat to him, and started trying to help him out a bit more on and off the field. We had a senior players' meeting at Cooper's house and

Battered and bruised after another NPC campaign with Otago. 2003 was a tough year.

he wanted answers. The consensus was that we weren't doing enough hard work at training and that we had become a bit soft. So we upped the intensity and won the next three games against Northland, Wellington and Taranaki.

The semi-final against Auckland at Carisbrook was a good game of rugby that Auckland won 39–33. At one point I threw a pass to Josh Blackie but he didn't try to catch it; he thought it was meant for someone else. The ball was scooped up and Auckland ran 70 m to score. I got subbed halfway through the second half. Up until then I thought it had been one of my best games and it was an extremely disappointing end to such a terrible year.

The season over, I went into 'make the most of it' mode for those few weeks every year before it was back into training for the next Super 12. I put in four 14-hour days painting my cottage in Central Otago. Then, after two weeks in Wellington with my partner, it was on to Auckland where I did a Cure Kids promotion. I watched the All Blacks' World Cup semi-final at Philips' offices (a major sponsor of Cure Kids) with a whole lot of sick children and their parents. After Australia won, the spectre of our loss to France at Twickenham came back to haunt me. I remembered the creep of bewilderment, the aura of disbelief and despair. My thoughts went out to our boys — I knew what they would be feeling — although this loss was more of a strangulation compared to the mugging the French had given us.

Next day, before I headed back south, I was having brunch in Ponsonby when I overheard a passer-by say, 'There's Anton Oliver; he must be laughing.' I wasn't, but it raised a smile.

The year had been a tough one, too, for my girlfriend, who was living and working in Wellington. We'd been trying to keep the relationship alive at a geographical distance — I'm not sure that she quite appreciated the extent of the pressures I'd been under, nor the importance to me of the issues. At the end of the year that relationship was over too. In a way if, at the start of the year, someone had offered me $30 and a dozen oysters to take 2003 down to the works and get rid of it, I reckon I would have taken it.

Chapter 14

An Atrocious Start to 2004

Until fairly recently — 2001 really — it seldom occurred to me that giving straight answers to questions isn't always appreciated. I saw candour as refreshing and desirable, and thought that those who talked of the need to be diplomatic had a point only if that meant avoiding being unduly insensitive or offensive. Unfortunately, 2004 started off in a rather unpleasant manner for me when an honest reply to a question from a journalist caused a bit of a stir.

At the Highlanders pre-season camp in Queenstown I did my first interviews of the year; they were also the first interviews I had given where I had said anything about the previous year's problems. Nathan Burdon of the *Southland Times* asked a question along the lines of, 'So what is different about the Highlanders this year compared with last year?'

I said that from my point of view the playing environment in 2003 was 'atrocious'. At the time I didn't think, 'Whoops, I shouldn't have said that', or, 'Careful, fella, dangerous ground.' I just gave an honest answer and got on with my day.

After Burdon's piece appeared, someone representing Laurie Mains alerted the NZRU. The word 'atrocious' wasn't well received. Next thing I knew, my lawyer, Warren Alcock, came up to me at training and handed me a piece of paper from the NZRU accusing me of bringing the game into disrepute. I was angry with Laurie and saw him as trying to suppress comment on what had gone on in the Highlanders. At this point it seemed to me that the New Zealand union was siding with Laurie and that angered me. I couldn't see how my remarks were dishonouring or discrediting the game, and I wondered why so many seemed to be running scared. I thought, 'Does anyone have any balls round here?'

Of course, atrocious is a strong word. But so what? The fact that it popped out was an indication of the cumulative effect the team environment had had on me and many others the previous season. A little later it was suggested that the New Zealand union's advisers may have been of the view that by using the word 'atrocious' I may have been implying a link between that and Hornbrook's analogy with Dachau. I was not.

I could easily see that someone might take Hornbrook's analogy with Dachau as offensive but none of the players, including me, had ever said that or alluded to anything like it. Actually I thought it a ridiculous comparison. Many of us were fearful, though, of speaking our minds, and also aware that you had to be very careful about what you said and to whom. The walls in the prefab building housing the offices and the player's lounge at Logan Park are thin.

The NZRU clearly felt under pressure and I was informed that they were looking at whether my remark constituted serious or minor misconduct. I had to employ one of Alcock's colleagues, Diccon Sim, to represent me. The NZRU decided that my so-called 'breach' had been minor, so I received a warning and a note was put on my file, but I still had to pay my lawyer's fees of $2000. I thought the complaint was juvenile — like being in a sandpit arguing over who had the biggest digger — and still believe I had a right to say what I did.

Since when, I wondered, does robust public discussion bring a game into disrepute? Quite

The claret is in free-flow . . . and this was just a pre-season game before Super 12 2004.

the opposite, I'd have thought. Nevertheless, I can see why the rugby union would take the position that it pursued the issue of its own volition and was not influenced by any other party. How complicated legal arguments become.

Greg Cooper, the Highlanders' coach, was unfazed. But I apologised to Coops and said that the last thing I wanted to do was splatter our 2004 campaign with muck from the past. The 2004 Highlanders had a poor season. We were nearly there often but we gave away too many turnovers and our ball handling was poor at crucial times. And our defence wasn't as punishing as it had been during periods when we'd had more success. We won only four games of the 11 played, and drew one.

Cooper and Phil Young, his assistant coach, were, understandably, feeling their way a bit and when the going got tough I was asked to help out in all sorts of ways. I was the person with the most experience of the franchise. Donny Cameron, Pete Gallagher and Alex McKenzie have all said that I took on a few matters that a captain doesn't normally get burdened with and that the new coaching staff relied on me heavily. I got weighed down with these extra concerns and over the years I think this has been my Achilles heel at times. The result was that my enthusiasm for the game waned; I lacked some of my old zest. And while I played well enough I had played better and it was a relief when the season ended.

Our last game was against the Blues in Auckland where we got thrashed. When we got back to Dunedin Airport, Des Smith handed me his cell phone and said Graham Henry wanted to talk to me. Henry was the new All Black coach replacing Mitchell after the All Blacks' failed attempt at world rugby's Everest, the Webb Ellis Trophy. It was with much amusement that I watched Mitchell try to retain his coaching job of the All Blacks. He had trumpeted that his tenure would be judged on his results and that was fine by him. With no World Cup in the NZRU Wellington headquarters he was judged all right, and no matter how successful the All Blacks had been up until that point his tenure depended on bringing back the World Cup to New Zealand.

Back on the phone to the new All Black coach, Henry said that I wasn't in his All Black team and that the Barbarians selectors had been chasing him, wanting to know if I would be available to play for them in matches in the UK.

I wasn't surprised to be told I wasn't in the All Blacks. In my heart I knew that in order to be worthy of being an All Black I had to play better and that was all that mattered to me.

Everything had become a huge struggle. I was altogether too equivocal about rugby and its importance to me — in fact its importance in general. Cynicism and bemusement . . . those things were there in far greater measure than ever before. I'd tired of the rugby kitchen and it was partly, too, because I'd become aware of other kitchens that looked damned interesting and attractive. Rugby had become insufficiently nourishing; I'd gone off the ingredients and didn't at all fancy the behaviour of some of the cooks.

So I flew off to the UK to join the Baabaas feeling pretty sure that the 2004 NPC would mark the end of my rugby career. But I got a boost from the tour. I had some fun and the trip made me realise that I wasn't sour on rugby in general, it was rugby in New Zealand that I was not enamoured with. Maybe I still had some desire left; maybe playing rugby outside New Zealand wasn't the negative experience that I had perceived it to be.

We assembled at Pennyhill Park Hotel in Surrey. I remembered it from the 1999 World Cup. Former Wallaby coach Bob Dwyer was in charge and Taine Randell was the captain. At our first meeting, Dwyer said that we'd been chosen because of our individual records and the respect that we had earned from the wider rugby community, the sort of respect that comes from performance over many years. He said that in the eyes of our peers we could lose or tarnish all of that in the next three weeks if our attitude wasn't right. That meant if we drank too much and failed to prepare properly for our games.

Dwyer's remarks hit home with a thump. When I thought of my career in rugby, and how it looked as if it was going to end with a whimper, I saw how important it had been for me to be respected both as a person and as a player. Nothing else compared or counted anywhere near as much. And while I had no idea what the players from other nations in the Barbarians thought of me, I wasn't going to let myself down by behaving like an idiot.

Then there was the realisation that the trip gave me the chance to meet lots of players I had only ever played against. Here was a fantastic opportunity to mix and mingle and get to know the personalities behind the mouth guards.

Matt Burke, Mark Andrews and Ollie le Roux were great storytellers and amusing all-round characters. I liked the Australian Nathan Grey too — a good man — and the Irish boys were lots of fun and always up for a pint. And I roomed with Taine Randell for a few days. Relations between us had become strained the previous year. Before the 2003 Super 12 competition began, Laurie had helped Taine obtain extra money as an incentive to encourage him to stay on in Otago. When news of this payment spread through the squad later it caused ripples. In Otago, in the late 1990s a transparent tiered system had been set up whereby everyone knew what tier their mates were on and, thus, what payments others were getting. When myself and other players heard that Taine had been given an ex-gratia payment we were upset.

It was the first time I had talked to him since the fallout in the Highlanders. I knew we were polar opposites in this matter and I thought I would be angry with him. But you can never

Being selected for the Barbarians in the middle of 2004 gave me a chance to catch up with Taine Randell. It was the first time I had talked to him since the fallout in the Highlanders . . . you can never get angry with Taine.

get really angry with Taine; he is so indifferent, and sometimes oblivious, to so much that it is impossible to hold a grudge against him. I told him that I was writing a book with Brian Turner — which he knew — and that he, Mains and Mitchell were the only people who had declined to talk to Brian. He said he would rather let sleeping dogs lie.

I played in our first game against the Scots, which we won. Then we played Wales and got thrashed. I came off the bench to replace Matt Sexton who was to retire after the tour. Sexton was one person I would have liked to have had more to do with when playing in New Zealand. He struck me as an honest, sincere man and we got on extremely well. Our final game was against an English selection that we beat at Twickenham and I had the honour of captaining the side. I scrummed with Kobus Visagie and Jason Leonard and we combined well: both are down-to-earth, good people.

After the tour I went through the main art galleries in London and then on to both Oxford and Cambridge to inspect them so that I would have an idea of what they had to offer if I managed to secure a place to study in the UK in 2005 or 2006. Then I visited my brother Brent in Bordeaux and we spent a few days in San Sebastian in Spain before I came home.

I had to come back for pre-NPC training with Otago. We had only 12 players at the first training and just a handful of them were to be in the side. Returning from France and Spain to take part in that wasn't thrilling, but since it was part of my job as the new captain I didn't complain. I played half a dozen games as a loose forward for the Toko club and really enjoyed it. They were, I thought, my last appearances in club football in New Zealand. But those games made me feel I might still have enough enthusiasm and energy to play one more Super 12 season, become the first New Zealander to clock up 100 games there, and tidy up all the loose ends in rugby in my homeland.

Around this time I met Chris Lonsdale, a Canadian student who was playing club football with my flatmate Duncan Blaikie while doing a PhD in sports psychology at Otago. We decided he could help me motivate myself and build on the benefit I'd got from the Baabaas and the Toko club. This helped keep me afloat longer than would otherwise have been the case, but nothing could have plugged the leaks that sprung as the NPC season pitched and rolled along.

Winter came in late and hard in Dunedin. We trained in terrible conditions for about a month. Snow and hail several times, bog and mush all the time.

Coupled with this I picked up a bad flu, which made me lose five kilos and, through sickness, miss my first Otago or Highlanders practice in 11 years. The nasty weather conditions persisted and I suffered from that viral affliction for the first four or five games of the competition. I felt lethargic and struggled to put any weight back on.

Things went from bad to worse on and off the field. Our ranks were thinned by injuries and everyone was struggling: coaches, management, players, me! Wayne Graham and John Haggart were new to their coaching jobs. But I had learnt from the Super 12. I was not going to get bogged down, not get too involved with others' problems. I figured the best thing I could do was play well on the field and lead by example, so that is where I put all of my energies.

It was quite calculated and in some ways selfish, but I had been down the other path before and didn't want to go back there.

It paid off for me personally. My play was good, particularly in the second half of the competition. I was our top try scorer for the year (five out of 20) and was named Otago player of the season.

During the 2004 NPC I realised that I would have to make a big decision about 2005 and whether I wanted to come back for the Highlanders again. Time and again since 2001 rugby had lost much of its allure for me. Greg Cooper had been great after I didn't get picked for the All Blacks early in 2004. He rang me up and said that from there on I had to start making choices based on what was best for me, not everyone else. He said that for too long I had been putting other things first. It was a tremendous gesture and I will always be grateful to him for pointing that out.

Leading up to the last game of the year against Auckland I couldn't sleep. For four nights in a row I had to take sleeping pills to get to sleep and thought this can't go on. This was to be my last game for Otago, of that I was certain, and while I didn't want anyone making a big thing of it publicly, I was still highly emotional about it. And the reason I couldn't concentrate fully on the upcoming game was that I was agonising over whether I should have one final Super 12 series for the Highlanders. A lot of people, including Greg Cooper, and my old friend Tony Gilbert, who had returned to work for Otago from a coaching stint in Scotland, were keen to know. I felt intense pressure: would I be letting down the rugby fraternity in the province that I knew best and had played for from the time I arrived to attend university in the early 1990s? Would it be fair — or look bad — to leave when Otago seemed to be at a nadir? Even more importantly, what was best for me?

On the Tuesday night team-mates Carl Hayman, Neil Brew and I went for a surf at Aramoana — well, they surfed and I drowned, as surfing was new to me. I came in from the sea earlier than them, got changed and went for a walk. Once home, I rang a few friends and asked for their opinion but then realised that it really wasn't needed; I had listened to my heart and it said don't come back. I figured you have to look to be happy in life and I didn't want to devote another six months simply to reach the 100-game milestone and to sanction the belief that I might be able to help out a struggling franchise. The Highlanders would be okay without me. This was it, all done — spent.

I told my parents that night, swallowed another dose of sleeping pills and got some shut-eye. Next day I plucked up the courage and went to see Coops. It was damned hard driving down to Carisbrook. I was so emotional, but he was understanding and accepting. He didn't try to dissuade me.

I got on with the job and we played Auckland at Eden Park. Our forwards were committed, our lineout worked well, and our backs turned on easily their best performance of the season. It was Simon Maling's finale as well and the team wanted to play well for him and to try to make amends for a disastrous session and finish on a high. With three minutes to play we had an 11-point lead and few would have believed we could lose from there. Auckland kicked off and one of our forwards was penalised, said to have been slow to release the ball after taking it down from the restart.

They kicked it out in the corner and scored from the lineout. The conversion went over. Then with time up, after a lineout near halfway, one of our players went for an intercept, tipped it on and the ball was transferred to Joe Rokocoko who took it at full pace on the cut and scored under our posts. Another heartbreaking loss to Auckland. Devastated is too weak a word for what I felt. I hated watching the jubilation in the Auckland ranks and was one of the first back

Joe Rokocoko has just scored for Auckland in our final NPC match of 2004. The try denied us the opportunity of beating Auckland for the first time on Eden Park since 1976. At the time I thought this would be my last game in New Zealand.

inside our changing shed. Sighting a table laden with drinks and a chilly bin full of ice, I heaved it over and bottles and ice went everywhere. I then stormed off into a corner where I ran out of steam, found myself on the floor in a praying-to-Mecca position where I cried, a broken man. It was everything coming out, all the emotion from the last week, the season, the years of results like the one I had just experienced, and apparently I was muttering, 'Why can't we fucking win? Is it that hard?'

Back in Dunedin, I prepared to leave 11 years of life behind. It felt both dislocating and liberating. I pushed thoughts of 'It's over', 'Was it worth it?' and 'How important was it really?' into the background. On the Monday I drove into Central Otago again, saw a few old mates, worked on revising sections of this book, did some work around my cottage near St Bathans, had a few beers and a big meal at Mike and Jude Kavanagh's, licensees at St Bathans' Vulcan Hotel. I looked forward to a few fishing trips into the mountains, to places I'd never seen, to a bit more freedom and variety in my life. Rugby was done.

Apart from having to be back in Dunedin for a press conference on Friday to tell everyone that I was not coming back next year, and that that was it for me and rugby in New Zealand, there were no other commitments I could see. However, the great God Dilemma was, unbeknown to me, preparing another visitation. I was sitting in an old armchair on Brian Turner's porch on the Tuesday, reading a manuscript, when he said I was wanted on the phone. It was Des Smith. He said, 'Take this number down. It's Graham Henry's. He wants you to ring him straight away.'

Henry asked me if I wanted to be an All Black again: did I want to go on the end-of-year tour? I couldn't believe what was being proposed to me. He then went on to say that I'd been the best of the hookers in the NPC and that they wanted an old and experienced head to give leadership in a side that would include a number of young, new faces. My answer was quick, loud and rudimentary: 'Bloody oath,' and then added, 'I am delighted and surprised. It would be an honour to be an All Black again.'

After I put the phone down I was absolutely elated. It felt like complete vindication to me. When I was very publicly dropped from the All Blacks before the Tri-nations in 2003 Mitchell had basically said I was not a good enough player, giving his four technical reasons for my non-selection. My steep slide continued which saw me plummet from number one to possibly number six in the hooking pecking order. The whole Highlander saga of 2003 had painted the picture that I was a negative influence on a team and that I destabilised team unity. So the vindication was sweet on both counts, because not only had the current coaches said my form was the best in the NPC, but they also wanted to utilise my experience and leadership on and off the field to help grow and guide some of the younger All Blacks. The best thing about it was that I didn't have to say a word, I kept my mouth shut in the media and was dignified in my responses to queries like 'Does it feel great to have proved them all wrong?' These questions didn't need answering. I sat back and enjoyed the feeling, a feeling that I hadn't experienced for a long, long time. I felt good about myself.

Brian and I opened Nana Sloane's tin of shortbread that she had made for me and that Peter had delivered after our Otago loss to Auckland four days earlier. We ate some of that with tea. Then we went and saw Grahame Sydney and he opened a bottle of bubbly. I was jubilant, but then — talk about a never-ending story — I began to feel uneasy. I hadn't told Henry that prior to his call I had made up my mind to retire, that I had decided not to re-sign for the Highlanders in 2005 and my gut told me that he should know that. So the next morning I rang Henry and told him of my intention not to re-sign with the NZRU for 2005. Henry said that was a problem. There was no point taking anyone away on tour if they were not going to be around next year for the Lions series at least, so if I wanted to go on the tour I would have to sign with the NZRU and play for the Highlanders in 2005, therefore making myself eligible for selection in the Lions series. I said that a few days would be needed to clear my head and think about his offer as I had just made a commitment to myself to stop playing rugby in New Zealand and that the decision had taken me an agonising two months to make. Graham was fine with that and I had till Friday morning to make up my mind; it was then Wednesday lunchtime. It was now up to me to decide what I wanted to do; the parameters were very clear.

Down with the phone and enter utter turmoil. My thoughts were all over the place. Not knowing quite what I should do, I rang several people, including Tony Gilbert, Peter Sloane, my father and others. Brian Turner said that at the time I made the decision not to re-sign with the Highlanders I had not been in a position to factor in the fact that I was in line for a return to the All Blacks, and, he said, there was no virtue in being intractable. Tony Gilbert was of a similar mind. Sloane took a different tack, thought that I should be wary of being 'used' again by those high up in our rugby.

It was such a surprise to be wanted in the team again because I wasn't selected for any of the tests played that year under the new coaching regime, the Highlanders had played poorly and my own form was adequate but not my best. The Otago season was an abomination. I had looked past the fact that I was the Otago player of the year and focused more on the poor results of a team with a proud history and of which I was the captain. And of course there was the 'troublemaker' moniker that had been my shadow companion for a few years now. Why on earth would an All Black recall even be contemplated? When I spoke to Wayne Smith he echoed Henry's comments to me in that they were impressed with my NPC form and I made the team on merit and they also wanted my leadership abilities. A week or two later, Smithy said that when he was coaching in England he had been unaware of the intensity of the debate surrounding me and the way in which I was being depicted.

Having made the decision not to play any more rugby in New Zealand, I had begun to anticipate the prospect of an enlarged and, hopefully, more interesting and stimulating world. But slowly, surely, I realised that the wish to play for the All Blacks had been the prime reason why I was in rugby, really. The honour, the pinnacle, the glory — that was some of it. And I could feel the urge to play overseas for the All Blacks again, the desire to go away and look around Rome, Cardiff, Paris and London. Get some rejuvenation and enjoyment out of rugby again before I left it behind. There was also the possibility, if things went well, of playing against the Lions in New Zealand in 2005 . . .

But I wasn't looking that far ahead. On the Thursday night I told Henry I'd be happy to tour. Then I called Greg Cooper and, feeling a bit chastened if not silly, left a message on his phone, saying, 'Have you got room in the Highlanders for me for another season? Have you got room for an old guy like me?'

You know the answer.

Chapter 15

Players and Coaches, Power and Performance

I n recent years, and especially since the advent of the Players' Association, there's been frequent talk about player power. But when hasn't this been the case? It is inaccurate to say that players of yesteryear had little to say for themselves in respect to tactics, training methods, management, coaching — that they shut up and did what they were told. That simply wasn't the case. Players have always had views on such things. Why wouldn't they? Think back to the days of, say, All Blacks like Andy Leslie and Ian Kirkpatrick, or Wilson Whineray. They had few support staff: a manager, a doctor and that was it. Coaches were of variable ability, were said to have been less well prepared than those of today. Back then the captain, his senior players and the manager ran the shop. So players have always had influence: contrary to popular belief players had far more influence in the past than they do today.

Nowadays, given the greater amount of rugby being played, given the financial rewards and the fact that rugby has become a job as well as a game — and perhaps a job first and a game second — players expect to have a say in what goes on, and how teams are run. That, surely, is not only natural, but, seeing that we are employees, right and proper.

I accept the need for boundaries — in fact I am a great believer in them — and I agree that ultimate authority must reside with the coach and the manager. Nevertheless, I think any player has a right, and should feel he has the right, to go to a coach and discuss any issues relating to rugby on and off the field. A player needs to feel he can freely discuss his game and other issues with the coach. A good coach welcomes that and often becomes a kind of father figure — understanding but firm — who makes players feel as if he cares about them personally and doesn't regard them solely as some sort of unfeeling machine whose job it is to switch on and off and do what he's told at all times without demur.

Essentially, the coach is the boss. The circumstances have to be exceptional before players should set out to undermine or challenge the authority of the coach. As a captain or senior player, for instance, I would never challenge the coach in front of other members of the team.

It's been said that in 2003, on one occasion I was critical of Taine Randell's actions, or lack of action, in the presence of other members of the team. I can't recall having done that. If I did, it was remiss of me. It's possible that, when discussing matters with other members of the back seat, I may have expressed dissatisfaction or exasperation in respect of certain issues, but anything regarding team matters is open to discussion among the back-seat boys. However, nothing gets said or done by them until a consensus is reached. Sometimes the consensus is to do nothing; often an individual back-seat member's views get shot down, and he's told he's wrong and to pull his head in. That's certainly happened to me.

In respect of Laurie Mains' return from South Africa and reappointment to Otago in 2001, I was, in late 2003, advised that Mains had been told that there were concerns about the amount of player power in the province and that he needed to do something about it. I don't subscribe to the view that it was ever a serious issue in Otago rugby. Nevertheless, some believe that Laurie was told that it was a concern to a few and given instructions to stamp it out. By the end of his reign he had apparently come to see me as the devil incarnate, Mr Player Power himself.

Mains was to reassert the old-style values that mist eyes and would assuredly, it was implied, return us to winning ways.

So those values, then, referred to by Otago stalwarts, what are they? Honesty, loyalty, hard work, uncompromising and unpretentious effort and commitment to the Otago cause

---

Coaches: a final word – Gordon Hunter

The key to Gordon's coaching was that he made the team feel, and play, like *a team*. He got us to believe in him and that made us want to play for him. Gordon was passionate about Otago and winning. But when he was appointed an assistant All Black coach he was not in a position to exert the same influence there. He had the same passion but, understandably, because he was not head coach, he wasn't able to have the same effect on the team. And when he went to coach in Auckland I am not sure how successful he was at developing the same culture in the north. I suspect they simply didn't 'get it'.

Gordon never got bogged down in detail; even his police friends will tell you that paperwork was not his specialty! Nevertheless, he set up computer equipment at home and learnt to use it regularly for analysis, especially when he was part of the All Black coaching team. But when he was coaching Otago we didn't have assistant managers and specialist coaches for this and that, so the onus was put on players to 'get it right'. Gordon expected us to think for ourselves and act in the interests of the team and Otago rugby.

In hindsight, we were lucky in that we had some very experienced and talented players, particularly in the backs. As far as I recall, they mainly coached themselves. So Gordon spent most of his time with the forwards. At times he nearly had us crying for mercy. We practised only twice a week in those days, so Gordon flogged us hard, for he couldn't be sure that all of the players would have been doing what was required on their own. After all the sweat was washed off and a big roast of beef had replenished tired bodies, us fatties — as the

---

are some of them. There's always been an element of romanticism about this sort of talk and this has influenced the perception that Otago teams have been hugely successful for many years. The successes that Otago's teams have had have come, so it's asserted, because we have that something extra that other provinces and their sides don't have. Winning reinforces the belief that the origins of success are found in a sense of provincial worth and pride. The reality is that when the archives are consulted, the story they tell is not one the southern rugby public would like portrayed. We have failed to be consistent performers and the big rugby titles have been few and far between relative to Auckland and Canterbury and more recently Wellington. Therein lies a key concept: relativity. When comparing Otago to all other teams other than Auckland, Wellington and Canterbury we have a proud record and have managed to raise our game on the odd big occasion, such as Lions 1993 and Springboks 1994. However, when looking at Otago's history relative to the big three, well that record isn't as impressive.

I have been in Otago and Highlanders teams that have been barked at and told that if we're not winning it's because we've been 'playing like pansies', won't do the 'hard yakker', 'lack guts', don't care enough about, or lack respect for, those who preceded us. Such is desperate talk, has rarely been true, and arises out of a regional, underdog sensitivity that occasionally tips towards sentimentality. It has also served to undermine any confidence that the team was building. I thought we were our own worst enemies for many years.

This is not just an Otago rugby phenomenon; it is part of the social fabric that makes up

tight forwards were known — accepted the hard work was necessary. But at the time it was bloody tiring!

Gordon was an excellent orator. Some of his speeches are legendary and the guys who played under him still smile and share their memories of his marvellous theatrical performances. Not everyone 'got' what Gordon was saying — I'm not sure he always knew himself — but he could be compelling. It was almost impossible to predict what Gordon would say. No wonder he was called The Riddler. It took time and effort to adjust to Gordon's style, and I found that those who said they found him riddling usually weren't listening carefully enough. Mostly, even when he was speaking plainly and using simple language, there was a deeper meaning underlying it all. Admittedly, some of his connections were rather oblique and I am sure that, every now and then, and for his own amusement, he threw one in that had no relevance at all, but generally his words carried deep significance.

For the Otago team of 1994-95 and the Highlanders team of 1996 his words were the fuel with which we drove our collective engine.

Gordon wasn't what is sometimes called a technical coach; his strength was in his philosophy on how to play the game, which for that matter was how he approached life. Summed up I'd say it was: do the hard work, get stuck in, always be positive, and attack. When young, Gordon had been seriously ill for a time and, later, he lost an eye when hit by a piece of metal, so it's no wonder that, when he coached rugby teams, there was never any talk of an easy way. He once said to me that when he lost his eye people felt sorry for him but he couldn't understand why. He prodded me and said, 'Lad, what do you do when you fire a rifle?' I thought about it and responded, 'You close one of your eyes.' He smiled at me and said, 'Exactly.'

That was Gordon Hunter in a nutshell.

living in the south: don't get too big for your boots, beware the tall poppy, self-deprecation and understatement are essential. This kind of self-mutilation only served to make rugby life harder for it always felt as if we were up against it. Instead of harnessing the collective confidence that the team created from good performances, we looked to suppress any gains made.

As for Otago's successes in national competition — if by successes we mean wins — it's been aeons since the province held the Ranfurly Shield, and we've won the NPC twice. In 1991 we won it under Mains when it was a round robin and the powerful Auckland side had 14 World Cup All Blacks out; we won it again under the current semi-final, final system when Tony Gilbert was coach in 1998. Otago's record, then, has been respectable rather than outstanding, that's all.

Memories of Otago's glory days will never die with the faithful of Otago rugby, and there is a craving for more days like those remembered from the past. For instance, older generations speak of Otago's 'proud record' against overseas teams at Carisbrook. Perhaps a southern underdog feeling is behind a craving for more victories in national and international competitions. But how much success, if success is measured soley by wins on the field, can a province like Otago expect in a nation where the population imbalance and the financial resources available to those who don't live in the more heavily populated regions are ever-widening.

The better and more successful teams I've been part of have had a lot of talented players in them. Without such talent, no team is going to perform exceptionally well. Generally, these teams have enjoyed playing together, been prepared to put the team's interests first, and trained hard. The players have had input into game plans — tactics generally — and had a coach who was firm without being overly dictatorial, egotistical or petty. I'm not a proponent of pampering, where just about every service imaginable is provided. That undermines self-reliance and can give

Coaches: a final word – Tony Gilbert

If ever a man was the antithesis of your stereotypical old-style rugby coach, Tony Gilbert is it. When I came to write this I thought, Tony was our back coach for a few years . . . I think. (Tony took the backs when Gordon Hunter was coach. Also, in 1998 he took the forwards for the Highlanders and the backs for the NPC.) The fact that I had to check that is telling. He was so unobtrusive that I was barely aware of his presence. Generally, that is how Tony operated. He never paraded, ranted or raved. In fact he was quite the opposite. I don't think I have heard Tony lower himself to swear in front of the guys. Everyone seemed to respect him because he was a good, honest, caring person. He had, and still has, an aura of wisdom that came from years of dealing with people in schools, be it parents or pupils, and also the players that he coached.

He understood the basics of human behaviour; he had a fantastic ability to understand each and every player in his team. He quickly worked out which guys needed a cuddle now and then, and which needed a size 12 up the jacksie more often than not! Consequently – and this was critically important – he was able to make those individual cells operate as a cohesive unit. We were an incredibly happy and harmonious team under Tony Gilbert. He made it look like he had a hands-off approach, which cultivated and facilitated an amazingly vibrant team culture.

individuals unrealistic and inflated ideas of their importance in the overall scheme of things. In the Highlanders in 2004, we decided that the guys should wash their own jerseys. It was only a small thing, but there was a message in that.

I believe that management and players need to treat each other with mutual respect. Also, that while some players require little maintenance by way of cajoling and reassurance, some need quite a lot. Some players just do what they are told irrespective; others like, and expect, to have their say.

I agree that running a professional rugby team is not easy. The balance in terms of results and morale is always shifting. At times there's so much talk it becomes exasperating; it's then that I can understand someone saying, in effect, 'Shut up and get on with it.' Some people, journalists and commentators among them, and some fans, will claim to have the answer to what makes a team successful. Likewise coaches and players work together before and during a campaign to come up with the right formula. Me, I keep coming back to the thought arrived at in 2004: there is no absolute answer. Quality personnel is the starting point. Combining quality with a healthy mix of experience and youth and a suitable game plan to match the talent are the on-field fundamentals for a good team. Off the field, mutual respect between players and management, open lines of communication, rigour of thought and action, and an absence of hypocrisy are all desirable and necessary components. And there's always the thought that all of us should be looking within ourselves as much — or more — than to others for answers.

When I started playing NPC and Super 10 rugby, over a decade ago, we trained only twice a week, on Tuesdays and Thursdays. Now, we train twice every day. Of course, as a young player back in the early 1990s, I was very much like all young players are, even today, in that I took little interest in anything other than playing and trying to cement my place in the team. To most

---

Again we had some excellent players; in fact it was at this stage that Otago teams played some of their most classically complete games, with strong, dominant forward play providing good ball for a skilful, fast, enterprising backline. And we won many games we shouldn't have because of the strength of spirit that resided deep within the team. Tony also set up a think tank comprising himself, Randell, Wilson, Kronfeld and myself. We debriefed after games and devised tactics for the next one.

Like Gordon Hunter, Tony wasn't what I would consider a technical coach. That said, I found him to have a deep understanding of the game and an ability to see strengths and weaknesses. But he wouldn't sit down with me and show me how to scrum. Perhaps he did that with other players, but in the main Tony left me to my own devices.

Some people find it odd to discover that modern-day coaches often spend more than half their time on matters unrelated directly to coaching. By that I mean PR work of one kind or another, and also dealing with internal politics. One could say that politics has been a festering sore – or was – in Otago rugby for years. Tony would have preferred just to coach but he found it necessary to work hard, though subtly, at calming the turbulent, flotsam-full, local political waters. This was one of Tony's strengths. He was so astute that for the first time in years there appeared to be some unity in the management of the game in the province. Tony was shrewd with a listening ear and had many an earthy anecdote on hand to help get his message across. Tony, like no other coach I have played under, had the ability to communicate with every ethnic group in the team, and we had plenty.

I like and respect Tony Gilbert.

young players everything is fresh, exciting. But the truth is that it's rare to find a young player who is genuinely concerned about the team as a whole. Mostly, the younger guys are focused on holding a spot in the team and enjoying what is often the first step towards the realisation of a dream — high pay and a long career in professional rugby with all its so-called glories. As a player gets older, has been in the team longer, he is given more responsibility and the team starts to feel like something to which he has contributed over many years. This is when players start to really care about who and what they are playing for; a sense of connection and ownership has taken place and their performances, especially in the big games, recognise this.

The world of Otago rugby in 1994 seems far off. Though still amateurs, the Otago team started staying together in a hotel on the nights before matches. At the time there were lots of students in the side and by shoving us into a hotel we avoided the noise of loud parties and were more likely to get a decent night's sleep. We had a coach, assistant coach, manager, and baggage man/ rubber (masseur). They went with us on away games along with a physio, whose job included strapping ankles and the like. None of them were paid.

Trainers were almost non-existent. They did the odd warm-up but that was basically it. I did all of my training by myself or with my brother Brent. We worked from our own programmes or ones obtained from other sources. These days the team trainer is seen in some lights as the most important person in the team. He has to get us physically prepared for high-intensity football and can have a disproportionate say in team structure if the coach lacks experience or defers too much to the trainer. If a trainer says the boys need more work and the coach doesn't have the knowledge to assess the merits of the advice, a team can end up being over-trained. From my experience that is the greatest danger, that trainers want to do too much.

Back in Otago in 1994 and 1995 there was none of this; indeed, in 1996, the first year of the Super 12, we still trained only twice a week as a team although the trainer was starting to have more influence and we did the odd extra session with him outside of rugby practices. Fitness work was always combined with training on a Tuesday where the forwards in particular had gruelling two-hour workouts of scrums and scrum rucks, down-and-ups and tackle bags. That was real rugby-specific stuff, and while at the end of it we were absolutely knackered we all felt good about doing hard work together and it definitely contributed to Otago's fitness on the field. At practice the team did little or no contact training as tackle suits hadn't been invented then. Now most sessions involve trying to simulate a game as closely as possible and consequently more injuries occur at training than in the past. Ten years ago we used to strap up, jump in our cars and drive down to Tahuna Park next to the beach and train there as the sand-based surface was always good. Pre-match analysis consisted of a talk the night before the game when Gordon Hunter would ask players for their views on how to approach the match and their opposites. There was no computer analysis but I know Gordon watched a lot of video footage for there was no one else to help him with the workload.

Paradoxically, today, too large a staff is the biggest danger for a professional team's management structure. Nowadays there are scrum and defence coaches, rubbers, nutritionalists, managers, assistant managers, kicking coaches, throwing coaches, computer analysts, trainers, physios, doctors (who have the easiest ride of the lot) and media liaison officers. The last are there to satisfy the insatiable media employees and their thirst for interviews. With so many in the management team, all feel they must justify their existence. All work to fulfil their job descriptions in order to justify and protect their jobs, and also to satisfy their need to believe that they are making a valuable contribution to the greater *team vision*. I'm not saying most of the support staff are dispensable; many do a good job. But unless their input is carefully controlled a team can be pulled in all directions and much of the fun disappears. The very worst thing about professional rugby — and I can say this without any equivocation — is recovery baths. Immersion in ice-cold tubs is the single biggest impediment to enjoyment known to humankind!

In my view a coach needs to keep some distance between him and the players and try to avoid showing favouritism. But just how far that distance should be is hard to decide. Let's say it keeps changing according to the team's, and individuals', morale. It's a tough job trying to do the impossible, being all things to all players. Coaches should be far enough away to still be the boss — like in a workplace — yet approachable. I've seen coaches socialising with some guys and not others to the point where the professional relationship — the line — becomes blurry. Then, when selections are made, and some get dropped, there's a lingering feeling that an element of favouritism was involved. If a coach gets too friendly with a player in the context of the rugby team, it makes both persons' jobs more difficult. Given that the balance in this area is so fine, unless there's a measure of distance, the player-coach relationship probably isn't working really well. Some players like, and need, regular dialogue with their coach. Others prefer very little contact; as long as they are playing they're happy to get on with it. Then there are some who worry about how the coach is interacting with the team as a whole. Some might say that it's a wonder there aren't more explosions, or implosions, than there are. A coach can be too consultative, or too authoritative. But when a coach decides he's going to do something he should do it. Vacillation or uncertainty often cause more trouble. To strive for perfection is admirable; to expect to achieve it is seldom realistic.

A coach shouldn't hide truths from players, however unpalatable they may be. If a player asks a coach why he's not playing, and it's because he's been missing tackles, he should be told. It always worries me if a coach is unwilling to talk about selections with players. A player who is not given reasons is left out in the cold. I've heard players saying, after being dropped, 'I thought I played well last week.' Most players won't improve unless they are told what they have to work on and rectify.

To assist in monitoring the feeling of the team a good coach needs to develop a rapport with two or three of the more astute senior players in order to gauge the way a team, and, in some cases, certain individuals, are coping with the pressures of training and playing.

And it's true — though not as true as some would like to believe — that a few players quite enjoy being ranted at, bullied even, and respond well to that. Put a sadistic coach with a bunch of masochistic rugby players and, hey presto, you're in business. But such a combination is incredibly rare.

'Anton has been wasted in All Black rugby' – Tony Gilbert

In September 2004, before the All Black team was announced, Tony Gilbert said:
'I hoped the selectors knew about his passion for the ABs, the leadership he provides and mental toughness he would bring to a rudderless pack. It's galling. Some Otago forwards rely too much on him.

'I was also informed that after Oliver had ruptured his Achilles in 2002, David Rutherford, the NZRU's [now former] CEO, was so impressed with Oliver that he wanted to find a way of bringing him into the NZRU administrative and commercial environment during his rehabilitation, in order that he might learn more about the business. Rutherford was convinced that Oliver could have added value.'

In bars throughout the land, though, particularly in rugby's traditional heartlands, it's not hard to find hard-core rugby fans who say, 'Rugby's a no-nonsense game. The players are too soft, there's too much poofy stuff going on. They're too precious.'

Of course rugby's a tough game, tough physically and mentally. Always has been. But I don't buy the argument that players are softer today. Players are bigger, faster and stronger now, and play and train more often. They may not be as durable, but even that's open to serious debate. If some seem precious, as critics allege, it's because, in most cases, the stakes are infinitely higher. One's livelihood depends on getting and keeping a contract to play. Players have to know what their employer wants them to do. More weights? Hit rucks? Run with the ball?

But I haven't seen much sign of a descent to the point whereby rugby's administrators and coaches look like being compliant to every footie player's wish. Settle down, guys, the tails aren't wagging the dogs in Otago rugby.

I can see that when I was a member of the back seat, prior to becoming captain, I was a bit of a unionist in that occasionally I saw the world as employees — players — against the bosses. I'd like to think that I had the good sense to act as a receptacle and saw to it that rubbish stopped at me. The back seat works best when it is occupied by smart men, who understand personalities, and who have been around the game for a good while. If the back seat doesn't filter information, absorb grizzles, then the coach is needlessly burdened with distracting issues.

A coach needs a very good knowledge of techniques and an ability to devise and develop varied attacking and defensive strategies. And he has to be able to communicate and get his ideas across to the players. Most coaches are stronger at one than the other. So which is the more important? I believe it is the ability to communicate. Take John Boe as an example: he is said to have an excellent knowledge of rugby strategies and techniques but isn't quite so good at putting them across. By contrast, Gordon Hunter's strength was his ability to communicate and urge players to give of their best. When Gordon took over in Otago he had a broad plan and

---

Coaches: a final word – John Hart

I have already discussed John at length in earlier chapters so I will try not to tread on a path already traversed. John is a very intelligent man, with a perceptive ability to read a game and understand it. This was clearly evident when I listened to him commentate on TV during the 2003 World Cup. He was light years ahead of any other commentator: concise, astute and insightful; he described in detail subversive events within a game that most were unaware of.

When John was All Black coach he was criticised for, at times, talking too often and for too long. Some of that criticism was fair; however, he was an excellent communicator and a good orator. John had a vision for the All Blacks, which was to make them thoroughly professional and raise the standards required of the players both on and off the field. One can argue over how successful he was but he was the first to try and he worked hard at it. He understood the critical role that sponsors played and sought to establish strong relationships with key financial backers. John had a fantastic eye for spotting talent and also was an astute selector. I think he was the right coach at the right time for New Zealand rugby when he took over in 1996.

relied on the likes of Stephen Bachop, Stu Forster, John Leslie, Arran Pene and others to work out the details. So players often act as technical and tactical advisers in their own right today. I only have to think of Simon Maling and Tony Brown, more recent examples, and their input into moves used by Otago and the Highlanders.

To sum up, in my experience no coach is perfect, and no player is perfect either.

In the Highlanders in 2004, Greg Cooper and Phil Young devised strategy and then talked to on-field decision makers — the likes of our halfback, first five, Maling for the lineouts, and myself. The day after a game the coaches would look closely at what had happened in the match, then they'd look at the team we were to play next, consider all that, and then talk to us. They looked at the various moves the other team had and, generally, worked with the backs on ways of countering them. In the end, of course, it's over to the coaches to pull it all together and say what a team is going to do.

Under Laurie Mains we had little or no say in strategy. I remember being irritated by Laurie's insistence that, just about all the time, we run straight at the opposition — using forwards as battering rams and not much else. One day Laurie stopped the whole training session and told Simon Maling he was 'not to touch the ball', except at lineout time, of course, which rather cut down his options to perform more than menial service. All Laurie seemed to want from his tight five was that we tackle or clear the opposition out of the way. We didn't like it, or agree with it, but we did it.

I reiterate: almost without exception under Mains we did what he wanted us to do. But to us it was too limiting because his defence-oriented style won't win the big games — semi-finals and finals. Most of the better-informed observers, and players, never gave us a bolter's chance of winning such games. What, then, is the point of sticking with that style?

Laurie had basically opted to go back to a type of 10-man footie that held little appeal for us or anyone else. I think that deep down, Mains and Randell felt that we didn't have the players to win the competition, but that by playing conservatively we would achieve respectable results. In other words, fourth or fifth for the year would satisfy most of the supporters. Sure, we won a few games on sheer passion alone, but you can't rely on that or keep it up over a four-month period. Players like myself, Tony Brown, Simon Maling, Kelvin Middleton and others were tired of being part of a side seen as 'worthy opponents', of being the 'nearly but not quites' who ended the year with a B or a B- on the report card.

In 2004 it was decided that the Highlanders would try to develop a style of play that would increase our chances of scoring more tries, and from further out. If a player saw a gap, he had the right to back himself and go for it; or make a couple of long passes to get the ball wider and open up attacking opportunities. If it hadn't been for a few handling errors at crucial moments we would have won more games and I hope that attitude persists and that the coaches have the courage to stick with ideological change and follow it through.

One hears it said of certain coaches that they are averse to being approached by players. Often that is a misconception. In the Highlanders in 2004, Sam Harding, a former All Black, and an energetic, dynamic and versatile loose forward, felt he didn't know where he stood with Cooper and Young. He was in and out of the team and his confidence was down. He was becoming disillusioned. I told Cooper and Young this. They said they'd explained why he wasn't first choice, that they had been through the video footage, and so on . . . I replied that I didn't need to see the footage, I just wanted to be sure that they had explained things clearly to Sam. There was definitely a gap between what Sam thought they were saying and what the coaches thought they were saying. I arranged a meeting between him and the coaches and I sat in to listen. At the end it was clear that while Sam didn't agree with some of their views on what they saw, they'd made it pretty clear what they wanted.

Sometimes players just have to accept that, whether they like it or not, they have to go out and do what they're told to do. As was the case when Laurie Mains told us, for instance, that if we saw two players in front of us and we were in any doubt as to what to do, we were to run at one of them in order to set up a better target. So I did, even though it went against all my — I trust better — rugby instincts. My instincts told me, at least go for the weaker side, get some leg drive going, stay on your feet a bit longer, get across the advantage line and give the support a little longer to arrive. It's called looking to dominate the contact area. Running straight at a opponent is what we call T-boning and when you do that too much of the advantage goes to the defender; he wants you to run straight at him. It is far harder, as a defender, to put a good tackle on a ball carrier who uses a step, targets an outside shoulder and uses a fend.

Former players from the pre-professional era, and longstanding supporters — categorised as 'old school' — are apt to say, 'Well, players get everything these days when compared with what we were given. Players talk about what they are entitled to, what their rights are, but when the discussion turns to where their responsibilities lie there's a silence.'

I think that those who came before me, before professionalism, have a valid point. Today's players are not so self-reliant. Just about everything is handed to them on a plate.

When I started playing, players were subjected to intense peer pressure from their team-mates; for example, we were made to feel, and did feel, ashamed if we turned up late. There was no need to impose monetary fines on players. Modern players, though, see monetary fines as a strong deterrent. Often it seems that monetary fines are the only things that work. That speaks volumes about the culture in top rugby today.

After playing against the Hurricanes at Carisbrook in April 2004, Tana Umaga and I had dinner together. He said that the Hurricanes were having trouble with many of their young

Coaches: a final word – Peter Sloane

I have a huge amount of respect for Peter Sloane. Of all the coaches I have played under he adapted best to the new professional environment and the demands made of a modern-day coach. Considering the era he played in and the climate in which he first cut his teeth as a coach, his was an amazing transition. Not only did he have to completely relearn all he knew about lineout play – for it is completely different with lifting and a one-metre gap – he also had to reassess scrummaging, which has changed immensely as a result of law changes. He also had to learn a completely different set of off-field skills. For instance, he had to learn how to use computers and become proficient with the analysis program that often beleaguers people of Peter's generation. He adjusted to the amount of paperwork required by the NZRU, which is both a function of employment law and the NZRU becoming more professional in its accountability procedures.

Sloane understood the significance of sponsors and other key financial relationships and welcomed and included sponsors' reps instead of excluding them. Peter moved with the times, was always looking for better ways of doing things, had a fantastic work ethic and was always very well organised. Unsurprisingly, and as is typical of most cancer survivors, he has a very positive outlook on life.

players who were happy to take anything and everything that was on offer, but whose willingness to contribute and care about their performance was open to question. Ironically, perhaps, the more efficiently a team is run and structured, the more likely it is that some players will take everything for granted and go through the motions.

Tana also told me that when guys were fined small amounts for breaches of their dress code they took no notice, but when the fines were doubled that worked straight away.

Is there too much rugby? Are players asked to play so often that the physical and mental wear and tear is excessive? I don't think we play too much rugby, when compared to UK sides, but we make too much of it. All the palaver — the incessant talkback, the panel discussions, the replays, the media speculation — a lot of it is intended to create controversy, stir contention. By contrast, careful analysis that results in insight requires time and thought and that's . . . what? 'Boring' is one answer from many of the punters and some in the media. The saturation coverage also has a lot to do with money making and employment. One can't complain too loudly about that, but does some of the tabloid and radio coverage have to be quite so juvenile? Players are told frequently that they need to 'lift their game'. So do those in the media.

It's easy to say — and some would term it ungrateful — but in the end it's only footie. Some see us as spoilt larrikins who run around bashing into each other and who, when not doing that, chase chicks, drive flash cars, and get paid large sums of money. Compare a professional sportsman's contribution to society with that of the multitude of mostly anonymous people who are paid far less relative to us, and it all looks distorted, unfair.

Do many of the players believe the hype and see themselves as super-special? When in our own little group, no. Players in teams are pretty good at dragging each other down, dismantling

I know Peter found it difficult at times when coaching in Dunedin. He was trying to make things happen and improve facilities but felt he wasn't getting much support from the Highlanders' administration.

Nevertheless he was always resoundingly optimistic. Peter was very knowledgeable on forward play. He was the first coach from whom I learnt something that helped me technically. He showed me where and how to hit in a way that improved my scrummaging. Clearly it helped that he had been a hooker as well.

Sloaney had a lot of sayings that I keep hearing and I share a good laugh with the boys whenever one pops out. They were mostly based on the uncompromising, no-nonsense approach he had to rugby. For example, Sloane was fond of saying, 'If you're going to give it to someone, make sure it's in the belly, not the back.'

We trained hard under Sloaney; there was lots of contact. He didn't allow any shirking and I liked that attitude. In the years since the advent of professional rugby, it's my impression that during practices the amount of hard contact has decreased. This is primarily because of greater workloads in other areas and the increased risk of injury that contact training brings. However, back then it was all on!

Sloaney was, and is, straight. He treated everyone with the same rough bark, which was far worse than his bite. Peter was a very good friend to me because he would tell me face to face where he thought I was at. I appreciated that very much at the time, and I will always appreciate that quality in him. The day he and I lose that is the day one of us is in a box.

pretensions — or any sign of them. In Otago, if a guy says something, or does something, publicly that is seen as silly, thoughtless, indiscreet — whatever — the rest of the team will remind him of it for weeks. I suppose a few of the lads, when away from the team, might succumb and strut a bit. That's a human weakness, but just how common that is, or how bad, I don't know. Personally, I am humbled by people who come up and say complimentary things, such as, 'Well played,' or 'Thank you for that performance.' Often people will say to me, 'You must get sick of that sort of thing,' and I reply, 'No, I don't, it is you who have taken time out of your day to say something complimentary, to give me a little piece of emotional energy, I should be thanking you!' Eleven years on I still feel humbled by such approaches from people who go out of their way to wish me well. I believe I have a duty to listen to people who pay me compliments. Often, too, I'm accepting compliments on behalf of the team rather than for me personally.

Luckily, I've had very few derisive remarks directed at me or the team. The ones you do get usually come from people who have had too many drinks. In Christchurch especially, it's common to have Canterbury fans tell you how 'useless' you are, and to 'go back home, you wankers', and worse. In the city on the plains, you have to be careful which bars you go into after matches, and be prepared to leave quickly.

When I started playing provincial rugby, I had no inkling that the game would be as it is today. I can't think of anyone who would have foreseen the amount of video analysis of games and of individual player performance that is carried out today. Every team examines videotapes of the others. Players have nowhere to hide; the replays show it all. Scrums, lineouts, who kicks and when and from where: it's all scrutinised and interpreted. Guesswork is all but eliminated. Strategies to counter another team's practices are constantly being devised — hence the fickle nature of teams' lineouts, for instance. Of course, the players still have to put their plan into practice, and that's where the interest, difficulty and inconsistency lie.

The Super 12 has changed massively over time. The first couple of years were dominated by the Auckland Blues who were innovative and attacking. Zinzan Brooke and Carlos Spencer had a lot to do with that. The game scores were very high and a lot of the Blues' emphasis was on scoring points: a team could put 30 points on them but they would rattle up 50 against them. Then came the Crusaders and Mehrtens was the key, along with their fantastic defence. The Crusaders lived off turnover ball and for a couple of years defence ruled. Then the Brumbies set the standard with an ultra-structured game. They'd call a move at lineout time that was meant to go through five phases, and they had a repertoire of such moves. But defence was still paramount. From 2003, teams (Auckland especially) became more attacking again, with ambitious off-loads a feature. Auckland and Canterbury have a greater pool of players with the ability to combine excellent attack with formidable defence. (In 2003, Auckland teams in the Super 12 and Ranfurly Shield had an intimidating defence.) And if a team doesn't have a good kicking game, Auckland and Canterbury will punish it on the counterattack.

In Otago, in 1998–99, I think we were ahead of most other centres when it came to smart player recruitment and fitness levels. We had a good tiered system whereby our development squad (B) players were fed into the top team. But we then stagnated; there were no clear pathways for succession for coaches and support staff.

In my playing years our most successful periods were with Gordon Hunter and Tony Gilbert. What successes we have had have mainly been because of the efforts of a pool of talented players. Over the years our training facilities and base amenities for players have improved, although relative to the major centres they remain embarrassingly inferior. I was one of the players who put some pressure on, pressure that resulted in the set-up we now have at Logan Park.

Good facilities, good players who are paid well commensurate to players elsewhere, plus a good coach . . . all that optimises a team's chances of success. But for all those things to happen there has to be first-rate administration.

I'm for carefully selecting a coach, appointing him for three or four years and, unless he seriously stuffs up, keeping him. In Otago coaches have felt that their necks were on the block much of the time.

As I see it, Otago's biggest problem has been off the field where the transition from amateur to professional rugby has been poorly handled. The players have been more adaptable and professional than the administration. For a long time it has looked to me that personal rivalries and petty club politics have interfered with and undermined the Otago board's ability to professionally manage rugby in the region. I believe the board should be a meritocracy and that long service and loyalty to clubs, while laudable, shouldn't be the principal criteria governing selection to the board.

John Hornbrook was Otago's chief administrator for many, many years. He took over well before the advent of professional rugby and was a loyal fan and servant of the game in the south. But the general feeling was that, for all his undoubted merits, Horny didn't have quite the range of skills needed to be CEO in the professional era. Hornbrook should have left earlier. There are many in and around Otago rugby who are adamant that infighting between individuals and clubs meant that elected members were more concerned with self-protection than with attending to the changes affecting the future of the game in the province.

Look at the list of coaches I have played under since I made the Otago side 11 years ago: Gordon Hunter, Glenn Ross, Tony Gilbert, Kevin Gloag, Laurie Mains, Greg Cooper, Wayne Graham. In the Highlanders there have been Hunter, Ross, Gilbert, Sloane, Mains and Cooper. The assistant coach turnover has been just as high. It has been quite astonishing. Some might say a nightmare, farcical. What does that say about the quality and consistency of the thinking by Otago and Highlanders' boards of administrators? How on earth can the teams be expected to perform consistently and well on the field when there's been this musical chairs arrangement off it? Players get picked on merit. If they fail to perform, out they go. The same cannot be said of our administrators.

There have been two independent reviews of Otago and Highlanders rugby since 2000 but the paying public — the loyal supporters — weren't told of the findings, nor were the players. The board declined to release them. No one in administration appeared willing to be accountable.

I rebut the allegation sometimes made that the players have been largely responsible for the high coach turnover in Otago. The issue in respect to Laurie Mains' term with the Highlanders is complicated and is dealt with elsewhere.

It is true that the players didn't have a lot of faith in Glenn Ross, but Glenn had little faith in himself. He was constantly changing his mind, was consistently inconsistent. It was hard to know where he was at and what he wanted. This is not to say he was an unpleasant or unintelligent man. He was articulate and eloquent. As head coach, though, a man has to have a bit more bottle than Glenn showed in Otago. I always thought that Glenn's talents were those of a good manager, a role in which Waikato employs Glenn today.

Kevin Gloag was conscientious and tried hard. At times he was uncertain and, in retrospect, I think it more than likely that was because he never felt he had the full confidence, hence the support, of the administration.

Peter Sloane was well liked and many were keen for him to remain but he felt the knives were out for him in administration. He thought he wasn't included and kept properly informed on what was being discussed and any innovation or idea that he brought to a meeting quickly got dismissed because 'that's not how we do things down here'.

Sloane was top dog, very much in charge. But he urged the team to come up with their own standards, a set of principles to live and play by, and he would ensure that we kept to them. If anything, in the end, he may have left too much to us. A couple of times Sloane told me to pull my head in, and said, 'Stop being a social worker, do your own job.' I have always gotten on well with Peter because of his honesty.

Overall, my biggest gripe with the Otago union has been its failure to nurture and bring on players to replace their best, long-standing talents. In the late 1990s we had a good balance of the experienced and the new. Fresh talent was coming through. But since then we've lost players and have failed to identify and secure talented newcomers. Without strong, good players and a stable environment the team performance suffers, crowds dwindle and sponsors are harder to attract and retain. Otago and the Highlanders looked good and enjoyed a lot of success in 1998–99 but then something happened — complacency, a resting on laurels? — and we frittered away our chance to build on that success. Ironically, during this period others (Canterbury and Wellington, the latter especially), were taking a good look at us, the way we played and trained,

---

Coaches: a final word — Laurie Mains

In 1995 Laurie was the first coach to select me as an All Black. I was only in the team for a week and didn't have any interaction with him whatsoever, so all of my comments are based on the Laurie Mains that coached the Otago team of 2001 and the Highlanders of 2002 and 2003.

I found Laurie enjoyed a hands-on approach to coaching. He was more of a technical coach and in this regard, in respect to forward play, he was just as good as Peter Sloane. And because of the length of time that Laurie had been coaching he was good at making decisions. If a player's form or fitness was 50/50 and someone needed to make a call, Laurie wouldn't vacillate, which many coaches who are unsure of their ground often do. Even if it was his star player, Mains had the ability to look at the overall picture and make the hard calls without dithering and uncertainty. This gave the whole canoe direction, which is very important; indecision can breed a loss of cohesion and confidence.

But Laurie could be a real Jekyll and Hyde. And a great deal of what he did or said was orchestrated. It was as if he couldn't help himself. But when he wasn't acting or playing petty, destabilising mind games, Mains could be a good speaker. Before we played Canterbury in 2001 he delivered a fine, rousing speech. Nothing profound, nothing daft or pretentious, simply relevant references to the best of Otago's traditions and the pride in unstinting collective effort. I can still remember that speech. I liked it at the time and told him so as we left the changing sheds.

Mostly, though, I find it hard not to be highly critical of Laurie's style and methods. He and Sloane couldn't have been more different in most respects. Laurie didn't have a clue how to operate a computer effectively – for rugby purposes he relied on videotapes – and had no real intention of ever learning. Laurie was apt to say that the computer stuff was

how we attracted players, and moved forward. We had the chance to protect our depth of player resources and ensure that we had players in line to replace retiring stalwarts but the administration failed to sort that out.

Look at the case of Tony Brown, our All Black first five and best goalkicker. It was well known that for some time he was having serious injury problems: his hamstrings were making it extremely difficult for him to play. He even had a back operation in an effort to rectify the problem. Brownie struggled for two or three seasons and when he finally went at the end of 2003, we had no one in line to replace him. All we had were a couple of promising but raw newcomers who, understandably, had a tough time. With No. 10 being, arguably, the most important player in a team, you'd have thought we'd have had two or three classy players lined up.

Then there's me; if I had left in 2004, as I was going to before being reselected for the All Blacks, we'd have had no obvious successor as hooker or captain. The selectors were going to look for two hookers in the draft.

In 2004 Tony Gilbert returned from Scotland and was re-employed to start work in an effort to solve our problems. In the process he has had to stand on a few toes and act fairly aggressively, but there was no point in procrastination.

---

overcomplicating matters and that the player evaluations as required by the NZRU were of little use. I think he believed that the time and trouble it took to obtain information gleaned from computer analysis and player evaluation work was disproportionate to its value, and that such work should not be required of a coach.

Many of us thought Laurie was poorly organised in comparison to other Super 12 and All Black coaches we worked under. Often our schedule for the day would change at his whim, or so it seemed. Even at trainings when Greg Cooper was given 30 minutes to work with the backs, if Laurie had finished with the forwards in 10 minutes, the backs' section would be prematurely curtailed. There appeared to be a lack of preparation for de-briefs. There were very few weekly management meetings because he didn't believe in them. We were a cavalier lot, flying by the seat of our pants. Laurie, in my opinion, was out of his depth in the professional environment. He was coaching in South Africa when professionalism was in its infancy, a time when South African teams were notorious for being miles behind others in most areas. In my view, Laurie basically coached from a template forged in the amateur days, a template that he declined to alter.

Laurie had a reputation in some quarters as the man you wheeled up in times of crisis, when organisations and teams were at rock bottom and had nowhere to go but up. So he was a bit of a shock-trooper and, to be fair, he enjoyed some success in that regard. Take the Cats in South Africa, for instance. Then, again, it can be argued that his were quick-fix methods destined to last no more than a couple of years. From my observation and experience, and I believe many would concur, Laurie left teams emotionally spent. And some would say that Laurie's presence didn't help quell the politicking within the regional administrations either; indeed, he seemed to have the opposite effect. I was one of several in the team who wearied of the way he operated: too many threats, too much growling, too many players treated as infants. Eventually apprehensiveness dissipates, the players turn off, and find themselves asking the question, 'Why were we here in the first place?'

I think Laurie could have been a good coach in the professional era if he had moved with the times as Sloane did. But Laurie's personality prevented him making the necessary changes.

It's been clear for some time, too, that a piecemeal redevelopment of Carisbrook wasn't going to be enough to satisfy the moguls further north. Sentiment and historical connection doesn't cut much ice with those who have most influence in rugby nationally and internationally today. I have no problem moving the home of Otago rugby if it means the preservation of the game in the south and I would support a new stadium somewhere down by the wharves or the foreshore if it meant we would still be guaranteed category A tests. The hard reality is that we have to at least match the facilities available elsewhere. I know money is hard to come by but it looks very like a case of cough up somehow or the game will die rather quickly in the south. Don't just see a new stadium as a rugby ground — see it and build it as a multi-purpose facility for the province as a whole. Otago has a strong spirit still. The province is full of good people. I'd hate to see us become second-raters with second-rate facilities and a second- or third-rate team. What a waste of a proud legacy that would be. And it is a very real possibility, far more real than most would allow themselves to believe.

From the start of my career, and for several years, my all-round skills were considered to be above average for a front-rower. Over time others have lifted their game to the point where it is expected that front-rowers run and catch the ball in open play. This is now the norm, no longer the exception. More practice, more training, better game plans . . . fatties' (tight forwards') fitness levels have gone through the roof; everyone has to be able to get around the track. If in trouble, all forwards are expected to stand at first receiver and make decisions too.

With respect to performance, players often aren't as honest with each other as they could, maybe should, be. It's hard, when you are playing with your friends all the time, to put the finger on them. But I do believe peer pressure plays a major role in the making of a great team. If a player is made aware that he's let his mates down — or fears doing so — that has more effect on performance than criticism from the coach. If a mate says, 'Hey, I needed you at that ruck, where the hell were you?', and others are prepared to say the same sort of thing, it can make a significant difference to a team's performance. But to say that sort of thing a player has to be damned sure that he is playing well himself.

One often hears someone described as 'good' in a certain position. So what makes a good hooker or prop? A good lock?

Former coach and All Black selector Peter Thorburn says today's hookers need to have: the ability to regularly reach the jumpers at lineouts; upper body strength at scrum to take unnecessary pressure off props; the ability to play as a fourth loose forward; a similar role at breakdowns to props, but with greater expectation of work rate; the ability to police the front of the lineout (a key role).

To me that's pretty close to the mark. I'd add that the loose-forward role applies both on attack and defence, tackling and running. When a hooker takes the ball when fed from a lineout, say, and runs it up, he's not actually trying to break the line and score himself, he's trying to get over the advantage line and provide quick ball for the next part of the planned sequence. If I can get some good leg drive going I may not go to ground so early. Many people get quite excited about a player busting ahead an extra yard and taking a player with him, but that can mean overlooking the fact that ball presentation is everything.

When it comes to lineout work, I am not the best thrower out there. I have never professed to be. Some are better, some are worse. Like all hookers, I have had games where I threw the ball perfectly, oozed confidence and we have won all our own ball. I have also had games when the lineouts were shambolic. That happens to every hooker too. Unfortunately for me, a few of those days have been in big games, in test football, the second test against Australia in 2001, for instance. Mud sticks.

When a side loses a few lineouts and the game, poor throwing is put under the microscope and magnified.

'Never took short cuts' – Mark Hammett

Mark Hammett regards Oliver as one of the 'best, most loyal guys I've ever had anything to do with in rugby. We've been friends from way back.' He always saw Oliver as having the potential to be the best hooker in world rugby and at his best he might well have been just that. Hammett was amazed when he heard that Oliver had been dropped and wasn't in the World Cup side in 2003. He says he rang him straight away because he was slightly embarrassed about it. Hammett says he felt uneasy to be picked ahead of Oliver because, 'let's face it, he was a better player than me'. He thinks that he may have been included to provide exactly the sort of leadership that Oliver offers.

The two hardest hookers Hammett has ever scrummed against were Matt Sexton and Anton Oliver.

Hammett says 'Oliver never took short cuts' and could be quite curt with guys that tried to.

According to Hammett, Oliver's 'all-round skills were fantastic'. He says he always felt sorry for the fuss they made about his lineout throwing. All hookers get put under great pressure there, he said, and he believes Oliver's throwing deficiencies became a fixation. 'Remember too, down in Otago he's always had to throw in to one of the shortest lineouts in the country, and usually with fewer options as well.'

It has always amused me to note the fulsome praise lineout jumpers receive whenever a team wins nearly all of its own throws. The jumpers are said to have dominated the lineout and they are also deemed to have had a good game around the field based on their lineout success. I've lost count of the number of times a lock or a loosie who has consistently won ball in two-handed splendour has been described as having had a great game even through he was quiet around the park. And guess who gets it first and foremost right in the neck if a team loses a few — the hooker.

So how do you know what went wrong when a team doesn't win its own throw? Clearly, if the ball is not straight, then the blame can only be aimed at the hooker, no arguments there. Unfortunately for me, if mine don't come out of the hand right they generally are not straight. I have thrown my share of them.

But if the throw is straight then we enter the strange, cryptic world of lineouts. What is going on there? For a start, the call can get lost in translation. It's pretty easy to tell that this has happened if the jumper leaps at the back with two lifters on him and the throw is lobbed to two in the line; or if there is only one lifter on a jumper, or if no one goes up at all. Sometimes the hooker is standing there cocked and ready to throw and things start to go haywire: there's movement everywhere in the lineout and confusion reigns; no one gets up, the referee is giving the hooker an earful, telling him to stop time wasting and get it in . . . but to what? To whom? It's then you either hold on to it and risk a free kick awarded against you, or you lob it somewhere and hope.

There are two key ingredients to a good lineout; one is consistency in the three components

Coaches: a final word – Wayne Smith

Wayne is without doubt the most technically proficient coach that I have known. Not only is he well versed in back play, but also he has a very thorough understanding of the fundamentals of forward play. Smith is superb, too, in crucial aspects such as the contact area, the breakdown and defence. Indeed, it was in the latter two areas that the Crusaders teams of the late 1990s proved to be supremely good. Smith deserves much credit for the way in which the Crusaders were, on the one hand, aggressive on the ball on the ground and, on the other hand, resolute and unyielding on defence. The Crusaders won their first two championships, in my opinion, by living off turnover ball to which were added touches of class from Mehrtens and a committed team spirit.

Smith is also a very good communicator, one of a plethora of ex-schoolteachers who are prominent in coaching in New Zealand. I guess successful teachers and top coaches require similar skills, and that both occupations demand that individuals be well organised, good talkers, good with people and good at imparting knowledge. In this regard, the words 'coaching' and 'teaching' are synonymous.

Wayne was one of the first to recognise how useful computers can be for analysing players' strengths and weaknesses. And also for devising tactics to counter, or unravel, opposing players and teams. Smith quickly gained the nickname 'Techno', partly because of his devotion to computers, but also because of his belief that modern rugby is a complex game. In his view many players and fans of earlier eras are apt to have too simplistic a view of the game. I felt that if Wayne did have a weakness it was in his tendency to overcomplicate matters, to focus on minutiae to too great an extent. But then I concede that the argument is circular. Get the little things right and the bigger ones will look after themselves.

Smith has a tremendous work ethic, something which I believe has been to his own detriment in the past. In 2000 and 2001 we didn't have a full-time computer analyst and Wayne would lock himself away for hours doing the work that, for the likes of John Mitchell and Graham Henry, has been done by a full-time, paid rugby analyst. In hindsight, Smith was doing far too much. Someone else should have been doing that job so he could stay fresh, focused and positive while putting all of his energies into coaching a rugby team. Of course, a thorough and intelligent analysis of one's own team, and of other sides, is essential if weaknesses are to be exposed and smart tactics devised. Smith was, and is, very good at detecting errors and strengths and working out ways of fixing them or countering them.

Wayne is also a very honest man. That worked against him when he expressed doubts as to whether he was the right man to continue as All Black coach during his review after the 2001 Tri-nations series. Most people wouldn't have had the guts to be so open and honest, but Smith always puts the team first and is remarkably selfless. I am sure his hesitancy was based on a belief that the best men need to be in charge of the All Blacks and that, at the time, he felt that perhaps the results had shown he wasn't one of them. I think he was, but he never got a chance to show us what he was truly capable of, as he was not reappointed.

Smithy is a good little bugger, someone who showed faith in me, something that I will never forget.

We are great cobbers.

that make up a lineout — throwing, lifting and jumping — the other is having an intelligent man calling the right throw at the right time.

If the jumper likes a back lob (that is, three steps back, then the jump), the hooker and lifters train for that. It can't be two steps and it can't be four, it has to be three. The same thing applies to lifting: a hooker knows instantly if a lifter has 'missed' his jumper. By 'missed' I mean that the lifters and the jumper haven't synchronised their efforts, haven't worked in unison. For instance, if one lifter is late the result usually is that the jumper can't get up to the required height and possession is often lost.

But if the lifters and the jumper have done their bit right it's over to the hooker to throw accurately. So if a throw is short or long look at the lifters and jumpers. Are the lifters' arms at full extension? Is the jumper jumping straight up? Has he locked the core of his body in so all of the force that is being put through him is transferred to height and not lost? Good jumpers don't really jump; they do a kind of half squat and accelerate vertically from there. It is really hard for a lifter to lift a jumper if the jumper is not set when he jumps and is still on the move forward or back in the line, or if he squats down too low or doesn't jump at all.

Every now and then, if a lock wants a back lob and his marker is right on him, he may subconsciously take an extra step or two and leave a good throw short. But more often than not with me, if the throw is short it is because I haven't given it enough. Which is okay if the opposition is not competing, but terrible if they are.

If a throw is too high and long it may be because a lifter has missed his jumper, or more likely it is because he has got entangled in the opposition and the obstruction prevents the jumper getting up as high as he needs to. But I have thrown plenty too long in my day as well.

All of the above can be spot on, but if the opposition are marked up where the throw is going it's a lottery. So I can't emphasise this point enough. If you are to have a successful lineout, the key is having a player with brains calling the right throws at the right times. Some people have the knack, some don't. It is better to have the guy calling the lineout stationed at the tail or in the middle so he can see how the opposition is defending. It is almost impossible to call lineouts from the front.

I was extremely lucky to have had Simon Maling calling lineouts for Otago and the Highlanders from 2000 onwards. We managed to survive with the shortest lineout in the competition. Next to Maling, our tallest forward was our tighthead prop Carl Hayman. Filipo Levi, our other first-choice lock at the time, was, and is, almost unliftable if he is tired or decides not to jump.

Most good lineouts have a player like Maling in them, a player who studies and dreams lineouts and delivers them to the team. As a hooker you have to trust the man calling the throw and I trusted Maling implicitly.

With regard to scrums, a tighthead prop has to have the right attitude, and without that technique isn't much help. The props have got to want to do the work, want to attack scrums, best their opponents. Every time it came to scrum training, Olo Brown just ignited. Away from rugby, Olo was a quiet, unassuming guy. One thing I learned on that tour to South Africa in 1996 was that when it came to training sessions, Craig Dowd and Olo upped their intensity and, boom, away they went. It was that desire to work, do it without thanks, without accolades, without reward. That's the most important thing.

A very close second is having the technical ability to be able to scrum. Size and strength count for little without technical ability. Historically, New Zealand props have survived against far bigger opponents by dint of superior technique. I suppose Joe McDonnell, whom I played with in Otago for some seasons, wouldn't have the best scrummaging technique around — after all he was a midfield back for years — but boy, he has good attitude. He's very attacking, gets pissed off and ratty.

'An old-style forward in a young man's body' – Colin Meads

Colin Meads said he first met Oliver on the plane to Australia in 1995 when he had been called in as a back-up hooker for the centennial test against the Wallabies. 'I was most impressed by him,' said Meads. 'I liked Oliver because he was an old-style forward in a young man's body. He was tough, uncompromising. No one took a flick at him and got away with it.

'Even then he had a reputation as a great guy.' Meads said he was 'astounded' when Oliver wasn't picked for the World Cup in 2003. 'If he wasn't one of the top two hookers in the country I'm a Dutchman.'

He was surprised to hear that Laurie Mains and Oliver had had a falling out because he saw Oliver as the sort of tough nut that Mains always went for.

Meads was also highly sceptical of John Mitchell's talk of needing a 'different style of hooker' and his claim that Oliver didn't fit the bill. 'Few people believe that. I think Oliver's everything you need in a hooker.'

As for locks, the first thing you want from a lock is for him to push. It's that basic. And he must have a physical presence. It helps to have the same questions get asked of scrums and front rows: who is dropping the scrum, and who is getting bested? Generally, players watching games know what is going on and if they are in doubt they ask one another. I have been in team rooms watching games on TV and a backline will pull an amazing move and score a try and I will ask the closest back, 'What happened there? Who did what?' A lot of spectators wouldn't have a clue, although they are not short of an opinion.

Locks with different skills complement each other. The way rugby is now, you have one who is a bit more athletic, and one who is more of a grafter. Ian Jones attracted a lot of attention for his leaping, whereas, when he was fit, Robin Brooke had a hard edge to him. A good lock has to be a man with courage who keeps at it and is uncompromising.

I am not yet 30 years old. My experience of life has been an extraordinary and unpredictable mixture of success and failure, of privilege and hardship, of effort sometimes recognised and sometimes not. All of my adult years have been played out in an uncommon degree of public spotlight. The roller-coaster ride of approval and disdain has taught me that nothing matters more than my own conscience, my own sense of what I value in myself and in others, and the knowledge that, above all, I am ultimately accountable to myself.

I experienced some tough times when my personal life and rugby failures collided. There were many times I was left bewildered and couldn't distinguish what was important any more. However, I refused to dwell on the 'dark side' and attempted to be positive. I didn't want to stop trying or become lost in self-pity.

Sure, there was a risk of humiliation and hurt by stepping into the fray again, but I would rather that than not try anything at all. I have always had the support of family and friends but *I* am responsible for my decisions and ultimately the consequences of my actions. Step up or step back? We all have to make such decisions. That's experience. That's life. Know yourself.